W9-BLM-592

HIDDEN AMERICA

ALSO BY JEANNE MARIE LASKAS

The Balloon Lady and Other People I Know

We Remember: Women Born at the Turn of the Century Tell the Stories of Their Lives in Words and Pictures

Fifty Acres and a Poodle: A Story of Love, Livestock, and Finding Myself on a Farm

The Exact Same Moon: Fifty Acres and a Family

Growing Girls: The Mother of All Adventures

HIDDEN AMERICA

From Coal Miners to Cowboys, an Extraordinary Exploration of the Unseen People Who Make This Country Work

JEANNE MARIE LASKAS

G. P. Putnam's Sons ★ New York

PUTNAM

G. P. PUTNAM'S SONS
Publishers Since 1838
Published by the Penguin Group
Penguin Group (USA) Inc., 375 Hudson Street, New York, New York 10014, USA • Penguin Group (Canada), 90 Eglinton Avenue East, Suite 700, Toronto, Ontario M4P 2Y3, Canada (a division of Pearson Penguin Canada Inc.) • Penguin Books Ltd, 80 Strand, London WC2R 0RL, England • Penguin Ireland, 25 St Stephen's Green, Dublin 2, Ireland (a division of Penguin Books Ltd) • Penguin Group (Australia), 250 Camberwell Road, Camberwell, Victoria 3124, Australia (a division of Pearson Australia Group Pty Ltd) • Penguin Books India Pvt Ltd, 11 Community Centre, Panchsheel Park, New Delhi–110 017, India • Penguin Group (NZ), 67 Apollo Drive, Rosedale, North Shore 0632, New Zealand (a division of Pearson New Zealand Ltd) • Penguin Books (South Africa) (Pty) Ltd, 24 Sturdee Avenue, Rosebank, Johannesburg 2196, South Africa

Penguin Books Ltd, Registered Offices: 80 Strand, London WC2R 0RL, England

Published simultaneously in Canada

The following chapters have previously been published in *GQ*, in different form: "Underworld," "Hecho en América," "G-L-O-R-Y," "Traffic," "The Rig," and "This Is Paradise."
"Beef" was previously published in *Smithsonian*, in different form.

Library of Congress Cataloging-in-Publication Data

Laskas, Jeanne Marie, date.
Hidden America : from coal miners to cowboys, an extraordinary exploration of the unseen people who make this country work / Jeanne Marie Laskas.
p. cm.
ISBN 978-0-399-15900-8
1. Working class—United States—Social conditions. 2. Working class—United States—Biography. 3. Working class—United States—Social life and customs. 4. Manual work—Social aspects—United States. 5. Subculture—United States. 6. Laskas, Jeanne Marie, 1958—Travel—United States. 7. United States—Description and travel. 8. United States—Social conditions—1980– 9. United States—Social life and customs—1971– I. Title.
HD8072.5.L37 2012 2012025457
305.5'.620973—dc23

Printed in the United States of America
10 9 8 7 6 5 4 3 2 1

This book is printed on acid-free paper. ♾

Book design by Meighan Cavanaugh

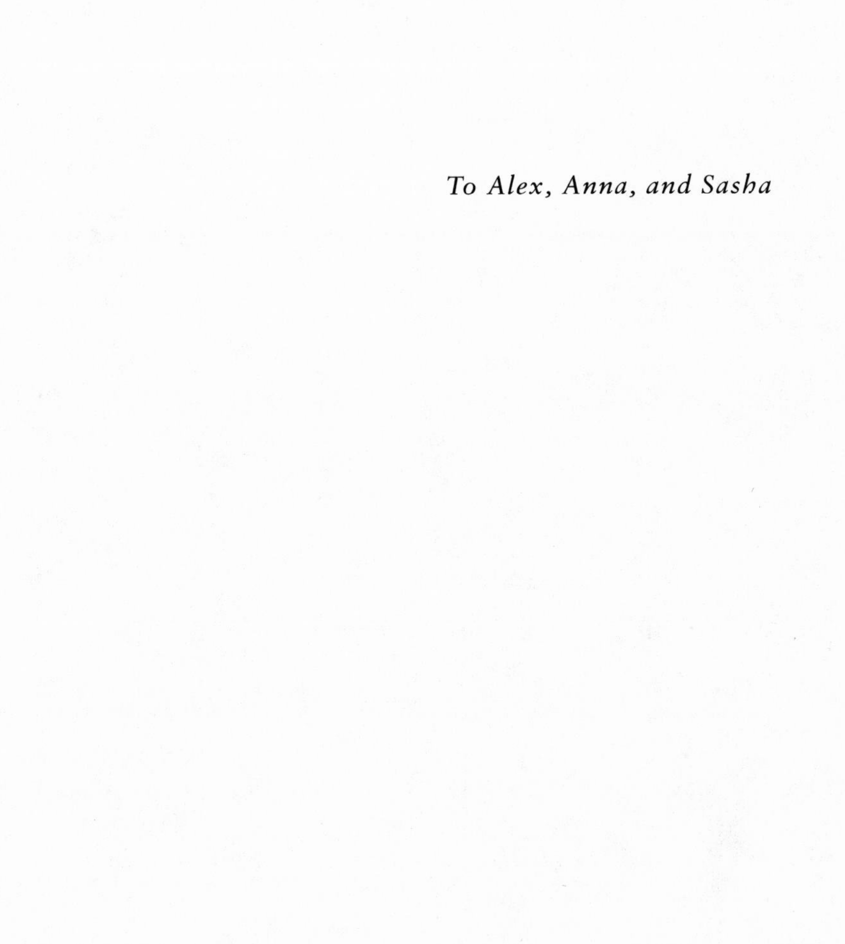

To Alex, Anna, and Sasha

AMERICAN mouth-songs!
Those of mechanics—each one singing his, as it should be, blithe and strong,
The carpenter singing his, as he measures his plank or beam,
The mason singing his, as he makes ready for work, or leaves off work,
The boatman singing what belongs to him in his boat—the deck-hand singing on the steamboat deck,
The shoemaker singing as he sits on his bench—the hatter singing as he stands,
The wood-cutter's song—the ploughboy's, on his way in the morning, or at the noon intermission, or at sundown;
The delicious singing of the mother—or of the young wife at work—or the girl sewing or washing—Each singing what belongs to her, and to none else,
The day what belongs to the day—At night, the party of young fellows, robust, friendly, clean-blooded, singing with melodious voices, melodious thoughts.

Come! some of you! still be flooding The States with hundreds and thousands of mouth-songs, fit for The States only.

—WALT WHITMAN, FROM *LEAVES OF GRASS,* 1860 EDITION

CONTENTS

HIDDEN AMERICA

INTRODUCTION

The idea for this book began forming in a coal mine, about five hundred feet underneath Ohio, when I was rolling through pitch-black darkness on a "mantrip," a small, squat, topless train car. My hip was wedged into the back of the miner next to me, my feet propped on somebody else, all of us tangled together, ducking low to avoid scraping our hard hats on the impossibly low ceiling. A pinpoint of light shining from my hat revealed little beyond a ramshackle system of posts and beams keeping the entire operation from collapsing. *This is not a place for people, this is not a place for people, this is not a place for people,* I thought, in rhythmic beats roughly in time with the clunk and clatter of the mantrip.

Everyone imagines going *down* when they think of a coal mine, but the real surprise is going *in*. The tunnel took our little knotted group farther and farther inside the earth, a mile, two miles, eventually about six miles away from the elevator shaft that had dropped us down. When the mantrip stopped, we rolled off it and righted ourselves and stood up—sort of. The ceiling of the mine was just five feet high. We were now at the face of it, where, bent over like broken saplings, the guys worked ten-hour shifts digging coal.

I tried to take the situation in stride, as you might, politely, when visiting a neighbor's sadly dilapidated home, or when listening to a child scratch out a tune on a violin; but the combination of the darkness, the six-mile commute away from our only escape hatch, and the fact that the earth all around us was bleeding deadly methane that could with the slightest encouragement explode—all of these aspects combined to steal from me any sense of decorum. *ARE YOU FREAKIN' KIDDING ME?* is what I said, many times over, in those first few days of a months-long journey in and out of the mine. *"They should make the ceiling higher!"* I said, stupidly. *"It's like the size of a small city down here; they couldn't put another stinkin' elevator in?"* Eventually, I just kept saying, *"Dude, this is ridiculous."*

The miners responded to my commentary with bored expressions. A flat gaze. An exhausted double blink that had a language all its own. It was a look that held the evocative message that would ultimately keep me in its grasp and set me off on the nine separate journeys over a two-year period that form the foundation of this book.

What is the matter with you? those miners seemed to say. *How is it that you know nothing about us, our lives, this world?*

Here was coal, a $27 billion industry, the fastest-growing energy source on the planet. And here were the guys who dug it. Every time we flip on a light switch, we burn a lump of coal. My daily life was intimately connected to these people—*dependent* on them—

and yet, up until my time in that mine, I knew nothing about them or their world.

It was humiliating. It seemed wrong in some inexplicable way. In writing *Hidden America*, I wanted to make that wrongness explicable. I wanted to connect my life to the people who make it livable and, maybe, reintroduce America to some of its forgotten self.

Who are the people who pick our vegetables, grow our beef, haul our stuff to the marketplace, make our trash disappear? Moreover, how did *that* become such a difficult question to answer? It seems to me we used to know the people who made our lives livable. We were more than likely related to them. In a preindustrial America, and in a small-town America, there was Uncle Charlie with his cows, Cousin Mike coming by with his truckload of hay, Aunt Sarah and her basket of lima beans, and, of course, the milkman. The raw material and the labor of the everyday had personalities associated with them, as well as culture and history.

That's all gone now. We live in cities, suburbs. We are busy. We expect electricity, a temperature-controlled environment, food, speed, and minimal inconvenience (i.e., not a stinky horse) in getting from here to there. We expect somebody to take our garbage away and do something with it so we don't have to think about it. We expect the shelves in our malls to be stocked with the things we need, when we need them. We have work to do, papers to sign, mortgages to make. We are civilized. We don't meet the cattle whose briskets we eat, we don't know the shape or the color of the hands that pick our lettuce, peaches, or celery. If the disconnect between us (the people who demand) and them (the people who supply) says anything about us, it's probably not flattering.

And yet, in *Hidden America* I am not advocating for some so-called simpler time, all of us chopping our own wood to fuel the stove, wringing the necks of chickens in order to feed our kids, gathering wheat, rolling oats, spinning cotton or wool. As anyone with a flat-screen knows, the simpler time is now, and I'm all for it.

Instead, I'm inviting America to steal a glance into these worlds, some hugely complicated industries, some tiny and private contributions, to wander with me and consider the everyday anew. Everything you know about America—all the history, all the politics, all the lessons from all the economic indicators, all the arguments from the red states and the blue—is irrelevant when you are sitting in a coal mine, or staring at a radar screen showing thousands of airplanes flying at once, or wrangling five hundred pregnant Red Angus cows beneath a blazing hot desert sunrise.

SOME MONTHS AFTER I left the coal mine, I was about 250 miles above the Arctic Circle, a few miles off the shore of Alaska in the frozen Beaufort Sea on a man-made island where the temperature hung around minus 45 degrees. I tilted my fur-lined hood in such a way as to deflect the wind as I listened to a guy talk about a stuck drill bit, making no mention of the fact that his mustache had turned into a bristle of ice. The small society of workers I got to know on that frozen island—where no one left for weeks and sometimes months at a time—enacted a drama underscoring the intensity of America's thirst for oil, of course, but also gave me insight into a certain kind of love, a brotherhood born of survival, and allowed me to witness private acts of heroism in combinations that shifted, yet again, my relationship to the everyday conveniences of modern life.

I went to Los Angeles County, California, where I tumbled atop a mighty machine rolling down steep cliffs of garbage nearly as high as the coal mine in Ohio was deep and pondered the quietly brilliant work of American engineers who fifty years ago set out to conquer the physics of trash, a conundrum so vast as to become philosophical: trash is *matter*, and matter never leaves. You can change its form, move it from here to there, plop it into the ocean, burn it, bury it, but it will always be with us. The people who manage trash became, to me, weirdly spiritual.

The aim of my research presumed that the people of Hidden America *wanted* to be known, a naïve miscalculation that occurred to me only as I discovered those who were indifferent to it, and, most notably, those who didn't want to be known at all. I lived in a migrant worker camp in Maine and set out with the workers before dawn to the blueberry barrens and learned about the lives of the people who pick our food. They had come from Mexico, Peru, Colombia, and points far south of the border; some were documented, some were not, and most of them lived in shame in the shadows, hiding, violating our laws as they toiled in the fields, picking the very berries with which I've long topped my Shredded Wheat each morning. Now that I know these people, I don't approach the table in the same way. Now there is personal gratitude, anger, frustration, and responsibility.

Being known, becoming invisible, being celebrated, hiding: these were constantly shifting objectives I confronted as I researched this book. In the control tower at New York's LaGuardia Airport,

I learned about invisibility as a goal unto itself: here was a team of technically trained soldiers caring for an unsuspecting public that needed them more than it would ever know. Only when an air traffic controller fails does he get notice; like so many characters in Hidden America, the better these people were at their jobs, the more invisible they became.

Hidden America is a look at America from the inside out, and that shift in paradigm is not a subtle one. The perspective is, in fact, the exact opposite of the view we've become accustomed to taking in our celebrity-driven culture. *Get on TV! Make millions! Win awards!* We become so familiar with the narrative we forget that there are any others happening at all.

I wondered about fame, tried to see if there was any place at all for it in a book about Hidden America. I thought about entertainment, our biggest stage, our most celebrated spectacle. The NFL generates $9 billion annually, pays its actors handsomely to run and jump and crash into each other while catching and throwing balls. Meantime, smiling cheerleaders dance on the sidelines, begging for notice. What would happen if we stopped and said hello to these folks, too? What I discovered with the Ben-Gals cheerleading squad was a different kind of invisibility, a distinctively female one. Dress identically, wear identical orange lipstick, move in identical sequence, become the *same* in order to become your best self. Moreover, the cheerleaders demonstrated nationalism at its most basic level, every Sunday embodying a contradiction I came to understand as uniquely American.

Sisterhood in *Hidden America* appeared as a slight variation of the brotherhood that became such a common theme—the value system in so many of those worlds held teamwork and support in paramount regard—while motherhood was a whole different animal altogether. A trucker named Sputter opened that examination for me, somewhere in Iowa, and hauling tractor parts with Sputter turned into a surprising personal journey.

My own political views have no place in this book, and I deliberately steered away from making pleas on behalf of anyone—undocumented immigrants, environmentalists, or other interest groups, even the progesterone-juiced cows pumping out perfect calves in West Texas. And yet, it seemed incomplete to ignore the fact that America continues to split itself into political extremes. How could I begin to make sense of that divide in a way that was consistent with the goals of *Hidden America*? I decided to set off to meet the people of a Hidden America I believed I had the *least* chance of ever understanding: gun owners. I needed to jump across the divide, full-on, and sit awhile. How, anyway, did America become a nation of some 300 million guns and 80 million gun owners? I don't mean politically, or even historically. I mean, *how*? Who are the people who arm America? Who are the clerks who stand behind the counter explaining, showing, doling out firearms? I went to Yuma, Arizona, and worked behind the counter at a gun store to learn. I sold assault rifles and pistols, semiautos and revolvers, while I listened and learned to speak a language I have yet to fully figure out how to translate to the people who inhabit the side of the American divide where I come from. The world of guns is the one culture in this book that remains for me the most inexplicable rabbit hole.

I could of course have gone on and on. I wonder about corn, about cotton, shipping ports, bridges and tall buildings, and about the whispers of unnamed soldiers buried beneath tiny flags. Hidden America only gets bigger and more complex the more you peck away at it and try to understand it.

It is important to note, I think, that *Hidden America*, like any book, has a sound track against which it is written and read. If America is singing right now, in 2012, the music is loud, cacophonous, all percussion and unyielding refrain:

> *Don't blame Wall Street, don't blame the big banks, if you don't have a job and you're not rich, blame yourself!*
>
> *STOP THE WAR ON WORKERS!*
>
> As business leaders, we know what it takes to create jobs. Let us explain how to put America back to work.
>
> We are the 99 percent.
>
> *Don't tax our job creators more!*

This book has no new slogans to add to the shouting, offers no charged rhetoric to the cause of the 99 percenters or the 1 percent. If Hidden America takes any position at all, it is necessarily from the sidelines, underneath, above, or inside. It speaks from these vantage points—captures the quiet, nuanced conversations that the shouting and the sloganeering drown out. Hidden America doesn't have an argument to make. Hidden America is busy. Hidden America is tired. Hidden America doesn't have a lot of time to sit around and watch debates on TV. Hidden America needs a beer and to get to bed. These are the people who keep America alive and ticking. The people who, were they to walk off the job tomorrow, would bring life as we know it to a halt.

I've thought about why any of this research or any of these stories matter: Why should I care who powers my lights, why my steak tastes so good, how my flight gets to the ground? I just want my damn lights to work, my steaks to be tender, and to get from here to there safely and on time. Like anyone, I have more important things to do than concern myself with the guts of the operation. (There is, after all, a reason we put doors on our furnace rooms and cover our engines with shiny hoods.) I think about how my eyes have been opened, again and again, over the past few years researching this book, and about all the perfectly fine years I lived with them closed. Which is better?

The image I come up with is that of the child who is never asked to set the table, whip the potatoes, or take out the trash. The child who wants a new toy and gets it, a new set of gloves, a hat. It comes to her because she asks for it, and so she asks for more. This goes on until expectation sets in, privilege and entitlement. Then the child discovers one day, eventually, and if she is lucky, that her parents work to provide her with food, shelter, clothing, entertainment, a comfortable life. She learns of the family's larger function, that her desires are just a piece of the puzzle; the world is infinitely larger, richer, and worthy of her contribution, too.

It happens all the time, I suppose, whether you are talking about a child's role in a family, a citizen's in a country, or if you consider just any old customer in a deli ordering ham. Pull the curtain back and show the action backstage, how it's done and how much brain power and brawn and sacrifice goes into making the systems work, and it becomes remarkable and fabulous and awesome.

UNDERWORLD

Hopedale Mining
Cadiz, Ohio

He handed me a salt-and-vinegar potato chip. We were more than five hundred feet underground, sitting on a blanket of powdered limestone, up in section two and a half south. I asked him if there was anything he enjoyed about coal mining.

He thought a moment. "I'm gonna say no," he said.

"Oh, come on," I said.

"You gotta stop shining your freakin' light in my eye," he said. "What did I tell you about that?"

He told me that the one thing that was going to piss off Billy, Smitty, Pap, Ragu, and the rest of the guys in the crew was if I pointed my light directly in their eyes. It's a common early mistake. The normal human urge is to look a person in the eye, and when your only visibility is from a hard hat shining a pinpoint of light through the darkness, naturally you're going to aim that sucker right at the eyeball.

"Sorry," I said.

"Go for the shoulder," he said. "Or the chin."

I asked him how he got the nickname Foot.

"The first day I went into the coal mine, a guy looked down and said, 'Damn, how big are your feet?' I said, 'Fifteen.' He said, 'You're a big-footed son of a bitch.' And that was it. One guy had a huge head, so of course we called him Pumpkin. One guy had a big red birthmark on his face, so of course his name was Spot. They don't cut you any slack. They'll get right on you. A coal miner will get right on you."

I shined my light on his boots and he wagged them, like puppets.

It was tough getting used to identifying people, in the darkness, just as feet, shoulders, chin, teeth. As for Foot, he was a truck of a man, forty-nine years old, a wide load in both girth and spirit. He had a messy mop of gray hair and a rugged, intelligent face that often wore one expression: *You gotta be kidding me.* He was proud of a lot of what he'd done with his life—his three kids, his stint as a county commissioner, his coal-mining expertise—but his heart, he said, belonged to his fifty-two head of beef cattle: Pork Chop, Frick and Frack, and, aw, Bonehead, with the amazing white eyelashes.

He'd been in and out of coal mines since graduating from high school and had just been promoted to assistant safety director of the Hopedale Mining coal company in Cadiz, Ohio, a small operation in the eastern part of the state, just beyond the panhandle of West Virginia. Aboveground, the area looks a lot more New England—rolling farmland dotted with tall oaks, white church steeples, geranium pots hanging on front porches—than it does the tar-paper-shack Appalachia that people tend to associate with coal mining. Underground, I wasn't permitted to go anywhere without Foot, even though I did. He got sick of me, and I got sick of him, and so he got even *more* sick of me in what became, over a four-month period, an easy friendship.

"It's kind of peaceful down here," I said to him.

"Yeah," he said.

We were not at the face, not "up on section," where the bellow and whir and *hucka-chucka-hucka-chucka* of the toothy, goofy, phallic continuous miner machine was extracting coal and dumping it, load after load, onto buggies that zoomed like lunatic roaches through the darkness. We were over in B entry, or A entry, or perhaps room 3; I had no idea. I rarely knew where I was in that endless catacomb of tunnels, on and on and on, about fifteen square miles in all, where the quiet, when you found it, felt like an embrace. You could sit there. You could shut your light off, sit there in the perfectly dark silence. Nothing. Just—nothing.

Until: *Pop!*

Hisssss.

A crackle like a fireplace.

Hisssss.

When you're inside the earth, this is what it sounds like. The earth isn't some stupid rock, isn't inert, isn't just a solid mass for people to stand on. The earth is always moving, constantly stretching and squawking and repositioning itself like anyone else trying to get comfortable.

"Down here," I said to Foot, "it's like you're away from all your problems. Do you think that's part of the allure for you guys—that you escape your problems down here?"

He looked at me, laughed. "This *is* our problem," he said.

I LIVE ON TOP of a massive vein of medium-sulfur bituminous coal—the very famous Pittsburgh Number 8 Seam that extends from eastern Ohio to western Maryland, where coal has played a vital role in the economy and culture for over a century. The fact that it still does takes a lot of people by surprise. *We still have coal mines?* I got that question a lot when I told people that I was hanging out in a coal mine.

In this way, I was slightly ahead of the learning curve: I knew coal mines *existed*. And not just in pockets of some America that never caught up, not as funky remnants of a bygone era, but as current places of work, day after day, guys with lunch buckets heading in and heading out, taking home sixty, seventy, eighty thousand dollars a year. To live where I live, in western Pennsylvania, is to occasionally get stuck behind a coal truck, to be vaguely cognizant of boxcars full of coal snaking in between the hills, to see a guy covered in coal dust up at the Toot-N-Scoot paying for an iced tea.

Coal, if it disappeared from the nation's consciousness, never went away. This is America, and this is *our* fossil fuel, a $27.6 billion industry that employs nearly eighty thousand miners in twenty-six states. We are sitting on 25 percent of the world's supply—the Saudi Arabia of coal!—and lately we've been grabbing it in record amounts, gorging on the black rock the Bush administration once called "freedom fuel."

The question I had going in was almost ridiculous in nature: If coal is really this big, and all these people really exist, how is it that I know nothing about them?

It took me months to even gain access to a coal mine: this is not an industry that welcomes publicity, perhaps because the publicity it gets is always so horrific. Coal mines make the news only when they explode, collapse, kill. It's exciting! Tragedy! Fodder for a cable news frenzy. *Look at these poor, stupid rednecks who work these awful jobs. Trapped! Suffocating! Buried alive!*

Repeatedly, the guys at the Hopedale Mining company asked that I not portray them as poor, stupid rednecks. This characterization, they said, would only display my own ignorance. They were shy at first, eager to impress, and, with little other apparent motivation, they welcomed me in. I followed one crew, the "E rotation"—Billy, Smitty, Scotty, Pap, Rick, Chris, Kevin, Hook, Duke, Ragu, Sparky, Charlie—who worked in the Cadiz portal, one of two the company owned. I followed them underground, home, to church, to the strip club where they drink and gossip and taunt and jab and worry about one another. I listened while they worried about Smitty, the loner of the group, who had just ordered himself a mail-order woman. Smitty had been talking to her on the Internet for more than a year; he was shipping her over from Russia and she was supposed to arrive, beautifully, on the first day of buck season. I listened while they mercilessly mocked Scotty, a disarmingly cheerful guy who often talked to himself, especially in the bathhouse, where the guys gathered after each shift to wash off the filth before reentering life aboveground. Scotty would be scrubbing away, smiling, telling himself all about this and all about that, and sometimes he'd come out with a laugh that would about bust your ear off. "What the hell is wrong with you, Scotty?" said Foot, who was showering next to Scotty when he recently did this.

"I'm going to be in jail tomorrow for murder," Scotty said to Foot.

"For what?"

"I'm gonna kill this son of a bitch I'm fighting, I'm gonna *kill* him!"

"Yeah, well, don't get too far ahead of yourself there, buddy," Foot said. Fight Night XV at Wheeling Island Racetrack & Gaming Center would feature its first-ever junior-middleweight championship, pitting Scott "the Rock" Tullius against Todd Manning, and a lot of the guys from the mine were going.

These were men who lived underground together for ten-hour shifts, five days at a stretch, often spending more time with one another than they did with their families, so they knew everything about one another. They knew all about Billy's brand-new house and the barn siding he used to panel his basement, all about Chris's kid getting his second bone-marrow transplant, all about Pap's wife getting her damn knee replaced—and they knew there was no sense in asking Pap what the hell he was doing, a sixty-two-year-old man still mining coal. Pap should have retired long ago. Or he should have had a job outside. A lot of guys put in years underground with the hope of moving aboveground; Pap could have had almost any job he wanted outside. But he chose to stay under, working what was widely regarded as the worst job of all: roof bolting. He was the guy drilling six-foot rods up into the top of the mine as the coal got dug out and the earth complained, hissing its hissy methane fits and collapsing more or less on a regular basis.

Of course I asked him why. Every which way I could think of, I asked Pap why he chose to stay under, but he, like so many of the miners I met, had a way of talking in circles. I asked Pap's wife, Nancy, the woman he called "the old bag I live with," why Pap still worked underground. She had no idea what I was talking about. "I don't know nothing about nothing that goes on in that mine," she said. (She did not mind being called an old bag and referred to Pap as "my Frankie" or, sometimes, "Lucifer.") She, like so many of the people I visited, always gave me a care package to take home, a few chunks of Edam cheese and a pear. Pap gave me two bottles of homemade blackberry wine to take home to my husband. I never once mentioned that I *had* a husband, but everyone kept sending home presents for him. Family was the assumption. Family-to-family interaction was the natural order of communication.

I spent months trying to position myself and my world around these people—people who seem stuck in a bygone era that isn't bygone at all. If anyone is gone, it's us, the consumer. We forgot, or we lost touch, or we grew up with our lives already sanitized. We live over *here* and they live over *there*, and we have almost no access to a way of life that we are so unwittingly dependent on. What disturbed me was nothing I found so much as the nature of the experiment itself: How is it that our own neighbors are the stuff of *anthropology*? If that says anything about us, it's definitely not flattering.

"*Why do we even have coal mines?*" said some blond-haired TV news lady in 2006, when twelve miners famously trapped in West Virginia's Sago mine were first pronounced alive and then—whoops—dead. All of a sudden, the nation's attention was on coal miners, zoo animals—specimens of humanity—while the coal miners looked back.

Why do we even have coal mines? The miners I talked to remembered listening and laughing, having great fun with that one. "Whenever you plug your vibrator in and it doesn't work, okay, that's why we have coal mines!" one of them shouted at the

TV. Okay, that might not have been the best example, seeing as your sex-toy industry is more or less dependent on batteries, which have nothing to do with coal. But the point is: power. Coal is power. "Yeah, turn the lights on, lady. That's why you need coal mines. Where do you think electricity comes from?"

Every time we flip on a light switch, we burn a lump of coal, each of us consuming about twenty pounds of those lumps a day. Fully half of our electricity comes from coal—and that's nothing compared with China, which leads the world in both the production and the consumption of coal, accounting for a whopping 70 percent of that country's total energy consumption. Coal is the fastest-growing energy source on the planet (much to the planet's reported gasping dismay).

And so, the coal miner. He shows up in country-music songs and poetry, a working-class hero. He works a job that has killed more than one hundred thousand since we started, over a century ago, sending people underground. It's enough to make you shake your head, sigh a grateful sigh, and go on and bond with the guys over at ABC News waxing philosophical: *"If there is such a thing as a mystique associated with a hard, dirty, and dangerous life, that mystique is attached to the miners who are such a part of the nation's consciousness and soul."*

That's where we start. That's where I started. I wanted the mystique. I wanted to discover that the guys who make their living underground do it because of some attachment to the earth, or to history, or to their own ancestry, or to further some fundamental masculine need for brotherhood, or—yes!—on behalf of the nation's consciousness and soul.

You talk like that in a coal mine, you'll get your lunch bucket nailed shut. Seriously. That's a beauty.

IF YOU WANT A JOB at the Hopedale Mining company, the first thing they do is bring you down for a tour to see if you can mentally handle it. You pretty much know instantly if you can take the confinement, the lack of light, the very real worry about the roof caving in or the air supply shutting off or something blowing up. And if you don't know instantly, there's a team of guys watching you to see if you twitch, shake, turn pale. Some guys say, "Yeah, never mind," and ask to leave. One guy recently passed out.

When Billy Cermak Jr. first went under, six years ago, he was trying to convince himself he was doing the right thing—*I can do this, I can do this, I can do this*—because coal mining was exactly the thing he swore he'd never do: he'd never allow the Cermaks to become *fourth-generation* coal miners. First his great-grandfather, recruited from what is now the Czech Republic by the coal companies; then his grandfather, who started working in the mines at age twelve and died of black lung; then Billy's dad, working most of his life in the strip mines. *That won't be me,* Billy grew up thinking. He would be a man of *his* generation, get himself a job somewhere at least air-conditioned. He'd become sick of the family farm, of a life so dependent on brawn. He went to college to study nursing, tried to pretend he didn't hate it, kept thinking, *It's gotta get better, it's gotta get better,* but it never did. He graduated, but ended up leaving the air-conditioned world for jobs in construction, on pipelines, and on the railroads. Muscles.

Might. Sweat. It just felt better. Soon he had a wife. He imagined sons on four-wheelers, boys raking hay. The farm. Leaving it only proved how much he loved it. And there he was, days at a time, off on that railroad. He just wanted to figure out a way to stay on the farm. And coal mining was right there in his backyard.

So in walks Billy Cermak to the Cadiz portal on Old Hopedale Road. *I can do this, I can do this, I can do this.* The building itself is blue corrugated steel with a big American flag hanging from a pole out front, struggling rhododendrons along the walkway, and a giant happy face painted on a fuel tank in the parking lot. The whir of the massive fan sucking bad air out of the mine is loud, obnoxious, and constant.

Billy gets suited up: coveralls, steel-reinforced boots, hard hat, light, and on his belt a battery pack, methane detector, and W65 self-rescuer respirator—a breathing mask intended to filter out carbon monoxide for about an hour. If there's an explosion or fire, you wrap that around your face until you can get yourself to an SCSR (self-contained self-rescue) apparatus, many of which are stationed throughout the mine, and which provide a full hour of actual oxygen. He's given a metal tag with his name on it and told where to hang it on the peg board. In case of a collapse, they want to know whom to go looking for. He gets on the elevator, plunges five hundred feet down—fifty stories, just—down. The elevator opens up and everything is white. That's the first weird thing. *White?*

Everyone, I was told, gets jolted by the white. You try to make sense of it. "They just paint this opening part white to cheer everyone up?" I said to Foot the first time I saw it. He didn't even dignify that guess with a response. "It's, like, a joke?" I said.

"Irony? A little humor to start your day before you move into black?" I figured we'd hit the black part of a coal mine as soon as we moved farther in. Foot looked at me in that way he came to look at me, a stillness, a flatness to his gaze, an expression that said, *You just keep turning into more of an idiot.* He said, "I think you'll find there are no aesthetic choices, nor is there irony, in a coal mine."

The white is on account of "rock dust," powdered limestone, a fire retardant that you throw on every exposed inch of coal—which, were it not rock-dusted, would be spontaneous combustion waiting to happen. One small explosion could trigger a series of explosions, on and on, *fwoom, fwoom, fwoom,* through the mine, but not if you've got it rock-dusted. Explosion is nothing to flirt with. I was not permitted even to use a tape recorder when we were at the face of the mine, where the coal was exposed and the methane was bleeding, nor could a photographer use a flash. The smallest spark could cause a blast.

So, five hundred feet down. White. That's just hello. You are not, technically, even at work yet. Once you step off the elevator, you climb onto a mantrip, a small train car. You don't sit so much as lie on that thing, a crawling convertible, as you lean way back on it so as to avoid scraping your head on the ceiling as you whiz on in through a cool, damp tunnel, mud, slush, *clunk, clunk, rattle, hiss.* You travel a mile in, two miles in, sometimes as far as six or seven miles in and away from the elevator shaft where you first dropped down. It depends on where they're digging coal. The guys, of course, are used to this, an everyday commute. Some of them break into their lunch buckets, Scotty sharing M&M's, Hook downing a Mountain Dew. They keep their lights off, conserving battery power, but the mantrip has a headlight, so you can watch the underworld whiz by, all of it crusty white, eerily frosty. Everything is crooked, bent, leaning; there are posts jammed in here and there to keep the top up, rusted reinforcement bolts jutting out, power cables hanging; the net effect is an endless crawl of abandonment and prayer. *Just keep the damn thing from caving in.* There is nothing aesthetic about a coal mine. There is no design, no geometry, no melody. A coal mine greets you with only one sentiment, then hammers it: *This is not a place for people, this is not a place for people, this is not a place for people.*

So, five hundred feet down, a couple of miles in. You are under somebody's house, or a grocery store, or, in this case, the Wendy's up there on Route 22. The guys joke about yelling up for a burger, maybe some chili. You roll off the mantrip and stand up. The ceiling is five feet high, and so you can't, actually, stand up. You look around and everyone is walking around like the freaks in *Being John Malkovich.*

"Okay, they should make it higher," I said to Foot the first time I experienced this. I wanted to call a congressman or something. This was ridiculous. There are *people* in here! Everyone's doing a duck walk, hands clasped behind their backs to give the body balance as they lean over and waddle. You work your whole ten-hour shift like that, duck-walking through the darkness, nothing but a pinpoint of light shining from your hat to tell you which rat tunnel is which. A rat. You feel like a rat.

I could not get used to the height. Every time I went down, I asked, "Is this lower than last time? Are we in a lower spot?"

"Same spot," Foot said, explaining that there was nothing to be done about the height. "A coal seam is a coal seam."

A coal seam is a coal seam, and this one was five feet high, and so that was how high the mine was. The height got decided a long time ago, like 300 million years ago, way before dinosaurs, when the coal seam was a ribbon of dead plants, slime. It sat there, buried sludge, covered up over millions of years. It turned to peat, lignite, then subbituminous, bituminous, or anthracite coal, depending on how many millions of years it had a chance to sit there and store energy and depending on the geologic forces surrounding it. A coal seam is an act of nature. If you want the coal, you just mine the coal. You don't mine above it or below it. Take any higher and you're mining rock, mixing rock in with the coal, a messy product that will have to get "washed." Take any lower and you're doing the same, plus probably hitting water and making yourself a mud hole, and Billy will have to go get the fucking sump pumps. You just take the coal. And shut up, because Foot could tell you about plenty of mines where the seam is thirty-six inches, thirty-two inches. Pap could tell you about working on his stomach—his *stomach*—down in Saginaw "scratch-your-back" mine.

There is good news. Every once in a while you find the good news, or hear about the good news: A glory hole! Come on over. A glory hole is a place where the "top" has opened up, forming a dome. Heaven. You can stand. Thank the Lord! Guys hang out in glory holes, Scotty stretching, Sparky rolling his neck around. Standing in a glory hole, you can feel your spine thank you even as you work on denying the fact that a glory hole is, technically, a cave-in, a place where the top fell down, maybe yesterday or maybe the day before.

The "top" is certainly the main topic of conversation in a coal mine. Bad top. Hey, that top over there is bad. Aw, this is some bad top here. Look out. Okay, that's coming down. Move. The top is falling. "Go on over to C entry at ten-plus-thirty and you'll see where the fucking top collapsed."

It's not always this bad. The top conditions in two and a half south, where the E rotation was mining, were especially crappy. Every coal miner I talked to had, in his history, at least one story of a cave-in. "Yeah, he got covered up" is a way coal miners refer to fathers and brothers and sons who got buried alive.

Air is probably the second most common topic of conversation in a coal mine. With every fresh cut of coal, the earth leaks explosive methane. You need to get that out of there. Guys up at the face are constantly getting off their machines to control and direct the airflow: tacking up tarps, taking them down, checking their methane detectors in an effort to keep fresh air sweeping across the face of the mine.

A coal miner is busy. A coal miner doesn't have time to sit around and ponder all of this: methane, bad top, no light, no standing, no bathroom, no water fountain, no phone, no radio, no windows, five hundred feet down, a couple of miles in. If I found that I could, in fact, mentally handle being inside a coal mine, it was only because I knew I was leaving. No matter how many times I went under, I would always be a tourist. I could ooh and I could ahh and I could leave. But Smitty and Kevin and Ragu couldn't, and Pap wouldn't. The Cadiz mine operates twenty-four hours a day, seven days a week.

The "face crew" works up at the face of the mine, operating the cacophony of machinery. At the head of the line you have Rick, the miner operator chewing off the coal with the *hucka-chucka-*

hucka-chucka continuous miner machine and its rolling drums of teeth. Behind him, two roof bolters, Pap and Charlie, with their mighty orange hydraulic jack machine that holds the top up with one arm, then slams four- or six-foot rods into that top, reinforcing it. Behind them zoom three buggy runners—Scotty, Ragu, Smitty—each capturing the coal and hauling it to conveyor belts. Behind them, the scoop man, Kevin, who pulls up in his scoop machine to capture the loose coal. Then Rick moves in with the miner again, making another cut, and the cycle repeats.

All of these men and all of these machines keep in constant motion, chewing, hauling, bolting, scooping, in what becomes a kind of dance. It's a factory that keeps going forward, sixty feet per shift, deeper into the mine and farther from the power center, the base of the operation. Every two weeks or so, you have to pack up the power center, move the whole factory forward.

Now, Billy Cermak, when he went down the first time, six years ago, to see if he could mentally handle it, he was elated. It wasn't so bad! It was . . . white! Kind of pleasant that way, really. Not all doom and gloom. And other than the height issue, it was just learning equipment—farm boys make the best miners, because farm boys know equipment—it wasn't bad at all. *I can handle it!* He started work the next week, a rising star from the moment he got there. He was put right up at the face, a roof bolter, and soon enough he shot up to crew chief. A boss. Smitty, Scotty, Pap, Rick, Chris, Kevin, Hook, Duke, Ragu, Sparky, Charlie—eleven workers under Billy's direction. The E rotation.

Billy was a gentleman. He wore cologne. If there's an upwardly mobile coal miner, it's Billy. He tries. He *believes*. He even shows up at the company picnics. Even his house, brand-new, with a big, bright porch and cats running around, says "winner." An eighteen-foot Playtime motorboat in the driveway, a shiny Dodge, and a Suburban. His house sits across from his dad's place, over from his brother's. The original family farm, intact. Billy has two boys now, and can't you just picture little Brody and Gage riding four-wheelers real soon? They have three miniature horses. Next year, an in-ground pool. For Billy, this whole thing is like the most unbelievable dream come true, even though he swore he'd never be a fourth-generation coal miner.

"The only thing I think about is the danger part of it," his wife, Tynae, said one day when we were all sitting in the living room, watching Brody tumble.

"It's not that bad," Billy said to her. "I mean, the danger isn't even a thought for me anymore."

"I know," she said, even though you could tell she didn't.

"Anything that happens is just a freak accident."

"I know."

"That's the only stuff that happens is *freak accidents*."

"I know."

Then she turned her attention to a Smurfs cartoon Brody had settled on, and nobody said anything.

A few days later, when I was in the mine, up on section, Billy said, "Look, I don't talk about the bad stuff in front of my wife, okay?"

Billy was there the day Albert got crushed. Billy was only two months into his happily-ever-after, just two months into learning that he could mentally handle it. An explosion. The power out. And the section foreman called, "We're gonna need some help!" It was over at the bottom of the slope, where supply cars travel from outside down into the mine, carrying tons of equipment. The cars had let loose, fallen through the air at maybe sixty miles an hour—one car, two cars, three loaded cars did a free fall on top of Albert, killing him instantly. Chip was the one who found him. Billy and Boomer helped dig. They found half of Albert. About half. Then they looked around for the rest. They wrapped what they found in blankets and drug it on out.

UP AT THE JOY SPOT, where the strippers were said to strip anytime, even nine o'clock in the morning if you wanted them to, a bunch of the E rotation guys were putting back a truly outstanding quantity of Coors Light while inviting me to consider the positive side of a coal miner's life. We sat engulfed by the blare of Metallica on the jukebox, beneath a sign advertising the day's featured shot: Jäger bombs, $4.50. On the positive side of coal mining, they said, there was the weather. Seriously, year-round, a steady average of 55 degrees underground. No rain. They sang the praises of working for Hopedale Mining, believing themselves to be the envy of area coal miners because of the five-and-three schedule (five days on, three days off; some mines are as high as six and one) and because it's a nonunion mine, meaning a lot less crap to deal with. The guys thought their pay, an average of $21.15 an hour for face rate, was excellent.

Sparky: "The paycheck is the reason we're there."

Hook: "You get your check and first thing is, I'll go straight down to Dillonvale. We got seven bars in one mile. Ain't nothing but opportunity right there."

Kevin: "Usually, I'll just buy twelve beers, and I'll go ride around and look at deer. I take my wife, my kid, hell, we usually see about seventy, eighty deer a night. It's all dirt roads; I ain't never passed a cop yet."

Rick: "Jackass, how many DUIs have you had?"

Kevin: "Two. But it wasn't looking for deer; it was for doing stupid shit, like doing burnouts in front of the bar and fucking going to the city drunk at three in the morning. Stupid shit. I don't do that now. I stick to dirt roads."

Sparky: "We're applauding."

Duke: "What does this have to do with mining coal? Tell her the good parts of mining coal."

Hook: "Okay, here's what it is: Everybody is there for the same reason. You mine coal, you get money, you go home."

Duke: "That's what it is. It's simple. Coal is your goal."

They ordered another round. They talked coal. They talked about how Rick, who runs the miner machine, was in charge. He wasn't the boss, but he was in charge and everyone knew it. Whoever runs the miner machine runs the show.

Duke: "He's got one priority, and that's penetrating. That's your job if you're on that miner. You're penetrating. And if you've got three shitbag buggy runners behind you loading off you and you gotta wait for them, you're not penetrating. And if you got shitbag bolters supposed to bolt these cuts behind you, then it's even worse. Then if you got a scoop man that cries all the time, it's real bad."

Sparky: "It's the dependency you have on each other. That's what it is."

Hook: "That's it."

They talked coal, ordered another round. They wondered why they just talk coal all the time.

Kevin: "If you're down there, you're trying to make everything all right for the next guy. Like, Pap brings me a sandwich every day, a bull coon sandwich. It's Amish salami or Amish ham. A lot of the guys bring extra food in case you get trapped. I always eat everything I bring, but Pap has something left. A bull coon sandwich. But come after lunchtime, Pap knows I'm ready to kill him. I tell him, 'You old fucking bastard.' You know. Everybody gets along in the beginning of the day. But anything after lunch, you're ready to fucking kill."

Hook: "If anybody wants to kill you, Kev, it's because you just busted something again."

Kevin: "That ain't true."

Sparky: "It's true."

Kevin: "Will you tell me, Rick, do I not do my job to the best of my ability?"

Rick: "No, you're a good scoop man. You scoop good."

Kevin: "Am I not the best scoop man you have ever had?"

Rick: "I told you, you scoop good."

Kevin: "See? I don't care what you mechanics think. If a machine is meant to fucking break and it's gonna break, well, guess what? You're looking at the fucking guy that's gonna break it. That's the way I've been my whole life."

Duke: "My priority is, I produce. When I worked the miner machine that's what I cared about. I produce. I don't care what the fuck else is going on or where anybody is, I produce."

Kevin: "But see, I do. I care. I do care. I care because *that* man cares. And *that* man cares. That man wants it rock-dusted, you bet your fucking ass if I got the opportunity and I can scoop it and rock-dust it, then I will scoop it and rock-dust it."

Hook: "It's the same as any family, bottom line."

Duke: "Bottom line. Because these fuckholes, every one that goes down there each and every day, depends on the next fuckhole. Bottom line."

Rick: "Bottom line is, he loves him and he loves him and he loves him and he loves him just like I love him."

Kevin: "You might hate them, but you love them."

Sparky: "Bottom line."

Hook: "That's it right there."

Kevin: "I'll tell you what I do a fucking good job at. I keep the fucking deadbeat fucking mechanics off their asses."

Rick: "A little rough there, Kevin, a little rough."

Kevin was not, in my estimation, any rougher than any of the others, but the deeper we got into drunkspeak, man love and man hate and bottom lines and fuckholes, Kevin was the one singled out. Rick slipped him a note. "I will not say the *f* word," it read. He told Kevin to put it in his pocket.

Kevin: "I have a four-year-old kid I don't say it in front of."

Rick: "All right. Well, you got a lady here."

Kevin: "I'm sorry."

Rick: "All right."

Kevin: "Now you think I'm a shitbag."

Rick: "No, I don't."

Kevin: "I know, Rick. I ain't good now, huh? You gave me a compliment and now you're taking it back."

Rick: "I'm not taking it back."

Kevin wanted to go home. Sparky said he'd drive him to his place, where he could just go ahead and pass out. Kevin refused. It was nearly midnight, and the guys had to be back at the mine by six.

Kevin: "I got a wife and a kid to get home to. I got two DUIs, and I'm a shitbag."

Sparky: "Seriously, you'll stay at my place. I'll even pack your lunch for tomorrow."

Kevin: "I got to go home with my family. That's why I'm going home, because I'm a shitbag."

With that, he took off. No one said much. No one even felt like bothering with the strippers.

Rick: "I thought we were gonna tell her the good parts about coal mining."

Hook: "We more or less covered most of it, wouldn't you say?"

EVERYONE I TALKED TO in the coal mine had a reason for being there that had nothing to do with coal, even if the reason was beer. Coal was currency, just as it is for the coal consumer, only in the case of the coal miner it is literally so. Coal is a good provider, but coal isn't free. Coal is dirty and dangerous—for the coal miner getting it out of the ground and for the planet burning it. Same deal. No kidding, no fooling, nothing subtle, nothing virtual. Coal doesn't play with you. The thing you can say about coal is, coal is honest.

"They say if you truly find a job you love, then you'll never work a day in your life," Foot told me, and he wasn't talking about coal mining. Fifty-two head of beef cattle, a brand-new Massey

Ferguson 390 tractor, a Krone KR 125 baler, and a Case IH 995 tractor with a loader on it—that's why he mined coal: to afford his farms, two of them, 280 acres in all. He was hoping to buy a third, because he had three kids and it only seemed right to leave each kid a farm. "There ain't nothing I like more than to smell that fresh-cut hay, throw that hay, rake that hay," he said. Sometimes neighbors offer to help him; they'll say, 'You work down in that mine all night and then you're out on that damn farm.' And I just tell them, 'If I was sitting here on the bank with a fishing pole in my hand, fishing, would you come to take it out of my hand?' 'Well, no.' And I say, 'Well, this is my fishing.' You know. This is my fishing."

I heard that kind of story over and over again. Only a few of the coal miners I met *didn't* own at least a hundred acres of Ohio farmland, chunks passed through the generations, added to, divided among brothers and sisters. Farming doesn't pay the bills, so you go into the coal mines. The deep, rich, plentiful mines of the Appalachia region are what have helped keep so many family farms east of the Mississippi intact for over a century.

If there was a threat to this natural order, it began over thirty years ago, when coal suffered its first serious reputation problem. The federal Clean Air Act of 1970 and its amendments in 1977 and 1990 placed stringent controls on the sulfur dioxide emissions from burned coal. Acid rain was the thing. Power plants were forced to turn to more expensive but cleaner-burning natural gas, while the industry flirted with nuclear technology.

Coal? Suddenly, you could hardly give away the stuff they mined in the East, the medium-sulfur bituminous coal of the Pittsburgh Number 8 seam and the similar-grade stuff of the 6A seam, where

I hung out with the E rotation guys in Cadiz. That coal burned dirty. Power companies turned to the far less efficient but cleaner coal out west, where very large-scale strip mines became coal's new cash crop. Mines throughout Pennsylvania, Ohio, Kentucky, and West Virginia closed as the industry in Appalachia went into a free fall.

Cadiz felt the punch. It was 1980, and Cadiz, home to what was once the largest shovel in America—the Silver Spade, twelve stories high, capable of scooping 315,000 pounds of earth in a single bite—struggled with its very identity. Even the coal festival held every summer, the Coal Queen pageant, the coal-shoveling contest, the heavy-mining-equipment parade—even that became a sour joke. They stopped calling it the Coal Festival. They changed the name to Heritage Days.

Guys scrambled for work, left town. Foot moved to Connecticut to manage two Wendy's fast-food restaurants—him in one, his wife, Jackie, in the other. It was ridiculous. It was like putting a buffalo in some kind of hat boutique or something. The suburbs were nice but oppressive. "You go to work, come home, and what do you do?" he said to me. No square bales to haul, no manure spreader to repair, no wandering steer to chase home under the light of the moon. *"How many movies can you go to?"* He lasted a year. Him and Jackie came back from Connecticut with their tails between their legs, moved in with her mom, who, at that time, owned the farm. The farm. That was all that mattered.

So when the eastern mines started reopening in the late 1990s, it seemed like God Himself was answering prayers. The mines reopened because the power plants had figured out how to burn that gloriously efficient dirty coal and wash the emissions, meeting EPA standards. They're still reopening today, at a fierce rate, thanks to "clean-coal technology," a controversial term if you talk to environmentalists who aren't buying the sudden image change. Scientists are figuring out how to convert coal into liquid fuel to power cars and jets. The country is in a decidedly passionate mood to let go of its dependency on foreign oil. This is America, and this is *our* fossil fuel. Freedom fuel! Coal.

For Scotty, the mine was a way of funding his boxing career, such as it was. It wasn't so much that Scott "the Rock" Tullius lost that fight to Todd Manning at Fight Night XV; it was that he was so widely expected to win, and not just in his own murderous heart, but even by the way the promoters were promoting it. On the radio. Talk shows. Scotty saying into the microphone, yeah, heck yeah, he was back, he took a year's hiatus but he was back. He took the hiatus on account of his hand getting crushed in the mine, smashed on the bolter. But it healed up. And he got back into fighting shape, eating nothing but raw eggs and chicken and water for weeks, no pop, no iced tea, nothing—and there you are, working in a coal mine. Hardly ideal conditions for an athlete. But he was back, and he had always wanted to fight Manning, and he was seriously worried about killing the poor bastard.

So it wasn't just that he lost. Worst of all—way worse than his mouth guard getting knocked clear out of his mouth in the second round, worse even than his eardrum getting busted in the third—worst of all was that the ref called the fight in the fifth. Called it. Now, Scotty had fought over a hundred fights and never had a fight called. Scott the Rock had started competing at sixteen, had amassed a 92–17 record, and there he was, thirty-one years old, down on one knee in the fifth when the ref called it. The place went nuts. “He got back up!” “He wasn’t down!” He had fans in the audience throwing their T-shirts into the ring, everyone screaming, and then there was Scotty’s mother up there chewing out the ref for calling that fight he should not have called. “He got back up!” “He wasn’t down!” And then out comes the championship belt, that belt was worth over $600, that belt is what you fight all your life for, and there was Todd Manning wearing it. It was bad. It was so ugly. Just . . . ugly.

The guys from the mine who were there saw Scotty getting whupped, and you can be sure he heard about it two days later when he showed up for work, all bruised and with a busted eardrum, and having to go back down five hundred feet under and run that buggy. The guys were, like, *Oh, Scotty thought there were four guys punching him in that ring; oh, Scotty got his ass kicked.* It was bad. It was ugly. It might have been the low point of his life, all around.

He decided it was over. He was going to retire from the ring. Hang up his gloves.

“Yeah, I’m done,” he told me. “I’m never gonna be a world champion. That’s what I always wanted to be, and I’m never gonna get there. I’m not. You know. I’m just . . . not.”

He didn’t look sad. Or he was the happiest sad man I’d ever met. It’s possible that Scotty had lived a previous life as a golden retriever, a tail-wagging pal who keeps coming back around no matter how mean you are to him.

“Boxing has given me a lot,” he said. We were at his house in a remote area of Wheeling, West Virginia, up a hill, where there’s nothing but woods out back, and so you can go on out and target-practice on pumpkins whenever you feel like it. His wife, Eddie, had a *Playboy* T-shirt stretched tight over her pregnant belly. She was about due. She was a boxer too. They had met at a fight.

"Boxing gave me a family," he said. "And I was close. Real close to going somewhere and getting the world title. But what are you gonna do? You're not good enough to make a living at it, so you gotta work."

He smiled, laughed into the air. "Jeez!"

He said anyway he was amassing a fortune. He laid out the numbers. The house needed work but was about paid off. Him and Eddie drove old cars. Between his job and hers at the plastics factory, they brought home $100,000 a year, most of which went straight to the bank. The plan was to work, save, and—as soon as they had enough cash on hand—quit. Retire. "We want to live our life. That's what our plans are."

I asked him what his life would look like once he started living it. He couldn't think of anything besides boxing, which was sort of where he had started out in the first place and what got him into this situation, so he didn't know.

The main thing was, he didn't want to be sixty years old working in a coal mine. He didn't want to be an old man like Pap, down there bolting every day. Nobody wanted to be Pap. Everyone spoke of Pap with respect, even kindness, but also with a certain amount of horror. The ghost of a future that was to be avoided.

"One day I was boltin', me and Pap, the roof was real bad," he said. "And all of a sudden it started sprinkling all around us, and it just come in behind us. About buried us alive. We was goin',

'Ptuh, ptuh.' We thought we was dead. I mean, we should have been dead. But we weren't."

He laughed. "*Ptuh, ptuh!* Aw, that was *bad!*"

I asked him if he thought that putting himself in such dangerous conditions upped the odds that he would die young—that he might, that is, never make it to retirement.

"You can't think like that," he said. "It's the chance you take. You don't think like that. I mean, sometimes you think about it, you know, you go, *Man!* Huh. Sometimes you do. But you get used to it. You get brave. You really do. I'm serious. You get brave."

He asked me if I wanted a drink of water or something like that. I said no, I was good. He asked me if I wanted to watch something on the big-screen TV, said maybe later we could watch tapes of some of his fights.

"Now, a buddy of mine, Robby Dutton, he's dead," he said. "We were pretty good friends. And we was on the same crew. And the miner machine, there was something wrong with it, a hose was leaking, and they were turning it and a bit got caught and come down and mangled his leg. We had to drag him outta there on a stretcher, all bleedin' *bad*. Aw, he was . . . we thought he was gonna die. Huh. But he didn't die."

"I thought you said he's dead," I said.

"Yeah. He come back like a year and a half later to the mine and he was having a hard time. Then, Memorial Day weekend. On his Harley. He was riding down the interstate and a woman was screamin' at her kid and pulled out, started screamin' at her kid, *POW!* Smothered him all over his Harley.

"Huh. *Pow!* Can you believe that?"

WITH THE OBVIOUS EXCEPTION of combat soldiers, I'd never been around people who knew so many dead people.

Pap's son was dead. Got smashed by a coal truck in 1993. Pap told me this with no break in his voice or release of his gaze. "It was quick," he said. "Oh, he never knew what hit him."

Death was a shame, a crying shame. Other than that, as a subject it wasn't near as interesting as Smitty's mail-order woman—who did not, by the way, arrive on schedule. There was a lot of chatter about this.

"She didn't show up?"

"She was sick. She couldn't board the plane."

"The way I heard it, there was a flu epidemic and they wouldn't let any planes out."

"Out of Russia?"

"That's the way I heard it—or maybe just the town she was in."

"It's her turn to come over, and everybody's got the flu and they can't come over? I think I would check into that. That would have been on the news somewhere."

"He said she was coming later."

"He already paid for her plane ticket?"

"That's the way I heard it."

"Aw, Smitty."

Pap was good friends with Smitty, thought of him as a kind soul. I rode with Pap in his pickup, through his hayfields. He was the only coal miner I met who had actual positive words to say about coal mining. Then again, Pap was a man of very, very many words, so this might have been a matter of odds. He was compact, rosy-cheeked, and his teeth were worn from left to right onward down a hill. "I come home from work," he said. "And I don't complain, 'Oh, John made me mad,' or 'Bob made me mad.' Like I tell my mom: 'The gloopies were there.' My mom, she knows. She always called them gloopies. Crazy coal miners. So I tell her, 'The gloopies were there,' and that's it."

As we drove around, it wasn't the gorgeous views he pointed out, the patchwork of hills rolling into the horizon, but instead various piles of rocks. Sometimes, he said, all you want to do is go out and pile up rocks. It's relaxing. It makes you feel good to know the hayfields are clear, to know your baler won't get banged up. He told me his wife used to help him on the farm, but ever since she got that job up at Sam's Club, she's too busy. Now *that*, he said, was a stupid job. "All them people do is eat," he said, blaming retail sales for Nancy's weight gain. Now, instead of just "the old bag I live with," he had started calling her Moo.

I asked him why he still worked in the mine, doing one of the hardest jobs.

"Oh, I don't know," he said. He talked about being "Little Frankie" in high school, only five feet tall, making the varsity football team. He said he was always very athletic. He was always a good worker. That started even earlier, in grade school, Father Coleman pulling him out, almost every day, just him and Dickie Angelo got pulled out every day after Mass to go on down and clean up the old cemetery. Tombstones were falling in, and it was all unlevel. So him and Dickie would wheelbarrow dirt in, smooth it out. Someone had to do it, and those boys were strong, good workers. Good workers. He worked instead of going to school, a choice decided for him by his church.

"I've always been a good worker," he said. "Me and Dickie were goats."

You work. If you're healthy, you work. You don't quit work until something bad happens, which is your sign to move on. Pap's own belligerent father sanctioned this pattern. "He got covered up two days after I got hired," he told me. "I took my physical on a Wednesday, I started on a Thursday, and Friday morning he got covered up. The boss working with him never made it. Crushed him. He was standing there, a guy knocked a post out, and the whole place tumbled. Killed the boss dead. Oh, they had to get jacks to get the stuff off my dad. Broke both his pelvises. He had pins in his pelvises, but it was the best thing that ever happened to my dad. He quit drinking after that, which was always his worst problem."

We drove past a doghouse that had *Buttercup* written on it. Buttercup, a yellow Lab, was a pup out of his son's dog's litter. "Ol' Buttercup," he said, tooting his horn.

"You want to go on up and meet my mom now?" he asked. She was eighty-seven, hadn't been sleeping well, but lately she had started eating a little bit. She lived in the original house, at the top of the hill, where Pap's grandparents had lived and died. There was pride in this: dying on the farm.

He rolled down his window, said it felt like spring was coming.

When we got to his mom's house, there were about twenty cats snaking on and around the porch. Inside was a small kitchen with a thin curtain leading to the living room where his mom was, in a hospital bed in front of a TV. She was tiny, swallowed up by that bed. On the opposite wall ticktocked a clock that had family members' pictures instead of numbers. She lit up when she saw him enter. He called her Bubba and spoke to her in Polish. When they switched to English, they talked about cabbage. The whole backyard used to be cabbage, and that's what the kids did: cut it, trampled it, put it in big barrels, and then it would foam up. They'd take the foam off every day, and when it quit foaming, you got your sauerkraut. "In the wintertime, that's what we ate about seventy percent of the time," he said. "Sauerkraut's what we ate. Isn't that right, Bubba?"

She closed her eyes, fell sound asleep.

"Okay, Bubba," he said. "Okay."

She was dying in that room. Of course she was. And there was nothing shameful, or odd, or worrisome about it.

I stood in the room with Pap and his mom, wondering what to say, where to look, and how it would be to live a life so coolly close to death.

ONE OF THE THINGS that happened was, way after I was finished researching coal mines, I kept going down into the coal mine. Explain that. I couldn't seem to quit. A couple of more hours down, a couple more, a full ten-hour shift. Friends would leave me voice mail: "You're not down in that coal mine again, are you?" My husband, despite being the recipient of many gifts, would call and say, "Okay, come on home now." My children missed me, and my mother was sick of this particular prayer added to her daily prayer ritual.

I had no explanation as to why I kept going back, other than that I was fooling myself into believing that I needed to go one more time. "It gets in your blood after a while, I think," Scotty said to me once. "You know what I mean? After a while, it kinda sticks with you a little bit."

Foot said, "Isn't it about time you got back to your life? I can't take babysitting you anymore."

"Yeah, okay," I said, pointing my light at his chin. I told him I wanted to leave, but I didn't want to leave. I started to go all *Wizard of Oz* on him. "I think I'm going to miss you most of all, Scarecrow," I said.

"Oh, Christ almighty."

I asked him if he wouldn't feel just a little bit nostalgic for the Cadiz portal, which first opened in the 1970s and would be closing soon, nearly all of the coal gone. By summer the E rotation guys would all be over in the company's other mine, in Hopedale. "You don't think it's kind of sad to say good-bye to this place?"

"Uh," he said. "No."

We were sitting at the power center, up on section, the place where they park all the generators and batteries running the equipment and the place where the microwave is and the couch. It was about 8:00 p.m., and some of the guys were taking dinner breaks, Rick with a Philly steak and cheese, cupcakes, Slim Jims. Chris had steak and a baked potato. Billy had homemade beef jerky. Foot was having chicken Alfredo, a Pepsi, and a Rice Krispies treat. The guys were, of course, covered in coal dust, their hands mostly black, but Billy said it wasn't like eating in *dirt* dirt. "It's *clean* dirt," he said. "It's just coal."

Hook, chewing Copenhagen, wanted to know if anyone thought Rod Stewart was gay.

No one did.

"Mick Jagger, he could go either way."

"He messed around with that what's-her-face all his life. Aw, come on. Help me out here. What's her name? That blonde? I'm narrowing it down here, ain't I?"

"Bianca!"

"No, that might have been their kid."

"Bianco, isn't that that black girl dancing around?"

"No, that's Beyoncé."

"We're not really doing too good here, are we?"

"Hey, I got the latest scoop on Smitty's woman. He said she got to be asking too many questions, so he told her to go fuck herself."

"What about the flu epidemic?"

"She wanted more money for a flu vaccine."

"Oh, man."

"He sent her $1,800 for the flight over. She does that to two or three guys a month, holy hell, she's making a good living."

"He's window-shopping again. He told me he's shopping again."

"Sooner or later, you gotta trust somebody."

They talked about killing coyotes. You make a cry like a wounded animal and you can call them in, shoot 'em dead.

They talked about Freddie Mercury wearing assless chaps.

They talked about why Smitty uses a spoon to eat grapes.

They talked about it being Billy's turn to relieve Pap on the bolter so Pap has a chance to eat.

Billy stood, ready for duty. "Okay, give me something to think about," he said, before heading out. He was a man who needed to keep his mind occupied while running equipment, to keep himself from going mad.

They thought about what to offer up to Billy's mind.

"Okay, I got one," Hook said. "If everyone is going to Wang Chung tonight, and everyone is going to have fun tonight, what is everyone doing?"

No one felt they could top that one.

Scotty came over, sat next to me. He told me his wife had had a baby boy. He told me how happy he was, holding his son. "It was just like looking at a little *me*," he said. He named him King.

At about midnight, Foot drove me out in our own private mantrip, him slouched down as he steered, me leaning on my side, trying to find the one spot of my hip best able to cushion the bumpy ride. We went rattling through the darkness, and I guess he could see me shivering. The drive out was always cold because you were moving into the wind, into all the fresh air whooshing through the mine. Foot grabbed somebody's jacket lying behind him, offered it to me. I cuddled under that sooty thing and thanked him. "Yeah, okay," he said. "I don't know why you never listened to me and brought a damn jacket in." He said he was glad our time was up so he could get back to his normal life, just dealing with the state inspectors he had to drag through the mine four and five days a week. I flipped my light on for one last look at the coal seam all frosted white, moving the light around with my head, drawing with that light on the walls.

Oftentimes, but only on the drive out of the mine, Foot got to philosophizing. This time he mused on how it was a man became a good man. Not that he was calling himself a good man, but he felt more and more that he'd been leaning in the direction.

"You're away from your kids," he said. "You work all kinds of crazy hours. Now, what happens when you work those kinda hours?"

I wasn't sure where he was going, so I didn't answer.

"What happens is you come home and your kids say they love you. Now, they're not saying that because they *know* you. They're saying that because of what their mom instilled in them kids. She's instilled in them kids that this is a good man."

"I guess so," I said.

"Because my kids didn't know me. You know what I mean? I wasn't there. So, why do my kids think so much of their dad? It's because of what their mom has instilled in them. Now, my portion of that is that everything she says about me, I have to make it more or less be true. That's my portion of the equation.

"Do you see? Do you know what I mean? If I'm a good man, it's because of the people I got around me expecting *good* out of me."

"Yeah, okay," I said, considering the theory.

"Down here, this kind of shit kicks in," he said.

HECHO EN AMÉRICA

Migrant Labor Camp
Cherryfield, Maine

Pedro awoke suddenly in the middle of the night, his eyes on fire. Out of nowhere, sharp, blazing pain. He sat up, rubbed his face, kept trying to unglue his eyes. He reached for his dad or his brother, fumbling frantically in the darkness of the damp tent. "Daddy! Juan! Daddy!"

Juan is Pedro's twin. They are exact replicas: slim, brown, shy, equally oblivious to the powers of their teen-idol good looks—the kind of twins who can survive by bamboozling people, taking tests for each other, talking to girls for each other. Juan felt Pedro's panic as if it were his own. He grabbed a flashlight. "Daddy!" he hollered, waking his father, who reached into the light and pried open one of Pedro's eyes. It was yellow, the eyeball hidden beneath a thick curtain of pus. "I can't see!" Pedro screamed. "Daddy, I can't see."

There are systems in place, of course: family doctors, pharmacies, and twenty-four-hour urgent-care centers in strip malls across America. But a lot of those amenities are not immediately within reach if you're a migrant worker living out of your car.

You're in a camp, beside some ready rows of broccoli or some bulging sweet potatoes under the stars, nothing but you and the full-throttle crickets—and maybe you should have put a plan in place for your kid suddenly waking up blind, but you didn't. You just didn't.

Up here, in Maine, the blueberry scent lay like a fog over carpets of balsam, and the mosquitoes were fat and in charge. Sixty-some people lived in the camp, at the end of a dirt road called Blueberry Circle, a deceptively quaint name for a place like this: a ramshackle settlement under a canopy of firs, laundry hanging from the trees, overturned buckets for chairs. Everyone said it wasn't half bad. First of all, it was free: if growers want the good rakers, they have to provide housing. There were two outdoor showers, two flush toilets, and electricity for lights, radios, TVs, anything you wanted. The cabins were plywood, weather-beaten and bowed, painted in cheerful, fading hues of red, green, gray, and brown, and fitted with bunk beds. If you got here too late to claim a bunk, you pitched a tent. The season would start whenever the blueberries decided, usually at the end of July, and last about four weeks.

Pedro and his father and his brother sat in the tent wondering what to do. It was nearly 4:00 a.m. and Consuelo, on the other side of camp, would be up soon to start the biscuits and the soup. Urbano, a compact, worn-out version of his sons, told his boys to stay in the tent, to be quiet and wait. They shouldn't disturb anyone's sleep. That was how he taught his boys. Keep a low profile. Don't ever make a scene. Not even if someone robs your tent; just hide your money better next time. If the family in the cabin next door is drunk and dancing and fighting and you can't sleep, put earplugs in. If the rain comes and soaks your bedroll, get up and sleep in the car.

Surely someone in Consuelo's huge clan—thirteen people crammed into two cabins—would know what to do for Pedro. So Urbano hushed his son, wrapped his arms around him, and rocked him even though, at fourteen, Pedro was way too old for something like that. "Shshshsh," Urbano said, swaying back and forth, his mind soon rolling with the thoughts that can rattle like loose cargo in the back of his head. He was a man who had awakened to a thousand mornings of bad news, but these, he knew, had only made him stronger. He had acquired wisdom. He had made peace with a sky filled with untold storms. And he understood how the world was divided: kings over here, peasants over there. Kings live in palaces and want berries on their cornflakes; peasants need the money so they work the fields. And you? You were born king or you were born peasant, and that got decided long before you fell out of your mama's womb, so don't bother worrying about it. Say your prayers, be thankful for what you've got, and hang a crucifix from your rearview mirror so Jesus will protect your family from the *chupacabras,* the goat suckers, and other spirits lurking in the woods.

Wash the apple before you bite into it, because that's the way you were raised. Germs, pesticides, dirt, worm-related matter, gunk, it doesn't matter: Just wash it. The fingerprints, too, go down the drain with the rest of the apple's history. The fingerprints are one of those aspects of American life that escape everyday thought: the fact that there are people, actual people, who pick our food. Sometimes, maybe, we are reminded of the seasons and the sun and the way of the apple tree, and if we multiply that by millions of apple trees, times millions of tomato plants, times all the other fruits and vegetables, we realize, holy potato chips, that's a lot of picking. Without one million people on the ground, on ladders, in bushes—armies of pickers swooping in like bees—all the tilling, planting, and fertilizing of America's $144 billion horticultural production is for naught. The fruit falls to the ground and rots.

There are machines, of course. Machines harvest corn, wheat, soy, barley, and plenty of crops that lie like luxurious carpets under a reliable sun. But machines can't climb trees, or tiptoe through forests, or reach delicately into caves; machines can't decide which orange is ready, which pepper is green enough, which peach has the proper fuzz, which mushroom has the wow factor. So much of the fresh produce in our supermarkets, as well as the fruits and vegetables floating in our canned goods and sitting stiff in bags in our freezers, so much of it is the result of judgment, reason, and other human gifts, to say nothing of muscle and sweat.

Most of the people who pick our food have brown skin. They come from Mexico and Central American nations and they lead nomadic lives, following the ripening crops northward in one of three streams. The western stream begins in Southern California and hugs the coast to Washington state, with a branch heading northeast from central California to North Dakota. The mid-western stream begins in southern Texas and divides off through every midwestern state. The eastern stream originates around

Fort Pierce, Florida, where workers pick oranges and strawberries in January, then move on to peaches and pecans and lettuce in Georgia, tobacco in Tennessee, New Jersey tomatoes and cucumbers, before arriving in Maine in late July for the blueberry harvest. After Maine, many from the eastern stream move on to New York and Pennsylvania for the apple harvests. Then it's a long trip down 1-95 to Florida for sugarcane, squash, and snap beans, and the cycle repeats.

These migrant workers blanket the entire country—not just the southern border states we tend to associate them with—and yet to most of us they are strangers so removed from our lives we hardly know they're here, people hunched over baskets in the flat distance as we drive down vacation highways. We don't run into them at the mall or the corner café. Rarely do we strike up a conversation at a bar with a person who introduces him- or herself as a person who harvests anything. We don't pal around with them on our college campuses and they are not invited to be pundits on TV.

Civilizations have for centuries worked hard to shield citizens from the world's unsightly infrastructure—the sewers and slaughterhouses and boiler rooms—and so it's easy to forget that there is anything going on behind the curtain at all. What we don't know can't hurt us.

More than 50 percent of the migrant farmworker population is in the U.S. illegally—the one piece of the story Americans hear quite a lot about, and are increasingly bothered by, or are urged to be. On TV and talk radio and especially during election years, we're told we must work together to stop this national crisis. These people are robbing our homes and trafficking drugs and raping our children right there in our JCPenney dressing rooms. The bad guys make headlines, as bad guys will, and the rest, we're told, are a more insidious blight: taking American jobs, giving birth to bastard "anchor babies" in what Pat Buchanan once called "the greatest invasion in human history." These people are here illegally, the reasoning goes, and are therefore lawbreakers; lawbreakers should be rounded up and jailed. (And surely America can pick its own stupid fruit.) Whether we buy into the heated rhetoric or not, one thing has been made clear: Immigration is a problem reaching a breaking point, and something must be done.

Except there really is no invasion, no growing national crisis. In fact, current statistics show that immigration from Mexico has actually gone down—and steeply so—over the past decade. (An estimated 80,000 unauthorized migrants crossed the Mexican border into the United States in 2010, down from 500,000 in 2000.) More to the point: There is nothing new about this story. Importing foreign labor has always been the American way, beginning with 4 million slaves from Africa. Later came the Jews and Poles, the Hungarians, Italians, and Irish, to work the mills and mines and factories—everything you learned in sixth-grade social studies about the great American melting pot. And with each group came a new wave of anti-immigrant, pro-Anglo rage—sometimes followed by outright expulsion. China was the first to fill the agricultural labor hole in California in the mid-1850s. Nearly 200,000 Chinese immigrants were legally contracted to cultivate fields there—until the Chinese Exclusion Act was created in 1882, thanks to the efforts of California's "Supreme Order of Caucasians." The "yellow peril" was shipped home. Japanese workers replaced the Chinese for a time, until the Immigration Act of 1924, which banned immigration from East Asia entirely. Meantime, the railroad between Mexico and the U.S. opened in the late 1880s, and the floodgates of a new labor force were opened. The U.S. Border Patrol was created in 1924 to control the flow, and the term "illegal alien" was born.

Our current debate over how to control the southern border is really just a rehashed version of a very old one cycling over the reach of history. It's a lively conversation about fairness and purity, about who belongs and who does not, and as a result, the people who pick our food are shamed into the shadows, nameless, mostly afraid, and certainly inconvenient to the experience of the satisfying first crunch and explosion of sugar that happens when we discover that, oh yes, this apple is awesome.

HUMBERTO WAS AWAKE even before Consuelo at the camp at the end of Blueberry Circle. He cleaned the kitchen in exchange for food. It was a special arrangement. (Meals usually went for about $6, depending on Consuelo's mood.) At sixty-three, Humberto was the oldest raker at the camp. He was a gentle man, unfailingly kind, and people whispered about him. He slept in an orange pup tent away from the rest, under a birch tree with branches perfect for hanging socks. He appeared sickly, wrinkled, his thin frame bent like scrap metal. People whispered he must be a homosexual, and he must have AIDS, and he must be contagious. This is a transient life where nobody really knows anybody unless they're family, so fear is always running things.

Humberto was finished sweeping when Consuelo breezed in, all hustle and purpose, firing up the oven and the grill. The kitchen was a plywood cabin slightly larger than the others, thick with unmoving heat on the outer edge of camp. It was for everyone at the camp to use, but few felt like cooking, and Consuelo had learned to capitalize on that fact years ago, back when she and her husband first started coming up here to rake.

It was about 4:30 a.m. when Urbano came into the kitchen with Juan and a stumbling Pedro, who could not see.

"Help," Urbano said, his face and neck wet with sweat.

"He needs a hospital!" Humberto shouted when he saw the boy's swollen eyes. He himself had no idea where the hospital was; he was, after all, a hitchhiking man.

"Where is the hospital?" Urbano pleaded to Consuelo, who had become engrossed as if in a complicated text on the folds of dough beneath her fists. She was a round woman who wore the constant smile of someone intent on avoiding all conflict, opinion, and consequence. Three of her four kids had come with her into the kitchen, and the baby was crying, while the nine-year-old was trying to give him his bottle, and the ten-year-old was cracking eggs, and the sun wasn't due up for two hours.

"Call that man," Consuelo offered, pointing to a business card taped to the wall. Soon her husband, Naud, wandered in, and his brother, Noel, still drunk from the night before. More kids, and Noel's woman, Tammy, with the bored, faraway look, and Tammy's daughter with the tattoos, and the daughter's boyfriend with the long dreads pulled up high in a ponytail. *Coffee. Was the coffee ready?* In a half hour the rakers would start lining their cars up to convoy out to the fields, and nobody had time for these two punk teenagers and their dad standing in the kitchen—*what did they want?*

Urbano gave up. He took the card off the wall and left. In truth, he was afraid of that whole gigantic Consuelo clan; he thought of them like the Mafia of the camp. You had to play by their rules, put up with their blaring music and with Mimi, their creepy Chihuahua, and with that nameless freak of a pit bull. That kitchen was supposed to be for *everyone* to use. A lot of the people in the camp appreciated Consuelo's sweet breads, her tamales, and especially her chicken mole, but Urbano and his boys knew how to cook for themselves, and they would have appreciated some use of the kitchen. They didn't come all the way up to Maine to *spend* money.

"Maybe this man knows where a hospital is," Urbano said to his sons, studying the business card.

The contact information was for Juan Perez-Febles, a beefy guy with a jet-black goatee who often came around handing out his card and telling people to call him if they had any trouble. Most people tossed the card as soon as he turned away. Could be some slimy lawyer drumming up business or a spy from Immigration. One thing you learn quick in this line of work is to trust no one.

Juan took the phone from his dad, as a fourteen-year-old will do, and dialed the number, while the three got into their car to go find a hospital. The phone rang into voice mail. "Can you help us?" Juan asked. "My brother is blind."

At the top of Blueberry Circle there's another camp, a better one, where the cabins have indoor plumbing and the workers stay on past the harvest. It's for the higher class of laborers, "the company Hispanics," those who have better skills—tractor experience, pesticide knowhow—or better luck and work an hourly wage instead of by the piece. One of the guys saw the car lights coming up the hill. He stepped out of his cabin to see who was leaving so unusually early. Urbano pulled over, and the man, who introduced himself as Luis, leaned into the car to see what was up. "Holy shit!" he said when he saw Pedro's oozing eyes, which really was the only humane response. "Wait here." He ran back to his cabin, where he grabbed his wallet and shoes, and jumped in the car, then took the terrified family to the hospital in Machias, twenty-five miles away.

Meantime, Perez-Febles was holding his phone, wondering who the caller was. The ring had awakened him, but he hadn't reached it in time, and the child who left the voice mail offered no name, the caller ID UNKNOWN. So a boy in one of the camps needed help? Was blind? Forty-five blueberry companies. Thousands of workers to oversee and protect. Perez-Febles dressed quickly, set out on his rounds, and felt a flash of the hopelessness that had a way of following him like a ghost.

"VACATIONLAND," THE LICENSE PLATE SAYS. Blueberries are one of Maine's largest crops, covering sixty thousand acres, and they're a symbol every bit as important as the lobster to the image of Maine as a happy, vital place. Maine is the largest producer of wild blueberries in the world. The woody plants occur naturally in the sandy gravel understory of Maine's coastal forests, where little else bothers even trying to grow. The plants thrive here because they have no real competition, and because of mycorrhiza, the symbiotic relationship between the blueberry plants and a fungus that regularly clings to their roots. It's a beneficial fungus, allowing the plants to extract nutrients from the otherwise lousy soil. In winter, the deep Maine snow acts as a blanket insulating the dormant plants. In spring, the melting snow provides all the water that greening perennials need. In summer, the large rocks tangled in the soil hold the heat that allows the berries to ripen. In fall, storms produce lightning that touches the earth, igniting whole fields, a perfect pruning. Wild blueberries have been surviving here for centuries like this, a vigorous conspiracy of nature.

As blueberries go, the wild variety ("lowbush") are the rock stars. The cultivated kind ("highbush") can be planted anywhere, and grow in huge fields in places like New Jersey and Michigan. You're as likely to find either topping your cereal. Sometimes you've got these big, fat berries bobbing in your milk, and other times you'll have tiny bold nuggets on your spoon. Do a taste test someday. The cultivated ones are watery and mealy compared with the tiny wild ones—intense bursts of candy-like fruit. Once you notice the difference, you will never buy the fat ones again.

The workers at the camp at the end of Blueberry Circle where Consuelo cooked, and Humberto pitched his tent, and Urbano and his sons slept, raked for Cherryfield Foods, the largest blueberry producer in the state and widely regarded as fair and accommodating. This was a world apart from the citrus groves of Florida or the vegetable fields of Georgia and the Carolinas, where working conditions have made shocking headlines since the late 1990s. Farmers in southern states have been prosecuted for modern-day slavery: holding migrant workers in debt and chaining them inside box trucks.

Maine, at least in recent years, has earned the opposite reputation. Farmers are known as honorable, and any migrant worth his callused hands finds a way to get here for blueberry season. The money is excellent and the locals don't treat you like shit. Something about Maine—poor, tucked up north out of the way, with that ragged, rocky coast of dramatic mood swings—something about this place is easier on misfits.

The question of legal status lingered in the sticky August air during my time in the camp, always present, like mosquitoes that kept biting no matter how many times you slapped your legs. All of the migrants who worked for Cherryfield Foods were legal in that they had passed E-Verify, the federally mandated screening test that runs your Social Security number and is supposed to tell whether or not it's legit. Companies face enormous fines if they hire workers who don't pass, and so it is nothing to take lightly.

And yet, at other camps around the state, migrants who spoke on the condition of (absurdly redundant) anonymity proudly let me see the Social Security cards they bought on the streets of Boston for $100 a pop. Fake green cards and driver's licenses, and a few showed me their "insurance"—paperwork for multiple identifications, just in case the first ones didn't work.

"And these pass E-Verify?" I asked.

"E-Verify is a joke," they said. "Everyone pretends."

False papers might be easy to come by, but the workers I spoke to said that getting into the United States was more difficult than ever. In 2010, President Obama signed a $600 million border-security bill into law, which included a thousand new Border Patrol agents, more Immigration and Customs Enforcement agents, updated communications equipment, and unmanned surveillance drones.

I heard dramatic tales of hiking for weeks across the Sonoran

Desert with skinny donkeys hauling bags of rehydration solution, and people paying thousands of dollars to "coyotes" to sneak them over the border. Crossing had become so difficult, in fact, that you couldn't go back and forth to see your family like you used to. Once in, you stayed, for years, not months, because you knew returning to the United States would be treacherous or impossible. Five years, six, maybe seven. You wired the money home until there was enough for a house or whatever you needed, and only then could you return to your family. To the people I talked to, a tighter border control was mostly a matter of a prolonged homesickness.

PEREZ-FEBLES WAS RAISED to salute the American flag and never look back. He grew up in Cuba, was sent by his parents to the home of friends in Pittsburgh when he was sixteen, and went on to embody an American mythology that is beginning to sound quaint if not downright Disney: a proud national narrative of a country of immigrants who come here and lift themselves up with hard work.

Having put himself through both college and graduate school, Perez-Febles was teaching high school Spanish when he learned of a job in Maine to work with the immigrant community he understood so well. This was back in the mid-nineties, on the heels of the state's infamous DeCoster Egg Farms scandal: the largest producer of brown eggs in the U.S. was deemed an agricultural sweatshop, the poster child of migrant-worker abuses. An OSHA investigation had revealed videos of workers cleaning manure with their hands and raw sewage bubbling from bathtubs and sinks.

Back then, Maine was known as one of the worst places in America for migrant-labor conditions, and as the new state monitor advocate, Perez-Febles was charged with reforming it. He documented violations all over the state, spent three years investigating a broccoli farm where he videotaped himself standing in an open pit of human waste. His work helped enact legislation to curb labor violations, and he became a regular in the blueberry barrens and camps. He set up the Rakers' Center next to the Columbia town hall during raking season, a gathering place with free services: donated canned goods and clothes, an education office, legal advice, and a migrant-health program that dispatches mobile units to the barrens. His efforts were hailed among labor advocates, who now hold up Maine as an example of a state that does the right thing.

As for the migrants themselves, the workers I spoke to rarely mentioned the services, or if they did, it was not their reason for coming to Maine. The reason was money.

Blueberries have always fetched the highest pay of any crop on the eastern stream. They're like the bonus round at the end of a pinball game: all of a sudden the points really start adding up. A good raker with a strong rhythm averages one hundred boxes a day. At $2.25 a box, it's not uncommon to see a weekly check for $1,350. Compare that with just $375 a week picking Georgia peaches, or $400 down in the orange groves of Florida.

Washington County, occupying the far eastern tip of the state, is where the majority of the blueberry barrens are located, and it has 12.2 percent unemployment, the highest in the state. And yet the money does not draw the local unemployed into the fields—an inexplicable dimension to the new American dream repeated nationwide. Raking is hard, backbreaking, and the sun is hot.

Just a generation ago, the harvest was a community effort. A ritual that brought all the locals out to the barrens. The blueberries were ripe! They had to be picked! There was so little time! You could make decent cash, help your farmer friends, have a good time gossiping with your neighbors, and shame the teenagers caught kissing behind the birch trees. Afterward you'd celebrate a successful harvest in town at the blueberry festival, compete for best jam, pie, candle, or soap.

The locals no longer do the raking, but the blueberry festivals still happen all over Maine, and the townspeople still celebrate, and the tourists still come.

The migrant workers I spoke to were well aware of the disconnect: they labored to support a culture they had virtually no part in, for people who had no part in theirs.

"Now, you see everyone here is brown," said Noel, Consuelo's brother-in-law, one morning in the barrens. He was a pretty man with a wide brow and long locks of wavy black hair, and he was cracking open a beer under a blazing sunrise. "When I first came here in 1998, there were white people raking blueberries. None now. White people got lazy and let the Spanish take over." There was still a chill in the air, but his shirt was off and he was sweating, having already combed ten boxes of blueberries from the endless green and purple brush. "White people are lazy. White people won't travel an hour or two away to work. Spanish will travel. Spanish didn't fight to take over. White people dropped their rakes and Spanish picked them up."

OUT IN THE FIELDS north of Pea Ridge Road, a tall truckload of fresh empties crept out of the horizon, and the workers sprinted like urgent bargain shoppers toward it. Yellow, green, blue, white plastic boxes identical in size, and so they stacked, Lego-style, ten, fifteen at a time. Lift the stack on your shoulder and run. You wanted as many empties as you could carry so you could be sure to have enough to fill as you raked. Your kids, those who were at least twelve, raked alongside you, pouring what they got into your boxes. Your kids, those under twelve, hid in the car, scratching their mosquito bites, waiting until nobody from the company was around, before they started raking. The company has zero tolerance about letting underage kids work, because there are laws in America. But your kids wanted to rake, and your family needed the money, so what was the problem?

Consuelo's husband, Naud, had claimed the far western edge of the barren, all of the family spread out in consecutive rows that had been marked off with twine by Pat, the crew chief, and the only white person here. You wanted the rows that lay flat and were free of rocks, not the valleys or hillsides or the gnarly, weedy spots. One of the ways to claim a spot in the barren was to park your truck and open all the windows and crank the stereo. Most of the music was Latin pop or traditional Mexican folk, the bass held tight and full by the moist air that smelled aggressively sweet.

A blueberry rake is a rectangular bucket of tines, a giant upturned fork, with a handle that can be short, long, or longer. Everyone had his own rake, many handmade to fit the body God gave you to rake with. A swipe with a rake is roughly the same motion as shoveling snow, but you do it faster, your arms swinging, the rake swooshing as it captures dozens of berries at a time. It takes about ten minutes of raking to fill a box; then you carry it to the road, put a piece of masking tape with your name on it, and start on the next empty. No one messes with another man's boxes, his rake, or even his masking tape: that was the code. Treated fairly, you didn't have to push and shove or cheat. This wasn't like Florida or Georgia, where half the time you pissed in your pants because they didn't allow bathroom breaks. This was fair: Rake as much as your body could take, stop when you needed to.

Cristo, a nine-year-old-boy, sat in the dirt alone in the barrens, watching the grown-ups compete for empties. His mom was here somewhere, and so was his dad. "We drove in the truck twelve hours from Florida, where we work lettuce," he said. "Me and my parents and my sister and my four brothers." He was a round boy dressed in a sweatshirt decorated with a Christmas wreath and a teddy bear, his head shaved bald on account of the heat. He said he had many responsibilities, but mostly his job was to take care of Dina, his seven-month-old baby sister. "She's back at the camp with my little brother now," he said. "We take turns." Cristo was in charge of rocking Dina at night if she cried, and if she got too loud, sometimes he would take her outside in the moonlight and climb with her into the hammock his father had strung between two white pines. There was not a lot to do back at camp. Sometimes he and his brothers played freeze tag or had water-pistol wars with some boys from Peru. "I would rather come to the barrens each day," he said. "My dad said I can rake, but if I get caught he will pretend he doesn't know me." One week Cristo made $120. He gave $100 of it to his mom, and the rest he took with him on a beer run with his dad to Milbridge, where he bought "memories" to take to his cousins in Florida: a deck of cards that said "Maine," a key chain with a lobster on it, and a little pillow that smelled of balsam. "When I grow up, I plan to become an engineer," he said. "Or a scientist, or a truck driver through the lettuce fields—but I will be frightened because sometimes you have to go through water."

Pat was ordering the grown-ups to go here and there with the empties, and Cristo had nothing to do but wait for the coast to be clear, so he rocked on his heels and held his rake like a guitar and pretended to be a Latin pop star, singing along with Romeo Santos crooning into the fog.

The sugary blueberry smell came out with a rhythmic punch as the brush was continually jostled, and the *shush, shush, shush* of the rakes was roughly in time with the thumping beat coming from the trucks. You could see necklaces swinging as the workers raked, glints of silver and gold catching the sun. The rocky fields fell into dips and deeper hollows, stretching into the horizon that moved past blood red and on to yellows and blues.

No one this morning talked about where Urbano and his boys were; it was likely no one even knew their names or noticed that they were gone. Except Humberto, the skinny man who cleaned the kitchen, who told the crew chief about the boy who'd shown up with the messed-up eyes. Otherwise it was business as usual: empties, rakes, masking tape, *shush, shush, shush*. There was no talk, for that matter, of life outside the barrens, of Cristo's school in Florida starting next week, of getting home to sign up for soccer or band. There was no talk of making it home in time for anything, no talk of the next crop, the next job, the next day, or even the tropical storm barreling up the East Coast, headed right here. Time in the barrens had no measure beyond the movement of the sun that warmed your back, then scorched it, then mercifully began letting go.

Noel needed a Monster Energy drink and so did Naud, and Consuelo wasn't here yet with the lunch truck. Cristo's mom, a wide woman with a high ponytail, came charging up to yell at him for wandering off, and then she bitched to no one in particular about her swollen ankles. "Are you talking to these men?" she said to Cristo, about Naud and Noel, who in truth presented no threat. "No, Mama, I'm not." She had found Cristo making new friends in the camp the night before, talking to guys who spoke ugly Spanish, a Spanish from some other part of the world, and she told him if any of them touched him she'd get a knife from the kitchen and stab them dead.

"No. Mama, no one touched me."

HUMBERTO WAS TAKING A BREAK, sitting on an upturned box, wearing a thin green T-shirt and jeans caked in purple. His way was to rake a few boxes, break, rake a few boxes. He simply didn't have the strength of the younger men and women. "Me, I'm slow," he said. His face was weathered as a fisherman's and he was unshaven. "Twenty, thirty, forty boxes a day. I never got to fifty, not once. That's what I wonder: how they get to a hundred. You're supposed to make so many boxes per hour, but I never do. But they keep letting me work. I don't know why. That's what I wonder too. The company is very nice to me."

He turned his rake upside down, began picking out weeds that had become entangled in the tines. He felt as welcome here as he did anywhere. Home for Humberto was not a place so much as a season. He knew nothing of the rhythms of a man who stayed somewhere after a harvest. He didn't have an address or a car or a telephone.

"That's my friend over there," he said, gesturing toward a group clearing a ravine. "The big one. And the other one. They look alike. I forget their names. I met them here. The lady in the kitchen is my friend too. She saves me my tent every year. That's how I have it every year: she brings it back for me. I bring my sleeping bag. My pillow. My toothbrush. The mattress I get from one of the cabins. I put my laundry on the trees. There's a basin. I have a new pair of boots. I have a shaving kit. I have some more things in Portland, where I have a locker. I have a radio. It goes off at four o'clock and it wakes me. If it's raining and we can't rake, I sit in my tent and listen to it."

Everything Humberto needed to know, he learned more than a half century ago from his father and his mother, whom he harvested alongside in the tomato fields in Mexico and then cabbage and spinach in Texas. When he got older, he found himself on the eastern stream. A friend of a friend. One day you're here and the next you are there. "I don't care if I stay in one place," he said. "I find some work. If I have the work, it's good. I keep busy. I don't stop."

His rake was clear and so he stood up, his body so thin it might have made a crackling sound. He felt his age. He couldn't haul stacks of empties on his shoulder like he used to. He carried his rake respectfully (not dragging it like the kids did) to the next row, which he then scanned and considered before entering. His boots were purple. Like a lot of people, he said he liked harvesting blueberries better than any crop. "Some camps you go to are better and some are worse," he said. "Georgia peaches are hard work, bad people. In New Jersey, there's a nursery I like. I go to Pennsylvania to work in the mushrooms. I come to Maine every year I can get a ride.

"I don't care if I stay in one place. I find some work. If I have the work, it's good. I keep busy. I don't stop. In Milbridge I catch the bus. Ellsworth. To Bangor. From there to Southbend. West Perry. I don't know if they're going to hire me or not in Geneva. That's what I wonder. I'll go to New York and look. Cabbage, onions, they have everything in New York.

"I was sick last year, so I skipped blueberries. The pain is coming in my chest; I was having heartburn and everything. Got to keep going. Keep going. Never stop! That's what I told myself. In Portland they give free medicine, injections, they have a clinic. I get all the medicine I need for a long time there."

Humberto began swiping the brush, bending over the earth with confidence and knowledge. "Also, I have a bank account," he said. "The bank is not around here. I have to travel to it. Somebody will give me a ride or I'll catch the bus. In the meantime I hide my money in the woods. I have many safe places."

It was hard to talk and rake at the same time. He could get only so many thoughts out before his breath gave out. After his rake was full, he poured the berries into a yellow box and then he ran his fingers gently over them, smoothing them.

The berries would go to Machias after that, in Pat's truck along with all the other berries, to a processing plant where they would be sent through the IQF freezer, then a laser scanner to sort them for size, then bagged and sent to supermarkets across the country and around the world.

"Lunchay! Lunchay!" some of the men in the barrens began shouting. Consuelo was rounding the bend in a white pickup packed with the day's offering—$4 for a tamale, $1 for a Monster Energy drink, $2 for a beer, $3 for scrambled eggs and sweet peppers in a cup—and the workers dropped their rakes and ran toward it. When Naud appeared, the line parted, and Consuelo served her husband first.

IT WAS MUCH LATER IN THE DAY, the sun beginning its surrender, when Perez-Febles finally tracked down the boy who had called about his brother being blind. He was making his rounds in the barrens when he lucked out and ran into Pat, who confirmed that a man in his crew had reported seeing such a boy. Pedro and Juan and Urbano were already back at their tent by the time Perez-Febles pulled up in his enormous black pickup. "Is this the boy?" he asked, hopping out. "Is he okay?"

Pinkeye, stupid pinkeye, a bad case of bacterial conjunctivitis. A complete nonissue for a kid with access to simple antibiotics; terrifying blindness for a kid without. Pedro got the medicine after the doctor pried his eyes open, assuring the family he would see again.

Perez-Febles apologized for not making it to the phone in time. He told them about the mobile medical units, about the Rakers'

Center, about all the free stuff available to them, and they thanked him, kept quiet, and did not complain. To them he appeared every bit as intimidating as the Mafia family—just one more person whose power they did not trust.

"Can I get something for you?" Perez-Febles said. "Can I bring you some food?" He was a hefty man, impeccably groomed, wearing jeans and the kind of dressy short-sleeve shirt that brings to mind cigars and nightclubs in Havana.

"We have plenty of food," Juan lied. "We are all set." He was leaning against their car, a dark green Passat. Urbano stood next to him, a shield protecting Pedro sitting inside.

"The rains are coming," Perez-Febles said. "You need a dry place, no?"

"We're all set."

"They are saying one more day of raking before the rains," Perez-Febles told them. "You should have a good day tomorrow."

"Thank you," Urbano said. "Okay, thank you."

In fact, Urbano wouldn't return to the fields until Pedro could see again. Urbano would not leave his boys alone at the camp—just no.

The family spent the next day waiting for Pedro's eyes to clear. The day after that, Pedro could see again, but the rains came down—a total washout. They went up to the other camp at the top of Blueberry Circle to see Luis, the man who'd helped them find the hospital and who was by now a friend. There was a TV in the kitchen, and so they watched movies. The next day, the same. The violent tip of the storm was wreaking havoc along the whole coast of New England. Four days straight of none of them raking meant no money coming in, a loss of at least $2,000. It was a problem. Urbano needed the money urgently.

He was forty-five years old, and it seemed as if everything he had worked so hard for was slipping away. He'd fled a life of poverty in Mexico as a teenager, eventually settling in North Carolina. This was back in the 1980s, when it was not unheard-of to get a green card legitimately. Urbano had *figured out* America, even if he'd never quite mastered the language. In the burgeoning South, he got steady work in construction, a bank account, a mortgage, and while his marriage didn't work out, he had good kids, smart-enough kids who never bothered anybody. He had never fallen behind in his house payments, not once, but then last year he got word that his dad had died back in Mexico, and so he went home to bury him.

"They shot my daddy," he said, sitting in the driver's seat of his car to stay dry while the rain beat violently down. He told the story without expression, his arm resting on the steering wheel, his gaze set uselessly on the windshield where a fly buzzed and bounced. "Somebody. A gun. Crazy people. The killer said he got confused—he wanted to kill somebody else. I said, 'Why confused? Because my daddy is an old guy. Is the other guy old?' He said, 'Yeah, I made a mistake.'"

The boys were up at the other camp with Luis. Urbano was down here by the tent, wondering if there was anything in there he should save from the rising water. The camp, so loud with dancing and drinking and gambling just a few days ago, had been transformed by the rain into a soggy, still sadness. Even the nameless pit bull was nowhere to be seen.

"When I went to Mexico to bury my daddy, I was on a bus," Urbano said. "This is a big problem: they know migrants from America are on the bus. Trucks came in the way. People with guns stopped the bus. 'All people get off the bus!' A gang. Necklaces. Rings. Forced it off. A lot of blood. Seven thousand dollars cash they got off me. It was all the money I had."

And so he ended up stuck in Mexico, penniless, with a father to grieve and to bury. "This was a big problem. I washed the cars. Cleared the fields for corn. It took a long time. Three months I was gone until I had enough money for the funeral and the trip back home."

He presented an exhausted smile, took a breath. "So when I finally got home to North Carolina, the mortgage man said I was behind. Every month behind while I was gone. I needed to make money fast. I knew about Maine. I worked there sometime before my sons were born. It's hard, fast money. I got in the car to come, and my son, he said, 'Hey, Daddy, I go with you to help work for the money,' and my other son, too: 'Hey, Daddy, what happen if you lost the house?' A lot of years working for the house. A lot of years. This is the point: maybe I can keep it. Maybe. I don't have the money yet. The mortgage man said he needed it all together or else he's putting the house for sale. My sons say, 'No, Daddy, we won't let it happen.'"

Pedro and Juan had never raked before; they knew nothing of a migrant's life. To them it felt like a duty but also an adventure. They would help their dad save the house, and then they would make more money for themselves. They would buy a motorcycle and give rides to girls.

Now, with four straight days of no raking and with blueberry season coming to an end, Urbano was losing hope of ever paying the mortgage man, and nobody talked about motorcycles or girls anymore.

In the car, Urbano swatted at the fly but missed. Suddenly he remembered Slim Jims: he had some Slim Jims in a ziplock bag in the tent. He dashed into the rain to retrieve them, then drove back up to the boys at the other camp. They were in the kitchen watching *The Price Is Right* with some ladies from town in skinny jeans and high heels fanning themselves from the sticky, wet heat.

When they saw their father, they marched up to him, excited. "We can stay here after blueberries and work other jobs," Juan told him. In the kitchen, the boys had learned about people staying in Maine into winter to work in the sea cucumber factories; it was a famously disgusting, slimy job that had a way of appealing to a fourteen-year-old. It was the end of summer, and the idea of going back to school was hitting them like a brick in the face.

Urbano listened and mostly heard foolishness. He knew his boys would soon start to miss home, their friends, the American teenager life he had built for them. He knew they longed to try out for football and go to the movies and kick back at the mall. They weren't rough-and-tumble migrant kids. They were gentle young men who probably didn't even understand about the prostitutes in the room.

"You have to go to school," Urbano said to his sons. "You can live with your mother."

"You think you're protecting us," Pedro said. "But really, it's the total *opposite,* Dad."

Some of the men in the kitchen laughed and made back-to-school jokes, but the boys did not want an audience for this conversation, so they fell silent.

"You have to go to school," Urbano said. "I make the decisions."

Perez-Febles was carrying cans of kidney beans and applesauce to his truck in the parking lot of the Rakers' Center, and he was getting worked up. He grabbed hold of two sacks of rice and heaved them into the back of the truck and then began driving toward Allen's farm. He knew this work was important—passing out food and medical supplies and information on legal services—but nothing was nearly as vital as the work he did translating. "I have to promise them: no *chupacabras*," he said. "*Chupacabra* is a devil in the woods, a mythical animal that sucks blood. Rapes lambs. It's evil-looking, like a coyote. A lot of the people who come here are afraid of the woods. Scared to death, some of them.

"We need a program for us to understand them as well as the reverse," he said. His brow sweat easily and his eyes scanned constantly, like a man of secrets. "All the cultural things. I don't even know where to begin. We refrigerate everything here. They're, like, 'What?' They don't have refrigerators back home, or if they do, the electricity is spotty. Then the employer gets fined because the employees leave food out. They don't know. They don't know to flush. They don't have plumbing. Flies. I have to put signs: *Please flush*. It's the little things. It's a whole cultural thing, you know.

"When I first came, there were a lot of problems," he said. "Women was one problem. Drinking another. Fights. Drinking and driving. Horrific. They had no idea about that. I tell them they'll be put in jail. It's a totally new way for them to think.

Speeding. Domestic violence. I try to educate them on the way we live. I say, 'People have rights here, and there is recourse with the law.' It's all new to them. And I tell them about DWM—driving while Mexican. I tell them that they will get stopped. They don't understand this law, and I tell them it's not a law; it's hard to explain." He sighed often, as if overwhelmed by the amount of information to convey, and when we passed Wyman's camp, a spick-and-span settlement of blue bunkhouses, he craned his neck to see if anyone was using the migrant soccer field.

"The average education for a migrant worker is fourth grade," he said. "A person in Mexico makes maybe $500 per year. And here in one month you can easily make $2,000. It's not comparable.

"Labor, labor, labor is everything.

"My premise is no human being is illegal," he said. "I call them undocumented workers or documented workers. It's a silent world. Truly an underground society. There are not enough documented workers to fill the needs—not nearly enough. America is dependent on its undocumented workers, and yet they live in fear and hiding." He rattled off immigration facts and figures the way another man would talk box scores. He said migrants pay into Social Security—money they'll never collect because their IDs are fake. "That's billions of dollars for the Treasury Department to keep. That's the other issue. It's really a good deal for the U.S. in many ways.

"I helped investigate a murder at a camp years ago. An axe opened the guy up. I wanted his widow in Mexico to get his money. He had seven hundred dollars, and I wanted to find her. We found seven IDs on him. We could not even identify the victim."

SHORTLY AFTER THE STORM PASSED, the sun returned, steam rose from the earth, and moods shifted dramatically. "You dump these buckets and I will get the sheets," Urbano was saying to Juan and Pedro. He was holding an empty laundry basket, standing in the cabin at the top of Blueberry Circle that had become the family's new home. Perez-Febles had continued to visit Urbano and his boys, and in time they began to trust him. The trust changed everything. Perez-Febles helped Urbano get a job with Cherryfield Foods. He could stay on and clean the fields, work the pesticides, become one of the "company Hispanics," like Luis. The job paid $9.50 an hour, and it would mean a chance to save the house in North Carolina.

The boys had just finished scrubbing the walls, mopping the floors, scouring the place with Pine-Sol so it smelled hospital clean. This cabin was bigger than anything down at the other camp, and it was just a few years old, solid, whitewashed, built to last. Right next door was the cabin that held the kitchen and the TV and bathrooms—with *indoor* plumbing—and the laundry room, where Urbano went to retrieve the sheets that were spun clean and dry. He pulled the linens from the dryer, savored the powdery smell and the warmth. He took the time to fold them corner to corner and then carried them back into the cabin, where the boys had each claimed a top bunk. Urbano thought about how many nights his boys had spent in the soggy tent and then the car, and something about the smell of the Pine-Sol and the sweetness of the clean fabric, just all of it combined, hit him and filled him with the kind of happiness that flows in bursts when a man feels any significant hope.

Another person might not have looked at a camp in the woods with indoor plumbing and felt overwhelmed with good fortune. But for Urbano it was like his luck was a weather vane that had been stuck for the longest time and then God sent a tropical storm to give it a mighty shove.

Juan and Pedro did not entirely share in their father's elation. Urbano had agreed to allow the boys to stay with him, but then he came up with the stupid idea of signing them up for school. The bus to Narraguagus High would pick them up at the top of Blueberry Circle. Both boys hated everything about the new school. They hated the name. Who could even pronounce it? They hated that it didn't have a football team. They hated that their dream of making money working with slimy fish and buying a motorcycle wasn't happening—the whole heroic adventure of staying in Maine to save their father from financial ruin was interrupted by the dull clamp of reality.

"We will play hooky every day," Juan said.

"We're not kidding, Dad," Pedro said. "We are not going."

Urbano paid them no mind and told them to get in the car, and then they all drove to the Walmart in Ellsworth to buy three-ring binders and paper and pencils so that everything would be ready for their first day. Pedro sat in the front, sucking a green lollipop, and Juan was in the back with his ball cap jammed low. He was wearing a T-shirt splattered with the signatures from last year's eighth-grade graduation—*I love ya, Juan! Shawna hearts ya! Ron was here!*—a history that now seemed like somebody else's. They were migrant kids now. "Loser kids," Pedro said to Juan. Under his ball cap, Juan was wondering if any kids up here even skateboarded. He wondered if Pedro was right: that the white kids were assholes to the migrants. He would fight for his family's honor if he had to. If he had to. His thoughts grew sour as fear solidified, and the towns along Route 182 rolled by the window. Most of them were tiny and quaint. They had pots of petunias hanging and American flags flapping and banners strung lamppost to lamppost advertising the blueberry festival in nearby Machias: a blueberry musical, a blueberry parade, a blueberry quilt exhibit, a tour of an actual working blueberry farm with a free shuttle.

G-L-O-R-Y

Paul Brown Stadium
Cincinnati, Ohio

Right now Adrienne might be sick. It isn't funny. It isn't her stomach so much as her nerves, her heart, her history. Rhonée, one of her closest cheerleader friends, has her eyes bugged out, standing outside the stall door, *"Adrienne? Adrienne, are you okay?"*

"I'm good," Adrienne is saying. "No, I'm good. I'm good."

She vomits. This is not good. Something is seriously wrong with Adrienne. At pregame practice in the gym an hour ago, she ran out crying—twice. Ran to the bathroom and slammed her fist into the stall door to get ahold of herself, to reclaim herself, to remember who she is: a Ben-Gal. Both times she returned to the gym with a smile, got in formation, front row, left center. "C-I-N!" she roared, "C-I-N! N-A-T-I! LET'S GO!"

She seemed *fine*. She seemed *Adrienne* again, five-feet-nine, a Thoroughbred of a woman, broad shoulders, booming voice, the biceps and forearms of a sailor. She is not the drama queen of the squad, not even close, not one of the girlie-girls with the super-yummy cleavages and the wee, wee waists and the sugary smiles.

She is the iron-willed, no-nonsense, no-curls straight shooter of the squad: six-pack abs, forlorn eyes, too busy with her own too-busy life to deal with a lot of crap.

"Is Adrienne okay?" shouts Shannon from the other end of the locker room. Shannon is perhaps best known for her extreme volume of sandy blond hair.

"What happened?" asks Shannon's very best friend and protégée, the demure Sarah.

"Is something wrong?" asks another as news of Adrienne's nausea filters through the din of cheerleader chatter.

Cheerleaders are all over the place, half naked, shrieking, sitting, squatting, kneeling in front of mirrors in the panic of an NFL Thursday night. National television! The game starts in just over an hour. This is crunch time, hair spray time, false eyelash time, Revlon Orange Flip lipstick time. *"WOULD SOMEBODY PLEASE HELP ME? I CANNOT FIND MY MULTIPLICITY ESCALATE VOLUME WHIP!"* Some cheerleaders are in curlers the size of Budweiser cans. The locker room, reserved just for them, is hardly equipped for the machinery of glamour, and so most have brought their own full-length mirrors, power strips, extension cords, suitcases of makeup, curling irons, hose. *"Try my Bouncy Spray Curl Activator. You can totally glop it on."* The cheerleaders are all scream and shout, jazzed with beauty adrenaline, in thongs and hose and push-up bras, stretching, bopping, bouncing, assisting one another with hair extensions, pasting over tattoos, spraying tans, announcing newly discovered cleavage-engineering solutions—"Duct tape, girls!"—hooting and hollering in a primpfest worthy of Miss Universe.

"We look so awesome."

"Oh my God, we do!"

Perhaps, fittingly, there is a big storm coming, right now a cold front dumping rain and snow on Chicago, moving swiftly east, headed exactly for Cincinnati, promising to turn a balmy 68-degree evening into instant winter in a way that no one anywhere near Paul Brown Stadium is prepared to believe. *Maybe the storm will be late? Maybe it will get . . . delayed?* Charlotte, the mother superior of the Ben-Gals, the one responsible for all the rules—all the line formations, all the dances, all the praise, all the punishments, all the outfits—has to make a difficult decision: teeny-weeny skirts with white go-go boots and halter tops, or catsuits that hardly provide any better winter cover. The gals vote: catsuits. *"Please! Please! Please!"* They love the catsuits. There is nothing sexier than the catsuits.

"Is Adrienne *okay*?"

"Did you hear she is throwing up?"

"Oh my God!"

Now, the men outside. The men are just super. Oh, the men think this whole thing is about them. That is so cute. That is enough to make any Ben-Gal roll her head to one side and get teary with admiration. *That is so sweet!*

Hello, men. Meet the cheerleaders. There are a lot of them. At first they are hard to tell apart in the same way kittens playing with a ball of yarn in a basket are hard to tell apart. Every single one of them you want to pick up and stroke and pinch and poke and take home. How can you *choose*? And what if you did take one home? Think it through. Where would you put the cheerleader? What would you feed it? Would you have time to play with it? Play with it in the way it longs to be played with? Yeah, that is one luscious volume of girl flesh.

The cheerleader is a fantasy. Let it go.

It. The cheerleader is an it. Are you aware that you have been thinking of this person as an *it*? Does that make you a pig? Nah. Or no more so than the next person, but that's not even the point. This is about the cheerleader. She is not trying to get your attention so much as she knows she has it. God, you're easy. You are not the reason she has been up since five working on her hair, spraying on her tan, squishing her breasts together and forcing them upward into a double-mushroom formation with the assistance of all manner of wired undergarments. Of course, you play a role in it. Of course. When you catch a glimpse. For barely a second on the TV. There on the sideline. Right after some blitz resulting in a crushing sack. She's there for you. Sharing your moment of glee. Bouncing up and down for you with her pom-poms, beckoning you to, yeah, pump-fake your way into her itty-bitty shorts.

Right. She knows you think this way, but there is more to the story: you are sorta beside the point. Oh, your weakness is *precious*.

This is good old-fashioned sex appeal. This is straight-up Marilyn Monroe pinup-girl shtick. Sexy-happy, happy-sexy. It's family-values sex appeal. Other than that, it has nothing to do with you.

This is America's entertainment, homegrown, full-on, nobody else has it. Football. Beefy men at war on the gridiron, pretty gals fretting on the sidelines. "De-fense!" Eighteen million people watch every NFL game, and well over 110 million tune in to the Super Bowl—our most watched television show every year. The NFL churns out $9 billion in annual revenue, and its thirty-two teams are valued at over $1 billion each. Taxpayers pour their own dollars into making sure football happens—ten of the nation's new $1 billion NFL stadiums are 100 percent government-financed, while another nineteen are at least 75 percent government-financed.

Within this gargantuan money machine stands the cheerleader. The one whose job it is to say, "Yay!" With all the cash floating around, people assume NFL cheerleaders are within some vague sniffing distance of the good life, but a Ben-Gal is paid seventy-five bucks per game. That is correct: seventy-five bucks for each of ten home games. The grand cash total per season does not keep most of them flush in hair spray, let alone gas money to and from practice.

The cheerleader is pure. The one actor in our most celebrated entertainment empire who gets nothing tangible in return. She is nationalism at the most basic level, every Sunday embodying the American contradiction. She parades around on our biggest national stage wearing the characteristics America loves about itself—loyal, devoted, confident, optimistic—and loathes: shallow, egocentric, materialistic, loud. She does not question her role and she does not stop smiling.

People assume a lot. People assume cheering in the NFL is also about a girl trying to snag herself a big hunk of a stinkin'-rich football player. That is not the case. The Ben-Gals are not even permitted to socialize with players, except at officially sanctioned appearances. This rule is strictly enforced. Zero tolerance. As for football itself, the game, the players, the stats, the formations—that stuff rarely rises to the level of actual conversation, because that is just background noise.

"We have a rule book that's, like, *this thick*," Charlotte will explain to any woman interested in becoming a Ben-Gal, stacking her hands four inches apart. "If you can demonstrate commitment and dedication and following-the-rules, you're good to go." It is not as easy as it sounds. Practices are Tuesdays and Thursdays at 7:00 p.m.—sharp—at which time a Ben-Gal must be in full uniform, full hair, full makeup, a state of readiness that can take two hours to achieve. She must then step on the scale. If she is more than three pounds over the target poundage assigned to her by Charlotte, she will have to attend the after-practice "fat camp," doing crunches and running laps for a half hour after everyone else is gone, and she may not be able to cheer in that week's game. There are many other reasons a cheerleader can get benched: If she misses a single mandatory practice, she will not cheer at that week's game. If she misses four practices, she's off the squad. She is permitted just two tardies per season. Within fifteen minutes, it's a tardy, but sixteen is a miss. Two tardies equal a miss. No excuse is greater than another. Death won't get you a free pass, unless it's your own.

Given all the rules and the lack of distinct perks, it is difficult to understand why so many beautiful young women would eagerly and longingly choose any of this.

Charlotte sees it as a gift. Charlotte sees herself as a fairy godmother with a magic wand under which only a few select gals earn the privilege of the wave. "My most precious thing I can do is take a person and give them the tools that the program offers and watch them grasp it and watch them mature," she says. "Now, not everyone does that. But you take a girl like Adrienne. I mean, she was . . . *whew!* She was kind of . . . alternate for a while. You know what I mean? And now, to watch her mature and develop into the program—she's a real special girl. She's had a hard life. She's the only single mom we have on the squad. Oh, I don't know why I'm talking about Adrienne. I mean she's not *Pro Bowl* yet. But still . . ."

Contrary to popular mythology, not all NFL cheerleaders are bimbos or strippers or bored pretty girls looking to get rich. The Ben-Gals offer proof. Neither a bimbo nor a stripper nor a bored pretty girl would survive the rigorous life of a Ben-Gal. The Ben-Gals all have jobs or school or both. Kat and Sarah are sales reps. Sunshine is a database administrator. Shannon works at a law firm. Tara is a cancer researcher working toward her Ph.D. Adrienne works construction, pouring cement.

MEET THE CHEERLEADER: RHONÉE

"This is my second year as a Ben-Gal. The first year, I commuted three hours from Liberty, Kentucky. That's how bad I wanted to cheer. I had never even heard of a switch leap before—where you do a leap and do splits and then switch legs? The first time I tried that, I felt like Peter Pan.

"I have a bachelor's in chemistry and a bachelor's in biology. I just finished my master's in public health with an emphasis in environmental health science. For two years, I worked on a project dealing with air quality within chemical-fume hoods. We came up with something called the smoke-particle-challenge method. I did monoclonal antibody research for BD Transduction Laboratories.

I worked for the U.S. government at the Center for Health Promotion and Preventative Medicine. We did soil sampling, water sampling, at military bases throughout Europe. That was the best job I ever had.

"When I first took my new job at PPD's global central labs, I didn't tell anybody I was a Ben-Gal.

"I met my boyfriend when I was fourteen. He was sixteen and I was fourteen. We took our time. We got engaged in 1998. He asked me to marry him in Paris, at the Eiffel Tower. I was, like, 'I'm melting!' That's been a long time ago. He's going to have to, you know, renew that. His job takes him to Chicago a lot, so I don't see him a whole lot.

"I don't feel thirty-two. I keep telling everybody you're only as old as you feel, and I don't feel thirty-two at all.

"For me the Ben-Gals is about fulfilling a dream. Not many people out there can say they're an NFL cheerleader. I have never been so proud to wear such an ugly color of lipstick.

"In Kentucky, cheerleading is big. But when a small-town girl tries out for NFL cheerleading and makes it, that's huge. I made the front page of our local newspaper. Last year I was Miss November in the Ben-Gals calendar. Everyone kept telling me they wanted a calendar. I didn't tell a lot of people I had them. Word of mouth, people asked. I ended up bringing over 350 calendars back to my hometown. This year I'm not a month, but I'm still in the calendar. You feel like a superstar. I had trouble doing the sexy look. They teach you how to do that, to look like you're mad at somebody. This year I don't look mad. Just like I'm halfway smiling. I'm wearing a Rudi Johnson youth-size small jersey that they cut up and made into a bathing suit. A youth size small.

"The Reindog Parade is this Saturday. There will be five hundred dogs dressed like reindeer. I have to be there at one. Judging begins no later than one thirty. The parade starts at two. I'll be walking in the parade with a reindog."

ADRIENNE COMES FLYING out of the stall. She is not done throwing up but refuses to continue. She will not give in to a day of senseless, stupid puking. She is Cheerleader of the Week! Okay, that news came days ago. So it's not *news* news, but tonight is the night, and so you could say reality is settling in. This is almost certainly at the center of the nausea Adrienne must conquer.

There are so many things that may or may not happen tonight. The storm may or may not come. The Bengals could score very many touchdowns. The Ravens could be called for holding or do an onsides-whatever kick. All kinds of . . . *football* things could or could not happen on this electrifying NFL Thursday night. But one thing is certain: Adrienne is going to be Cheerleader of the Week. She'll get her face on the JumboTron during the second quarter. Just her, dancing live, beside a sign listing her name and her hometown and her hobbies—in front of sixty thousand people in Paul Brown Stadium—for perhaps five or six or seven seconds.

Okay, listen. Adrienne poured the cement in Paul Brown Stadium. Way before she became a Ben-Gal. When she was just a regular person working under a hard hat in the freezing-cold wind blowing off the Ohio River. *She poured the forms.*

She does not feel worthy to be Cheerleader of the Week, and yet, at the same time, she does. (When in this life does *she* get a turn?) She is looking into the mirror, trying to get color into her cheeks. She is trying to get ahold of herself. *She is a Ben-Gal!* A good Ben-Gal. An obedient Ben-Gal. She stays in her target-weight zone, 144 to 147 pounds, higher than most because of her muscle, her height. She does not smoke. She does not chew gum. She has no visible tattoos or naughty piercings. She curls her hair when Charlotte or Mary tells her to curl it, sprays it when they say it needs to stand taller or wider, slaps on more makeup when they demand bigger glamour. She works as hard as any other Ben-Gal at becoming what the coaches call "the total package."

But Cheerleader of the Week? It is overwhelming.

"Come here," Rhonée tells her. "Look in this mirror. Isn't this a great mirror? It makes you look so skinny. It's an awesome esteem booster!"

"All right," says Adrienne.

"Oh, you look awesome," Shannon tells Adrienne.

"You *always* look awesome," Sarah tells her. "I wish I had your abs."

"I wish I had your boobs," Adrienne tells her.

"I wish I had your hair," Rhonée tells Shannon.

"*Everyone* wishes they had Shannon's hair," Sarah says.

"I wish I had your brains!" Shannon tells Rhonée.

"Oh, you girls are so awesome," Adrienne says.

Cheerleader of the Week. It is not something most people in the world ever get even close to being. For that matter, most people don't get close to being a regular Ben-Gal—just thirty per year, out of a field of a couple of hundred who try out. Chief among the characteristics required to make the squad—beyond raw dance talent, a degree of physical beauty, a soldier-like level of self-discipline—

is a specific consciousness. It is so obvious to those who have it, and yet so fleeting, if at all attainable, to others. Ask a person who does not have it why she wants to be a Ben-Gal and she will say things like "Because I love to cheer" or "I have cheered my whole life" or "For the camaraderie" or blah blah blah.

Now try this same question on a person who has within her the consciousness, the essence, of what it is to become a Ben-Gal.

"So, why do you want to be a Ben-Gal?"

She will look at you. She will look at you blankly, keeping her smile in place while her eyes tell the story: *What, are you from Transylvania or something?*

"Because it's a *Ben-Gal*," she will say, wondering politely and in her own generous way if you have perhaps suffered some brain injury at some point in your tragic life and if there is anything she can do to help make your world just a tiny bit brighter. Everyone, she thinks, wants to be a Ben-Gal. Pity the president of the United States, the queen of England, the winner of the Nobel Peace Prize, for not having the attributes necessary to become a Ben-Gal. It is difficult to accept that not everyone in this world has what it takes to become a Ben-Gal, and for those people, all she can do is pray.

That's what it takes to become a Ben-Gal. If a woman has any lesser sense of the glory, she will not make it.

Charlotte and her assistants, Mary and Traci, and the captain, Deanna, maintain and constantly feed the glorification. Each Tuesday at practice, they decide who will cheer that week and who will not. Six people per corner, four corners, twenty-four cheerleaders. Six get cut. It depends on weight, glamour-readiness, dance-preparedness, all the factors of the total package. Each Tuesday, as nonchalantly as possible, Charlotte reveals her choices for those who will cheer and those who will not, for those who have earned a coveted spot in the front of the formation and those who must go to the rear. "Sarah, you are in the back," Deanna will say, or "Shannon, I want you up front." *Nonchalantly.* Because it's stressful enough. It's devastating enough to be left out or put in the back, even though most girls sort of *know*, can sense, can see the signs in Charlotte's eyes or see the way Mary is whispering to Charlotte and nodding and pointing and wondering, *Who told Sunshine she could dye her hair that dark?!?!*

The choosing goes on all season. Everything is about the choosing. Whose picture will make the Ben-Gals calendar? Who will be Miss January? Who will make the front cover and who will make the back? These choices are revealed Academy Award–style at a special ceremony in September, with slide shows, at a restaurant, with families invited, and lots of hugs and lots of tears, celebration, consolation, grieving.

There is more choosing. There is the biggest honor of all: the Pro Bowl. One cheerleader per season per NFL squad is chosen to attend the Pro Bowl in Hawaii. All season long, the cheerleaders speculate about who will be chosen. Charlotte will tell no one until it is time; she is the decider. No one understands the total package better than she, herself a Ben-Gal from 1978 to 1989, a Pro Bowler, and a coach for thirteen years.

The choosing is the bait that keeps any Ben worth her Gal reaching toward her total-package goal. And each week there comes this choice: Cheerleader of the Week.

Who among the living would not vomit?

Now, THE MEN. The men are super-adorable. The game has not yet started, and some of the cheerleaders are glamour-ready, so they have left the locker room to sign calendars by the stadium gift shops. "Who-dey!" some of the men chant, soldiers coming to battle, stomping up stadium steps toward nachos, hot dogs, beer. "*Who*-dey!" The idiosyncratic growl is a Bengal original and all the more popular now that the team is actually semicompetitive. Marvin Lewis came as head coach in 2003, turned the team around, gave football back to a woefully depressed Cincinnati. From a cheerleader point of view, it's been super.

Who-dey!

The men are dressed in orange and black, some with striped faces, crazy wigs, naked bellies pouring over Bengals pajamas, furry tails hanging from their asses. Soon this platoon rounds a corner, comes upon a table behind which four cheerleaders sit. Daphne, Sunshine, Kat, Tiffany. Glimmery and shimmery kitty-cat babes signing calendars, $10 a pop. The men say OH MY GOD with their eyes, stop dead in their tracks.

"Who-dey!" the cheerleaders say, all sex and sweetness and growl.

The men suck in air, seem to have trouble releasing it. These gals are, well, *whoa*. These gals are—fuckin' A.

The cheerleaders give a thumbs-up. "Awesome outfits, guys!"

The men look at each other, at face paint, tails, fur. *Oh, sweet Jesus . . . we look like fucking idiots.*

"Who-dey!" the cheerleaders say.

The men dart away like roosters.

Outside in the parking lot, the men are more serious. Businessmen, banker types, tailgating, bonding. Somebody knew somebody and arranged for two cheerleaders—yeah, two real cheerleaders—to come to the tailgate party for two hundred bucks. Heh heh. *Where they at? Are they coming? Where they at?*

Holly (blond ringlets) and Stephanie (brunet innocence) arrive.

"Hi!" They have doe eyes and dewy smiles. They wear little string backpacks in which they carry pom-poms. They slip off their backpacks. They slip off their white satin Ben-Gals jackets. "Ooh, it's chilly!" Holly says, revealing her naked arms and abundant bosom. "Ooh, that storm is coming!"

"I've been looking at you girls on the Internet," one of the businessmen says.

"Dude," says his colleague. *"Dude."*

"I'm Holly," says Holly. "Nice to meet you. Thanks for having us."

"You want some beef barley soup?" one says to her. "Some kielbasy?"

"We have Chips Ahoy," says another.

"I'm good," says Holly.

"We're good," says Stephanie.

The conversation is not flowing. Just what *is* the purpose of this meeting?

The men give up trying to talk to the cheerleaders, turn to one another, laugh, grunt. Holly and Stephanie stand there smiling. Stephanie is shy, is a first-year, is taking lessons from Holly, who is also a first-year but who has so much more experience feeling gorgeous. "Would you guys like to learn a cheer?" Holly asks them.

"Uh, yeah."

"Come on, do it with us."

"Uh, no."

"Well, will you say it if we do it?"

"All right."

Of course, it starts to rain. The men dart under a tarp. Holly and Stephanie stay out in the rain, just a sprinkle, a trickle, a tickle, droplets for the cheeks.

"Let's go, Bengals—ooh, aah!" the cheerleaders chant. "Let's go, Bengals—ooh, aah!" They spin, throw their heads, offer ass. The men learn the words quickly. "Let's go, Bengals—ooh, aah!" The men hold up their beer cans, toast one another. Heh heh.

The cheerleaders finish and wave, taking their jackets and pom-poms with them.

"Well, that was worth it," says one of the men.

MEET THE CHEERLEADERS: SARAH AND SHANNON

Sarah: *"I work for Pepsi. I'm pretty much on call twenty-four/seven, so it's stressful. If somebody runs out of Mountain Dew and they're having a sale on it, they're calling me to get out there. I'm, like, I know, I know."*

Shannon: *"This apartment is two bedrooms, two baths. We met pretty much through Bath & Body Works in Lexington. We both went to the University of Kentucky."*

Sarah: *"I called Shannon 'Miss Hair.' I was, like, 'Do you know Miss Hair?' That was my first meeting of Shannon. We've been* *best friends ever since then. We're so laid-back. Nothing gets us really fired up too much."*

Shannon: *"I thought it would be awesome to be a Ben-Gal. You just put it way up here. You never really think you can get there."*

Sarah: *"We dared each other to try out. To be an NFL cheerleader, I think every girl dreams."*

Shannon: *"We use a great bra by Victoria's Secret. Body by Victoria Push-up Bra. We all had to get a bra that has a fixture that's real low. It's spandex and it's definitely tight, so it squishes and pulls. And then we have bronzing stuff to make it look more . . . You do it, like, right here in the V. It makes it look like there's a shadow, so it makes your chest look bigger."*

Sarah: *"Being a female, you gain water weight. You can go in there and think you're so thin, and it'll weigh you five pounds over. It gets frustrating. I eat lots of asparagus."*

Shannon: *"There's, like, seven or eight things on our grocery list. For breakfast it's egg whites and oats—dried oats."*

Sarah: *"People think we're so weird. You have to be very disciplined. And you have to get in that mind-set, because it is hard to follow. Very, very hard to follow. Like, a guy will ask you out on a date on a Wednesday night, and you can't say, 'I can't eat, because I have to weigh in tomorrow.' But you can't go and not eat, either. So it is hard."*

Shannon: *"I've been in situations with people who think, like, Oh, you're not having fun. Or, Why won't you go out? Because I don't want to eat."*

Sarah: *"I usually say to a guy, 'Let's wait until Friday night, because I have four days to get my weight back down after that.'"*

Shannon: *"You saw us in practice in the short booty shorts and, like, a sports bra or bikini top? That's so they can see your fitness level. The stomach, the legs, the butt."*

Sarah: *"They stand right in front of you with a clipboard. I don't like it, but it's a good idea. It has to be done."*

Shannon: *"It's about glamour, fitness, and always being ready: full hair, full makeup, giving 110 percent."*

Sarah: *"Of course, guys look at it as some type of sex symbol. But I don't think it's a thing that guys want their girlfriend to look like, you know what I mean? It's like a costume. It's not something I think a guy would like to look at every day."*

Shannon: *"Egg yolk is actually what carries most of the fat. I'll usually put one yolk and about six egg whites just to have some fat and not just the protein."*

Sarah: *"This month has been good. I mean, we gained a few pounds, but that helps you start again."*

Shannon: *"I'm not usually this color. I tanned yesterday."*

Sarah: *"If Shannon has her hair up in a ponytail, I swear, ninety-nine out of a hundred people would bet it's fake. It looks so perfect, and it's so big and thick. I bet ninety-nine out of a hundred would think it's fake. It's that good."*

Shannon: *"You want some water?"*

THERE'S MORE. For Adrienne, so much more. You have to understand at least one more important beat of the backstory: this is not the first time Adrienne has been named Cheerleader of the Week. The first time, she blew it. She may be the only Ben-Gal in history to screw up so royally. It happened three weeks earlier. Charlotte had told Adrienne, "This is it! You're going to be Cheerleader of the Week!" The night before the game, Adrienne was so excited she could barely sleep. Well, she did sleep. And sleep, and sleep, and sleep.

She awakened to the sound of her phone ringing. It was Missy, calling from the parking lot, where all the other cheerleaders had already gathered. "*Where are you?*" Adrienne hoped this was a bad dream. But, no, it was true. She had overslept. She threw on her clothes and rushed into the stadium, arriving not exactly Ben-Gal ready and more than sixteen minutes late.

"Tardy!"

The Cheerleader of the Week was . . . *tardy*? She was immediately dethroned. She would not be allowed to cheer, let alone be

Cheerleader of the Week, and she would be penalized two games. Hey, late is late. Rules are rules. All the gals, including Charlotte, embraced her, grieved with her, over the tragedy that seemed for her so typical, so many almosts, so much dumb luck, so much stupid, rotten, dumb luck.

"It's my own fault," Adrienne told her teammates on that dismal day. "It's nobody's fault but my own."

For all her mother-superior-style discipline, Charlotte is a kind soul. Now here it is, just three weeks after Adrienne's disaster, and Charlotte is giving her a second chance at being Cheerleader of the Week. *Here you go, Adrienne. Your sins are forgiven.*

So maybe it's the generosity that is making Adrienne sick. The outpouring of love. The second chance that in so many ways feels like the last. The thought of going out there, in front of all those screaming fans, appearing on the JumboTron in the stadium whose concrete you yourself once poured.

After serious consultation with Mary and Traci, Charlotte has an announcement. "Catsuits!" she bellows out into the locker room that by now is held in tight under a hanging cloud of aerosol. "Okay, girls, *catsuits!*"

"Catsuits!" the women shriek. There is nothing sexier than the catsuits.

Adrienne throws her head into the sink, runs the water at full blast, plunges. "Catsuits!" several tell her. "Catsuits!" They throw their arms around her, leap tiny leaps. "Catsuits!"

"Adrienne, honey, are you okay?"

MEET THE CHEERLEADER: ADRIENNE

"My mom was killed. She was murdered by my stepdad. I had just turned a year old. I break down sometimes. You can't think: Why me? Things happen for a reason. You just can't think about the unknown.

"This right here is a mud mat. It's just so we have a flat area to set our forms on. We poured all this today. We started back in the corner. Last pour, we did over three hundred yards.

"The finishers finish the concrete and make it look pretty. And the laborers, which would be us, rake it and pull it close to grade. The rod busters are the ones that put all the rebar in. They are just totally rebar. Oh, God, I would never want to be a rod buster.

"Cement is not the same as concrete. Cement's an ingredient in concrete. Cement is the glue in concrete.

"Working with all men, you realize that they really act like girls. They whine and cry. I'm not trying to be stereotypical, but they act different. I don't think of myself as a female at work. I think of myself as an employee. As a guy. Well, I don't want to be a guy. But I let them know: You're not allowed to call me names or treat me like dog crap.

"With the Ben-Gals, with thirty girls in one group, you'd think it'd be a bunch of backstabbers, cliques, but it's not like that. They say I'm this role model because I have a little girl I'm raising on my own and I work construction. They say I'm an inspiration. They say that they're amazed I do all this.

"I went to college, a full ride in track. I chose criminal justice. Afterward, I took a test in Lexington to become a cop. I got all the

way to what they call the 'rule of five,' when they compare you to four other applicants. I had four speeding tickets, because I commute a lot. That ruined my chances. That kinda bummed me out. I was, like, Screw this.

"Then I took the county exam and failed by two points. I did bad because the whole time I'm thinking how I'm gonna kill my boyfriend because he made me late. He had my car, didn't get it back to me in time. The whole time I was thinking about him.

"I had a change of heart. I decided I didn't want to be a cop. I didn't want someone to have to tell my kid someday that I'd been shot.

"In the beginning, when I started working construction, the guys were horrible. The first day, my boss said I was a lawsuit waiting to happen. He made me bust up a twelve-by-twelve slab of concrete alone, with a sledgehammer. Then I had to carry four-by-fours, one after another. But I stuck it out. I've been doing this eight years. My body goes through a lot.

"After my mom was killed, my aunt Pam wanted me. She really wanted me. After two years, she hitched a ride to Florida in the back of a truck to get me. People were upset with my grandma for letting me go. Pam was sixteen at the time. I call her my mom now. She ended up being a single mom with six kids. I think that's why I am the way I am today, because I was raised on love.

"I told Pam I wanted to go on Ricki Lake *and find my dad. I said I want to know who made me. She didn't want me to do that, but she talked to my aunts. I met him at a benefit. It was weird. I cried. Like, wow. We went out to dinner the next night, to F&N Steak House, in Dayton. I ate chicken, and he was so mad. 'I bring you to a steak house, and you order chicken?' I didn't want him to*

think I was money-hungry. He told me how beautiful my mom was, how much he loved her. He said he remembered the last time they made love was 1975, World Series game seven. He followed a newspaper story about me in high school but didn't know for sure that I was his.

"I don't regret anything that's ever happened. I did get the shit end of the deal with Mom dying, but that was out of my control.

"I never get hit on. A lot of my friends say I'm intimidating. Women who are successful or independent, guys are too scared to talk to. Which I hate. Because I'm a person.

"My one fear is failing at being a mother. I don't want her to go through the things I went through. I'm afraid she'll be a priss. Her dad spoils her, which I hate because it makes me look bad.

"Being a Ben-Gal in general is just awesome.

"Being Cheerleader of the Week is awesome.

"Taking photos for the calendar was awesome. It's a day that's all about you. Last year I ended up being Miss October. This year I was Miss December. It's heartbreaking when you don't make a month. People say, 'Why didn't you get a month?' We don't know. But when you are a month, you feel great. Awesome. Sexy. Amazing. You feel like you're somebody.

"Underneath this, I have jeans and long johns. And then I have two long-sleeves on, a sweatshirt, a sweater, and one of the poly sweatshirts that, like, covers you, and my Carhartts. You get cold. Your hands and feet and face and your nose. I'll thaw out later on tonight, like, a couple hours after I'm home I'll start thawing out.

"I've always wanted to be a nurse. Ever since I graduated from high school. So I'm just gonna go back and give it a shot. I'm a people person. That's my calling. I get home, and normally I pick

up my daughter, and we usually do homework. I have to study. I'm taking chemistry. In a couple years, I should be a nurse. I should graduate in three years.

"You're not supposed to put a lot of stickers on your hard hat, because sometimes OSHA will think that you're covering up a hole. If these get a hole, you can't use them, because something might land on your head and kill you. But I have this sticker that says HOTTIE. *And* DEWALT TOOLS. *The twin towers—one of the guys from the company, he was killed, so I have a sticker for him. And I have one that says* BITCH GODDESS.

"I spit, too, like boys. Oh, yeah. Just 'cause, I don't know. Your mouth gets dry or whatever. The guys are, like, 'Quit spittin'. That's not ladylike.' And I'm, like, 'I'm not a lady at work.' Charlotte doesn't know I spit. Charlotte would kill me."

"WHO-DEY! WHO-DEY! Who-dey think gonna beat dem Bengals?"

"Nobody!"

It is time. The gals have pranced like a pride of lionesses out of the locker room and are standing in the tunnel, peering out. There are enormous Bengals walking around back here, but the gals notice only one another. They are cold. Sarah is holding on to Shannon for warmth; she always seems to disappear next to Shannon, mostly due to Shannon's hair, currently a celebration, a testament to extremes, curls streaming like Niagara Falls down her back, crashing into the bend of her bottom. "I'm so freezing!" Sarah is saying.

"Get a grip, girl!" Shannon says. "It's showtime!"

The catsuits are sleek, sleeveless, with necklines plunging deep and tight, allowing for blasts of perfectly spherical honeydew breasts. Each gal wears a thin glitter belt around her hips and a pair of white satin wrist cuffs crisscrossed with orange laces. Hair is high, broad, glued in place. Makeup is paint, pasted on thick. Tans are air-sprayed, darker in the V to accentuate the total package. Perfect. Exactly perfect.

Of course, it might not *really* rain and ruin all their hard work. It might not. The storm is probably still over Indiana or something. It could hold off. The balmy 68 degrees has gone *kerplunk* to 52. Outside, in the stands, ponchos are starting to come out.

"I don't know about the eighties look, with all this hair," Lauren says. "Do you think we look like poodles?"

"I can't brush my hair after," Tiany says. "I have to wash it."

"I have to soak it," Brooke says.

"You guys!" team captain Deanna interrupts. "Think how lucky we are to be here, and savor every moment!"

"Sexy, ladies!" Rhonée shouts. "SEXY!"

"SEXY!"

"Wooo!"

With that, they fire out of the tunnel like bullets out of the barrel of a gun. One arm up, pom-pom shaking, "Let's Get It Started!" "Who-dey!" "Who-dey!" Fireworks shooting into the night sky. Any one of them could burst into tears of excitement. Some of them will. Adrienne will absolutely not. Adrienne is all game face, determination from a twisted gut. She's on the five-yard line, next to Maja and Tiffany, all the cheerleaders lined up forming a chute, a welcome path for the football players, who come chugging out like boxcars. "Who-dey! Who-dey!" The gals stand like ponies, one knee up, one arm down. Pom-poms shimmering.

They take to their corners, and the kicker kicks off, and the stadium erupts into "Welcome to the Jungle," Axl Rose crooning his timeless anthem, gals dancing stripper moves with hips, ass, roll head, whip hair. Then they just as quickly retreat into sweet pom-pom action. Sloopy. Feelgood. Hicktown. Worm. Tweety. All the dances have code names.

"We're on Pump, right?"

"We're on Worm!"

"Oh my God!"

Four sets of cheerleaders, one set in each stadium corner, Charlotte and Mary and Traci with walkie-talkies, demanding coordination, demanding precision: "Lines, ladies, *LINES!*"

Six minutes into a scoreless first quarter, most of the hair is . . . flat. That was quick. That is a shame. But that's okay. At halftime they'll charge back to the locker room and drop to their knees in front of mirrors waiting like lonesome cousins. Hot rollers. Curling irons. Makeup. Spray tan. Primp! There is not much time to re-create perfection, but they'll do their best.

Six-yard line. The football players are trying to pound the ball in. *Come on, football players!* The cheerleaders hold their arms up, smile, keep their arms high, and jiggle their pom-poms, shimmer shimmer shimmer. They have turned themselves into candles burning flames of hope.

A field goal. *Okay, we'll take it.* Who-dey! "Jungle Boogie." Celebrate with the cheerleaders; watch them bounce like balls.

It isn't until three minutes, twenty-six seconds into the third quarter that Carson Palmer completes a forty-yard flea-flicker touchdown pass to T. J. Houshmandzadeh, but that is not even the point. The sky has done it, finally opened up—sheets of rain.

The gals valiantly bump and grind to "Bang on the Drums," the touchdown song, in the glimmery downpour. Forget hair spray, forget makeup. It is all washing off now, washing down, soaking them. Wet cheerleaders! The JumboTron appears itself to experience the orgasm. Exploding wet cheerleaders! The cameras are all over the cheerleaders. The gals are screaming, laughing, howling, forgetting everything. Forgetting the fucking construction site, the man who murdered your mother, the store calling for more Mountain Dew, the chemical-fume hoods and the smoke-particle-challenge method, the men who don't call, and all those egg whites and protein shakes that have made this moment possible. Forget it all! This is it. This is a rain dance, a joy dance, a jet-propulsion explosion of cheerleader love, love to the crowd, love from the crowd, men in striped pajamas, wigs, tails, painted bellies washing clean, oh, those men are super, super-duper adorable. Who-dey drunk.

In the stands cheering for Adrienne is Pam, the woman who hitchhiked decades ago to Florida to scoop her up. Also, Adrienne's cousin Leslie, her aunt Nancy, her little aunt Sandy, and her regular aunt Sandy—the one who takes the picture. It is the first time they get a picture of Adrienne on the JumboTron. In the picture, Adrienne is smiling and looking up. It's just her face next to her name and her hometown and her hobbies. In that moment, she doesn't even know she is on the JumboTron. She is wet, out-of-her-mind joyful, free.

Hours go by, hugs, happiness. At home she gets into her PJs, shares the couch with a bowl of popcorn. She holds the picture of herself on the JumboTron. She has to get up tomorrow at six, and it's going to be cold out on the pad where she'll be pouring. Cold. She looks at the picture. She thinks she looks awesome. Like a real girl. Happy. She tries to hold on to the feeling. Like, right now she still has the feeling of what it is to be Cheerleader of the Week. Warm, explosive, a volcano inside you. She looks at the picture again and recognizes perfection. She wonders what to do with it. She is not the type to put a picture like that on display. She has her collection of tiny ceramic angels on display. In a few days she puts the picture in a box in the closet of her spare bedroom, a space for love letters.

TRAFFIC

Air Traffic Control Tower
LaGuardia Airport
New York, New York

To get to the air traffic control tower at New York's LaGuardia Airport, you have to walk through Concourse D in the Central Terminal, past the shiny shops and fat pretzels and premium brews, into and back out of streams of travelers yammering wirelessly at wives, lovers, brokers. You come to a thick steel battleship-gray door, shove it open with your hip. Step inside. You are now in . . . Leningrad? Bucharest? Cinderblock walls washed in dingy fluorescent light, a cramped elevator, slow and rickety, up to the tenth floor—*Sorry it's so cold, but this thermostat hasn't worked for shit in years*—through another gray door, up a knee-creaking set of concrete stairs: *Welcome to the LaGuardia tower cab. Would you like a doughnut? Check out the view!* The skyline demands all of you first, Manhattan spreading unobstructed like a mural written on the bottom of the sky. Airplanes everywhere, white, silver, crawling. Rikers Island sits alone on the upwind leg of runway 31. Shea Stadium, on the opposite end, is mere skeleton and guts, just now on a crisp October 2009 morning coming undone. *You don't see a view like this every day.*

Never mind the furniture, the duct-taped Archie Bunker couches in the break room, the ragged fold-up tables and the ancient, empty vending machine advertising Mike and Ike for twenty-five cents. Never mind the missing ceiling tiles, the warped paneling, the chipped Formica, the spectacular curls of peeling paint. Taped to the handset of a red phone is a sign reading BLACK PHONE. Some of the computer equipment brings to mind Tandy and Heathkit hobby kits. Some sections of the control console bring to mind the golden age of telephone operators wearing pointy bras. For a long time the roof here leaked so badly, they had giant diapers hanging, tarps tacked from here to there to catch the water; a garden hose took the water down a flight of stairs to a janitor's sink. Sometimes the bathroom plumbing goes, and when it goes it really *goes*: some controllers keep an extra shirt in their lockers in case of explosion. (Others have learned to flush with their foot and duck.) "But—check out the view!" people here say with pride intent or not intent on masking the obvious. *Yeah, this place is a dump.* This is the center of the universe, a tower serving 23 million passengers a year as they fly in and out of the most congested airspace in the world, and yeah, this tower, built in 1962, one of the oldest in America, is a dump.

The FAA promises a new tower next year. You can see it emerging next to the parking garage. It's *right there*. Is it fair to be skeptical? Some LaGuardia controllers remember hearing about a-new-tower-next-year as far back as 1984. "Next year." "Next year." "Why fix up the old tower when a new tower is coming next year?" A quarter of a century of no next-years is enough to make any worker with a spare shirt in his locker in case of toilet explosion feel . . . skeptical.

Cali loves it here; it sounds crazy at first, but he does love it. (In fact, most LaGuardia controllers kiss the mud-colored carpet tile they walk on. They could tell you about the alternatives. Stick around and they'll tell you about the alternatives.) At the moment, Cali is on Ground. It's 8:20 a.m. on a Friday, rush hour, every forty-five seconds another airplane landing, then another launching, then another landing, relentless as throbs of a throbbing headache. Twenty-six departures wait in line, all stoked up, backed up on Bravo clear down to Foxtrot. Twelve controllers maneuver the chaos. Brian is on Local, clearing for takeoff and clearing for landing, while Cali, on Ground, is managing the taxiways—a constantly moving puzzle of airplanes loaded with thousands and thousands of souls. Of all the positions, almost everyone here loves Ground most, *because it's so fucking complicated*. LaGuardia Airport is tiny compared with its sleek modern counterparts, like Atlanta or Denver with their endless parallel runways spread over thousands of acres. LaGuardia is jammed into just 680 urban acres; taxiways are tight; runways intersect; you can't launch a departure until the arrival on the other runway crosses the threshold or else the airplanes will . . . collide. There's also water on three sides to avoid falling into. There are also adjacent behemoths Newark and (especially) Kennedy airports, each launching and landing one plane every thirty-six seconds, constantly breathing down LaGuardia's neck. Kennedy, just twelve miles south, is obnoxious. If *Kennedy* goes into delays, it's LaGuardia that has to change its runway configuration to help *Kennedy* get out of delays. All in all, the complications make this place so much more awesome than a place like Atlanta or Denver. This, anyway, is the LaGuardia mystique. This-dump-rocks.

Cali sends a Dash 8 into the departure lineup, feels the thunder of a launching 757 soaring past the tower windows. He's keeping an eye on an Embraer jet and gate Charlie 9. He has a lot on his mind. His first name is Tom, but the guys call him Cali. He plays hockey. He used to be a short-order cook. He is proud of his gardens, especially his enormous orange canna lilies. His hair is buzzed, and his eyes are smart, and his nose is prominent, and his accent is Long Island. His movements are impatient gesticulation, yadda yadda yadda. His headset cord is long, enabling him to wander practically the full circle of the cramped tower cab. Like nearly everyone else here, he stands when he's on position. It's not a sit-down kind of job. "Swivelheads" is a nickname for tower controllers, because they're constantly scanning in all directions, like owls.

The 757 that just launched is headed to Chicago. That flight, like every commercial departure, has more to it than the commonly recognized components of pilot, flight plan, and fuel. Every flight has people watching over it, guardian-angel style, every step of the way. For example, shortly after Brian launched the 757, he handed it off, via radio, to a controller fifteen miles away at the Terminal Radar Approach Control (TRACON) in Westbury, Long Island, where it showed up as a blip on a radarscope. The 757 now becomes the charge of the TRACON controller, who guides it as high as 17,000 feet. At that point, it is handed off to yet another controller, this one at the Air Route Traffic Control Center in Islip, New York, where it shows up as a green blip on that controller's radarscope. Centers are spread out like a net across the United States, twenty-two in all, each filled with controllers watching, babysitting, passing off blips to one another. The New York Center controller, for example, will guide the 757 west and eventually pass it off to a controller at the Cleveland Center, who will guide it farther west and pass it off to the Indianapolis Center, who will likewise guide it and pass it off to the Chicago Center. As it nears its destination, the 757 will descend, get handed to the Chicago TRACON and then to a controller at the Chicago O'Hare tower, who will clear it for landing and steer it to its gate.

Nearly 30,000 commercial flights thus zoom across America's skies each day and never bash into each other. The "modern" air traffic control system, and the FAA itself, was created in the aftermath of one of the most dramatic commercial midair bashes, way back in 1956. On a warm summer morning, United Flight 718 from Los Angeles was headed to Chicago, and TWA Flight 2 from Los Angeles was headed to Kansas City. Over the Grand Canyon they met, at 21,000 feet, inside a cumulus cloud. After impact, both planes plunged into the canyon, taking 128 people to a most violent death.

You don't hear of accidents like that anymore. The FAA employs 15,000 controllers who make sure that midair collisions and a host of other horrible things don't happen. Controllers are choreographers, deciders, big-picture people with a knack for making split-second decisions based on physics, geometry, aerodynamics, and God-given guts. They're perched above runways in little glass rooms and hidden in radar rooms, physically cut off from us and yet completely connected, or so we hope. We'd know them better if they did a bad job. The better they are, the more invisible they become.

Hidden, too, is the cloud of anguish under which they work. There is bitterness and resentment, feuding and infighting. Here is a workforce in a festering standoff with management, again and again, and now again. The story of air traffic in America today is one of growing pockets of exhausted controllers working with ancient equipment in understaffed facilities. The stakes go well beyond the inconvenience of airport delays, which are getting famously worse. The stakes are millions of passengers going from here to there: the safe handling of an utterly vulnerable public.

At the moment, Cali is plugged-in. He's on his tiptoes, getting a better view. Plugged-in is what a controller calls it when he's on position. Plugging in means plugging out of the rest of your problems, or those of your union, or of a bunch of blabbermouth politicians in Washington, D.C. Plugged-in is its own dimension, hypertime and hyperthought and hyperawareness of airplanes loaded with people and all their problems. Cali glances down Zulu taxiway. Is it clear? He's probably going to need it. He's seeing four or five or twelve steps ahead.

What happens out on the tarmac is everybody wants to be first. Everybody wants to be next. Everybody wants to *go*. A 737 has just landed, touching down on runway 31. *Destination!* Destination, to a passenger, means *I'm done*. Get-off-the-plane. Shake the wrinkles off your overcoat and march on bloated feet into the next fragment of your day. Mentally, all the passengers on the 737 play out the scenario even as they sit obediently with their seat belts still buckled, tapping their tappy fingers while the plane taxis toward its assigned gate, Charlie 9.

But Charlie 9 is occupied, an Airbus taking forever to board. A whole different horde of passengers who want to be first, next, *go*. Shifting, settling in, folding overcoats, claiming elbow room, all the passengers on the Airbus play out a scenario of getting somewhere on time, or late.

Move! thinks the pilot of the 737.

Hurry! thinks the pilot of the Airbus.

Get me out of here! thinks everybody all at once.

Cali knows the story, over and over again the same me-first story no matter whose head he gets inside. *Me first!* There is only so much a controller working Ground can do. Cali shoots the 737 down toward Zulu. "Bravoshordazulu" he says, machine-gun fast, into his headset. Not "Taxi by Bravo and hold short of Zulu" but "Bravoshordazulu." The pilot hears Cali's command, thinks *Fuck*. Zulu is nowhere near Charlie 9. *Is this dipshit going to hold us all the way down there by Shea Stadium until our gate is cleared?* No, Cali's just moving the 737 out of the way. He's got a departing Dash 8 he's rolling up Alpha (*Me first!*), and he's got another arrival, an MD-80 to roll Bravoshordamike (*Me first!*), and he needs to do what he can to help Brian, next to him on Local, launch a twofer (two departures for one arrival) if LaGuardia has any hope of getting out of delays. Cali is seeing all of this at once, a matrix of decisions hurling without apology toward the threshold of another matrix of decisions and another and in an instant another. It's overdrive for even the most practiced brain, all those variables, all those planes, all those souls, all that responsibility, no chance of saying *Fuck it!* and walking away, no ghost of a chance at all of that until, finally, after about an hour, a replacement controller steps in and you plug out, go downstairs for about thirty minutes to the break room for some crackers or an egg sandwich from the concourse, give the brain a chance to empty, exhale, recharge.

Cali is the sort of person to constantly ask himself, *Well, how would I feel?* It guides him through his decisions. The last thing a passenger wants to feel after landing in an airplane, he knows, is the feeling of sitting on the tarmac. *But I have arrived at my destination. Why am I not moving on with my day? How long are we going to sit here?* So Cali won't just park the 737 down at Zulu while it waits for its gate. If at all possible, he'll keep the plane moving on the tarmac. He will pause it at Juliet, inch along, then hold for a moment at Lima. "Give the passengers the *illusion* of progress." That's his motto. It gives the people hope.

He turns the 737 up Alpha, tries to swing it so it arrives at Charlie 9 the second the gate becomes available. He nails it, thinks, *Yessss.*

Another controller might not have bothered with all that. Another controller might have just dumped the 737 down at Zulu, just left all those passengers stranded down there, hopeless and forlorn. To do it better doesn't matter in the scheme of things, doesn't get anyone anywhere any faster, does nothing to help LaGuardia's reputation as one of the world's most delayed airports. It's not heroic. It's not avoiding a midair collision. It's certainly not landing an Airbus A320 on the Hudson. It's just 120 passengers feeling slightly less awful about being stuck in an airplane. A little bit of humanity. A little bit of love. What of it?

EARLY ONE SUMMER, when I first visited the people at the National Air Traffic Controllers Association (NATCA) union offices in Washington, D.C., to inquire about meeting some controllers, they assumed I was there to talk about misery. Did I want to understand why controllers were so miserable? In fact, my driving curiosity was about the work and not the mood of controllers. They said it would be difficult to separate the two.

They whispered a strategy for dealing with the FAA, which they spoke of as if it were shrouded in Kremlin-style inscrutability. *Say this and don't say that.* I would have to go through the FAA if I wanted to get access to a facility, and I would have to be very careful about how I asked. The FAA had a reputation for granting precious few such requests, and it probably wouldn't grant this one. *Try this and don't try that.*

When I went down Fourteenth Street and talked to the people at the FAA about meeting some controllers, they assumed I was there to talk about misery. Had I spoken to anyone at NATCA? "What did they say?" They wanted to squelch rumors. They spoke of the union as if it were a bunch of bratty little girls throwing fits for a candy fix. They handed me a handsome four-color glossy report proving that controllers were happy, or if they weren't, they should be. Everything is *fine*. Don't panic. *Everything is under control.*

NATCA was a bunch of crybabies. The FAA was a big fat bully. *Spoiled brats! Meanies!* When moving between the union and the FAA, it is easy to feel like the only grown-up in the neighborhood.

At issue is a labor shortage. Air traffic controllers are retiring at a rate of nearly one thousand a year. A shriveling workforce, ever-increasing air traffic—somebody has to guide all those airplanes. *You guys have to suck it up,* the FAA says to the controllers. Work more hours, take fewer breaks—work six-day weeks if you have to. *Yeah, you have to.* Six-day workweeks are now the norm at the nation's busiest radar facilities, which are notoriously hard to staff. The fact that everyone saw this crunch coming long ago—and had been warning about it for years—makes the union nuts. Do the math. Controllers have to retire at fifty-six. Most experienced controllers were hired in the early 1980s after the then union went on strike and President Reagan famously fired their asses. Most of the people brought aboard back then are now in their fifties and being booted out the door. And so there's been a surge in controller retirements: nearly half the workforce will become eligible for retirement in the next three years. *We need more controllers!* The union has been saying it for years. *Our guys are falling apart here! They're gonna start making mistakes if you don't give them a break! Why won't you hire more controllers?* It's not a simple task. Training takes years. *We need more controllers in the pipeline!*

The FAA acted, finally, in 2006. This was in the wake of failed contract negotiations. *Forget it,* they said. *Here's your new contract. Take it or leave it.* The union took it, sort of. The union refuses to use the word "contract" when referring to the "imposed work rules" controllers now work under. Among the 2006 changes: a salary freeze and a two-band pay scale. All new controllers would be brought in at as much as 30 percent less than those hired before the imposed work rules. A certified controller just starting out at LaGuardia tower now, for example, makes about $63,000; under the old rules, he would have started at around $93,000.

And so it was at bargain prices that the FAA finally started hiring like gangbusters in 2006. The plan is to bring aboard nearly 17,000 controllers in the next decade. Finding all those warm bodies is an issue. Gone are the days when controllers were expected to have college degrees. Now people can walk in off the street—McDonald's or Piercing Pagoda or carnival washouts. Once hired, a recruit attends the FAA Academy in Oklahoma City for three months and then gets stationed at a tower or a TRACON or a

Center, where one of the already overworked controllers trains him on each position. Gone are the days when training to become fully certified at the nations' toughest facilities could take up to five years; new recruits are now fast-tracked in as little as two.

The union fears the worst. *Is anyone listening?* The union says America's skies are not safe if its controllers are exhausted, miserable, overworked, resentful, or inadequately schooled. The union says, *Please, everybody, please remember what's at stake.* The union says it's only a matter of time.

Oh, relax! says the FAA, citing stellar safety records and accusing the union of trying to whip the flying public into a fear frenzy to get them to support the union's whiny demands for a real contract.

The union says it's only a matter of time: serious runway incursions—those considered likeliest to cause a collision—are way up.

Say this and don't say that. Try this and don't try that. Who did you talk to and what did he say?

After months of deliberation, the FAA said okay, I could come into one of their facilities; they would pick one for me. The union was pleased—finally, maybe the real story of controllers would get some attention—but said the FAA would probably offer some little Podunk place with little traffic and little misery. A place that would show off some jazzy simulator or something that would make the FAA look good.

Finally, the FAA offered LaGuardia tower. The union said, "Really?" and "That's a good one." Then they told me that controllers could get fired if they dared to speak the truth about how miserable they were, so I'd better take that into consideration. By the time I got to LaGuardia, I was imagining scared rats hunkering in corners of a cage.

But of course that isn't what I have found. I have found Cali and Brian, Lars and Eric, Tim, Andy, Joe, Franklin, Camille, and the rest of the C team, one of three groups of twelve controllers who man the tower 24 hours a day, 365 days a year. There is little time here for pouting. Brian is my assigned guide. He is a compact man with ruddy skin and sharp blue eyes and a fatherly earnestness. Each day he brings a different coffee mug to work, on each mug a different photo of his four kids. "To remind myself why I'm doing this," he says. He does not appear even a tiny bit miserable, and neither, for the most part, does the rest of the C team. Joe, the (nonunion) supervisor, is distinguished from the rest of the (union) group only in that he wears a tie. He also wears a lanyard covered with pins: Snoopy, the logo from the seventies band Yes, a shamrock, a pink ribbon for breast cancer awareness he has been wearing ever since one of the guys' wives was diagnosed.

The tower conditions, to be sure, are laughable. The plumbing, the leaks, the tired equipment. Most people, if they saw this, would not feel encouraged.

Controllers here, as in a lot of towers, still use "strips." Strips are pieces of pale green paper with flight data written on them—one strip for each departing and each arriving flight. Franklin, a happy old man, sits Geppetto-style in the corner, printing out the strips. At his side is a big white plastic bucket, the kind you salvage after home remodeling projects, filled with plastic strip holders.

Strip holders look like the trays you put Scrabble tiles on. Franklin carefully threads each strip into its own little holder, hands them down to the guys working traffic. The guys slide the strips around in the holders to indicate things: a third out (or so) means you've contacted a pilot, half out (or so) means a plane is ready to launch, strips balanced over the console like diving boards mean something else. When they clear for takeoff, they slide the strip all the way out, stamp it with an old-timer time stamper—*bonk!*—then pitch the empty strip holder—*clunk!*—into another white bucket. *Bonk. Clunk! Bonk. Clunk!* The rhythm gets hypnotic after a while. You can close your eyes and tell how busy LaGuardia Airport is just by the *bonk!* and the *clunk!* It is a sound that makes you question what century you are, in fact, in.

"I don't quite know how to tell you this," I say to Brian one day. "They have *computers* that can do this sort of job for you." He looks at me. His eyes are all trust and innocence. I say even the local library long ago figured out how to ditch the card catalog. He nods. "We like the strips," he says.

Redundancy is a controller's friend. Short-term memory is almost always maxed out. If you can't remember what you told this pilot six commands ago or that pilot three commands ago, you can glance at the strips and know the story in an instant.

As for the rest of the equipment, Brian refers me to Lars, a controller with a computer-geek bent who can't help himself from desperately trying to keep the tower from suffering a complete analog collapse.

"Don't even get me started," says Lars, when I ask him about the odd assortment of computer equipment, the whole Commodore 64 vibe. He's a lanky man with a long, rubbery face topped with sandy-blond hair. After many sighs and shakes of his head, he finally finds words. "It's such a mess." He says the problem with the computers in the tower is that nothing matches, nothing is integrated, every piece of software comes with a dedicated monitor: *It's a fucking monitor farm in here.* "A Unix thing here, Windows-based stuff here, stand-alone stuff here. Some contractor talked somebody in the government into buying it, you know. You can smell the backroom deals going around. It's just . . . no big picture. No big picture. It drives me absolutely nuts."

I ask about the red phone labeled BLACK PHONE.

"Standard operating procedure," Lars says. "The book says use the black phone, but—"

"Oh, that phone doesn't work," a controller says to him.

"It doesn't?"

"It's been broken since I started training."

"The black phone?"

"Not the *black* red phone."

"No, the black phone."

"Not the red phone that's black?"

"There used to be a black phone that didn't work."

I stand and look at them, blinking confusion and worry.

"Look," Joe says to me, "the *red* black phone calls the police garage, like, for a medical emergency, someone needs paramedics at the gate, whereas the other red phone is, okay, the airplane is coming in with minimum fuel, can crash or whatever—the *real* red phone. Then the tan phone is the Queens fire department."

"That's the one that doesn't work. The tan phone."

"It doesn't?"

"Jesus Christ."

For the sake of adventure, Brian has asked the crew if they'd like to go out after work for some beer and good times. So after work we go. Brian has arranged for Phil to be the designated driver, and seven of us ride in Brian's silver minivan to a Holiday Inn in Queens.

"So this is how air traffic controllers party?" I say in the van, all of us sitting up good and straight with our seat belts on.

"We are so fucking responsible," says Cali.

I tell him it's actually very encouraging to learn that the people in charge of keeping all those airplanes from bashing into each other are dependable geeks in reasonably good moods. "Word down at headquarters is that you folks are miserable," I say.

"Oh, so you've been talking to NATCA," Lars says. The van erupts with laughter. They themselves are union members, but not "*that* kind." Not, that is, the hard-core kind that shoots itself in the foot by whining all the time. They tell stories blasting management and the union, blaming both for keeping this war going—especially at the TRACON. They tell of a union guy having a beer with a manager in a bar; another union guy walks in, sees this, *You can't drink with a manager*; they almost come to blows. A union guy gets promoted to management—crosses over!—and the other union guys key his car in the parking lot. Management plans to do a Thanksgiving turkey at the TRACON until the union hears about it: *You can't do that! Nobody eats turkey with management.*

"A Thanksgiving turkey at the New York TRACON, *are you shitting me?*"

"That's what I heard."

"Like the Pilgrims and the Indians are going to sit down and eat together, are you shitting me?"

"That's what I heard."

If there are hot spots of controller misery in America, the New York TRACON is, they say, among the hottest. They know this because many of them used to work there.

"It's two and a half years of my life I'll never get back."

"I got out. I escaped. I survived."

"You sell your soul to work there."

"They offered bonus money, like, $75,000, to get people to work there, and still they can't staff the place."

"Brutal."

"A black hole."

"A snake pit."

"You can't get out."

"A shithole."

No sign announces the New York TRACON, a two-story ash-white warehouse beneath a tower with antennae and satellite dishes sticking out like whiskers. The building is surrounded by a barbed-wire fence and is policed twenty-four hours a day by at least one remarkably gloomy security cop in a guard shack. Tall stacks spew dark stuff from a recycling plant on the other side of the parking lot. It is not a place that welcomes journalists—not for a long time now. I get in because Brian makes some calls. I feel an uncomfortable duty to be polite, like he's taking me to his creepy, crazy uncle's house and neither of us knows each other well enough to say, *Whew. Creepy.* Brian shamefully calls himself a TRACON washout. He tried to work radar two years ago, but couldn't cut it. Unlike every other TRACON washout I meet,

Brian expresses humiliation over his failure to succeed here. He *wanted* to make it. Surviving at the New York TRACON is, he says, the ultimate test of controller bravado. "But I hear all these other guys talk about washing out on purpose, and I guess I'm lucky."

Upstairs is where the action is: a windowless gymnasium-sized room, dark as night, sectioned off into sectors, each with lanes of glowing radarscopes. Supervisors (nonunion) sit perched on a raised throne in the middle, looking down upon rows of about fifty controllers (union) flopped in chairs like melting cheese, hunched over, mumbling into headsets. The supervisors are the ones taking me on the tour.

"We handle about 6,500 flights a day," one of them proudly tells me, "into and out of Kennedy, LaGuardia, and Newark, as well as forty-six smaller airports all within a 150-mile radius."

"It's an awesome responsibility," he says. "You get—I don't want to call it a God complex, because that's more for heart surgeons. But the ego starts. If you work here, you gotta start understanding where your ego's at."

The job of a TRACON controller is to organize the flow of traffic leaving and approaching the airports. Think of a highway. The TRACON controller handles the merge and the highway itself. There are dozens of other highways at dozens of altitudes he likewise manages. Now, say, at any given moment, ten of those planes zooming at those altitudes all want to use the same exit: LaGuardia Airport. The TRACON controller manages that confusion, gets everyone lined up to exit, one at a time, then hands the organized traffic off to the tower controller. Time is everything, space is everything, keep each airplane at least three miles apart, don't waste airspace, don't allow gaps. Quick: Turn ten random jets into a necklace of jets making a descent toward LaGuardia, each plane zooming one mile every eleven seconds. It is not a job for thinkers. You can't sit back and say, *Hmmm*. You can't be a person who analyzes or ponders or wonders about the implications of anything. Success as a radar controller is about intuition and guts, repetition and feeling.

"You gotta be able to dance," the supervisor with the ego tells me. "You gotta be able to inject imagination in a moment's notice. You can't say, 'Oh, this isn't working—what do I do now?' You gotta say, 'This isn't working—*do this*!' Know the plan and know when to change it. Always have an out. Do some crazy stuff. What if that guy loses an engine? You gotta know. You gotta have ideas. You gotta dance. I go home and my wife says, 'Don't boss me around like an airplane.' It's true! Here, you say something and it happens. It *happens*. It's not like that at home. You know, 'You can't talk to me like that! Shut up.' I always had that problem. You get used to it. I'm not going to call it a God complex, but . . . free spirits, a lot of us are. You gotta be able to dance."

At one point, but only after I ask, one of the supervisors agrees to walk me down among the controllers working traffic. I want to talk to them, meet them, maybe pull one aside and hang out in the cafeteria for a soda and ask if there is anything at all to the TRACON's reputation as a shithole, as the place where teams of disgruntled controllers sit and fume about their jobs—jobs that are about keeping thousands and thousands of otherwise helpless people safe as they're flung through the sky. The controllers I pass are, of course, busy. But even those plugging out for a break, or just plugging in after a break, avoid my eyes. I feel like I'm being escorted on a tour of the villagers by Castro or something.

"You're kidding, right?" explains an unplugged TRACON controller I meet later at a bar. "No one talks, no one looks up, if management is around. That's, like, *not done*."

The former and current TRACON controllers I talk to do so in whispers, saying please, please don't use their names. They don't want the FAA to know they're bad-mouthing them, nor do they want the union to know they are (less so, but not insignificantly) bad-mouthing *them*. They feel trapped in the cross fire, little kids scrambling to dodge the rocks the big boys hurl at each other. None of them complain about the job itself. They feel proud of the work they do. (They continually mention God and heart surgeons: "But we have *thousands* of lives in our hands every minute, and the heart surgeon has, what, two a day?") They hate everything else. They hate being treated like shit by the FAA, mandatory overtime, six days a week, no questions asked. They hate being exhausted. They hate spending so much time training young recruits, some of whom they feel to be lost causes. The dregs. "We're getting people now who might not have any other options. When you think about the number of lives you have in your hands every day and the people they're sending us to put through training, it's scary." They hate the mold or whatever the hell the black stuff was that used to pour out of the ceiling vents. They wonder if the black stuff is the reason so many of them have asthma. They have inhalers. They hate not being able to leave the building for lunch. "I just want to drive down the street to McDonald's. They're afraid I won't be back in time. I'm, like, I have hundreds of lives in my hands every second, and I get them where they need to be safely. You're telling me I can't get myself back from McDonald's?" They hate getting so little respect. They hate the chickenshit cowardice of their managers. "My manager won't come out to the control floor, won't show his face. I barely know what he looks like." They hate the paper that went around, like, three times that they had to keep signing: *You will not strike. It's against the law. You'll lose your job. It's against the law.* They hate plenty of the ways the union is handling the situation, expecting them to *not* impress management, to *not* go above and beyond the call of duty. "I was raised that you go to work and be the best possible that you can be. But it's not really like that. We're not supposed to impress our managers. We're only supposed to impress each other." Imagine being on a baseball team and you purposely stand there and take strikes just to piss off the coach while your teammates cheer.

Perhaps most of all, they hate being stuck. They can't leave this mess without quitting altogether. Any FAA controller can put in a bid for a job at another FAA facility, but your existing manager has to release you to take the new job. Woefully understaffed, the managers at the New York TRACON can't afford to release anybody. "You're stuck here. And they'll flat-out tell you that. You're not leaving. I got told the other day that maybe, *maybe*, I'll get out in five years."

Oh, they could have gone on and on with the complaints, so they did.

They hate the shame of it all. "It's such a good job. It's a lot of fun. But the FAA takes every hope of enjoyment out of it. They ruined the industry. When I first got in, everybody was all about doing everything possible to get as many planes in line, in the shortest amount of time. And over the years, the FAA has just pushed us and pushed us and pushed us, and now people are, like, 'I don't care.' They can hold the aircraft for hours, the aircraft will divert, and we don't care anymore. Now we just work until we think we have enough in, and we hold the rest. It's not the same mentality as it was. I'm sure you could look at the delays from five years ago to now and you'll see much bigger delays now. People have stopped caring."

Factors influencing flight delays are, of course, numerous: airline problems, such as pilot shortages and mechanical breakdowns, and weather issues that cause ripple effects across the country. FAA critics have long pointed the finger at antiquated technology, to which the FAA has responded with the promise of a new, $22 billion satellite-based system (current projection: 2025).

It's hard to quantify the human factor that goes into airport delays: teams of overworked, pissed-off, unmotivated controllers in radar centers that feel to them like prisons. It's hard to know if the human factor translates to real safety concerns, although the Office of the Inspector General (OIG) for the Department of Transportation has been warning about that one for a while. Testifying before Congress recently, the OIG reminded everyone that in 2003 it had reported that "almost 90 percent of controller operational errors [when a controller allows two aircraft to get too close] were due to human factors" such as fatigue and "situational awareness." In May 2007, the OIG reported that the FAA had "made little progress in this area." Progress, according to the recent congressional testimony, had come slightly, in the form of NATPRO, a program designed to sharpen controllers' "mental skills most closely associated with visual attention and scanning."

Visual attention and scanning are important, but so, you would think, is the other human factor: *These people are miserable.*

Does it matter? America has enough to worry about. So some radar controllers are cranky. So some of them have stopped caring.

ON FEBRUARY 24, 2009, a controller testified before Congress about a recent day at work, indicating the degree to which a controller's job can absorb the whims of worker apathy, or lethargy, or the moral conflict of a man who knows he *should* care but is too pissed off to bother. One month previously, pilot C. B. "Sully" Sullenberger had famously landed US Airways Flight 1549 on New York's Hudson River, saving the lives of all 155 people aboard the plane.

> *Good morning, Chairman Costello and Ranking Member Petri. My name is Patrick Harten. I have been an air traffic controller at the New York TRACON and a proud member of the National Air Traffic Controllers Association for the past ten years.*
>
> *While January 15, 2009, is forever etched in my memory, it began unremarkably. I arrived at work at 12:30 PM to begin my eight-hour shift. At 3:12 PM I was assigned to work the LaGuardia (LGA) departure RADAR position. This position handles all departures from LGA airport. At 3:25 PM, the LGA tower controller advised me that Cactus 1549 was the next departure rolling for takeoff.*
>
> *It was a routine westbound departure off of Runway 4 traveling due north on a 360-degree heading and climbing to 5,000 feet.*

I instructed Cactus to climb to 15,000 and turned my attention to give instructions to another aircraft under my control.

I then turned back to Cactus 1549 and instructed him to turn left to heading 270, heading the aircraft towards its destination. That is when the Captain advised me that they suffered a bird strike, lost thrust in both engines, and needed to return to LGA for an emergency landing.

I made a split-second decision to offer him Runway 13, which was the closest runway to his current position and turned him left at a 220 heading so he could return to the airport. I then immediately contacted LGA tower to ask them to stop departures and clear the runways for an emergency return.

While I have worked ten or twelve emergencies over the course of my career, I have never worked an aircraft with zero thrust capabilities. I understood how grave this situation was.

After I gave him his instructions, the Captain very calmly stated: "We're unable."

I quickly vectored an aircraft that was still in my airspace and then gave 1549 a second option: land on LGA Runway 31.

Again the Captain said, "Unable."

I then asked the Captain what he needed to do to land safely. At this point, my job was to coordinate and arrange for the pilot to be able to do whatever was necessary.

The pilot told me that he could not land on any runway at LGA, but asked if he could land in New Jersey and suggested Teterboro.

I had experienced working traffic into Teterboro from my time working in the Newark sector, and after coordinating with the controllers in Teterboro, we were able to determine that Runway 1 was the best option. It was the arrival runway, and clearing it for an emergency landing would be easier and faster. It also meant that 1549 would be landing into the wind, which could have assisted the pilot in making a safe landing. I called Teterboro and explained the situation. The controller at Teterboro reacted quickly and prepared Runway 1 for the emergency landing.

I then instructed the Captain to turn right on a 280 heading to land on Runway 1.

The Captain replied: "We can't do it."

I replied immediately, "Which runway would you like at Teterboro?"

The Captain replied: "We're gonna be in the Hudson."

I asked him to repeat himself, even though I heard him just fine. I simply could not wrap my mind around those words. I believed at that moment, I was going to be the last person to talk to anyone on that plane alive.

I then lost radio contact with 1549, and the target disappeared from my radar screen as he dropped below the tops of the New York City skyscrapers. I was in shock. I was sure the plane had gone down.

Less than a minute later, 1549 flickered back onto my radar scope. The aircraft was at a very low altitude, but its return to radar coverage meant that there was a possibility 1549 had regained the use of one of its engines. Grasping at that tiny glimmer of hope, I told 1549 that it could land at Newark, seven miles away, on Runway 29, but I received no response. I then lost radar contact again, this time for good.

It was the lowest low I had ever felt. I wanted to talk to my wife. But I knew if I tried to speak or even heard her voice, I would fall apart completely.

I settled for a hasty text message: "Had a Crash. Not ok. Can't talk now."

BRIAN, MY GUIDE, invites me home for dinner. Home is Blue Point, Long Island, over an hour away, a commute he does not mind. In the minivan, he tells me his Little League coach was a controller. He would look at him and think, *Wow.* In the 1980s, when *Top Gun* came out, Brian imagined himself a fighter pilot instead. He took flying lessons, anticipated glory. But reality won out over imagination, as it does for responsible men, and he found himself at the FAA Academy. A lot of the other controllers I talked to had fallen into the career, as if from outer space, a Plan B for dreamers. Joe studied to be a history teacher, Lars studied geology and chemistry, Andy was a graphic-arts major, and Cali, too, wanted to be an artist. He grew up on Long Island, and remembers passing LaGuardia tower often; from the road, it looks like a vase, gently narrowing in the middle. As far back as Cali can remember, he wanted to work in that tower, because the shape was so beautiful.

At home, Brian's wife, Kathy, makes spaghetti. Brian loosens the tie he is still getting used to, rolls his head around and around. "It feels like a leash." A few days ago, he got promoted to supervisor of LaGuardia's C team. The guys made fun of the tie, of course. What this means, though, is that Brian has left the ranks of the union and crossed over to management. *Crossed over.* This fact has hardly raised an eyebrow with Cali and Lars and Tim and the rest. Just a nice thing for Brian. Brian is washing out the mug he took to work today. This one says WE LOVE YOU, DAD. His own dad died when he was five. He's being the dad his dad never got to be. A breadwinner. A responsible man. And now a supervisor.

Kathy makes whopping quantities of extra pasta, having recently learned you can freeze it. She makes homemade sauce even though Brian consistently sings the praises of Ragú. She makes a homemade apple pie. The kids say please and thank you and admit they're showing off because their dad asked them to be superpolite. We sit down to eat, and my phone rings. I ignore the call, but then it rings two more times. I excuse myself to check the voice mail to find a message from an upset union rep who works at the TRACON. He and I had plans to meet later. He was going to talk to me on the record about conditions there. On my voice mail he says, "Forget it." He says he's learned that I am "speaking to management," and therefore he will not speak to me.

Management? Does he mean Brian? *Brian?* And how does this union guy know I am with Brian? Does he? Are my tires getting slashed somewhere? I close my phone and go back to the table. I don't tell Brian. I don't want to ruin anyone's appetite.

The next morning, just before dawn, I meet Lars, Cali, Tim, and Eric at the Family Dollar in East Northport and ride in the carpool lane with them to LaGuardia. Eric can't hear because of the Papa Roach concert he went to last night. Tim is mad at his busted Xbox. Cali is thinking about how much he enjoyed the book *Kitchen Confidential*. Lars is driving. I tell them about the voice mail.

"Get *out*! That is beautiful! Oh, that-is-beautiful!"

"I can't stand it!"

"That's the TRACON, baby! You didn't properly genuflect to the union!"

"They're so warm and cuddly I just love 'em. I just love 'em."

"That's why we still have no contract. That. THAT!"

"That's bullshit. NATCA used to be king of the jungle, and now they're not, so they're pissed."

"Even when they were kings, they were pissed-off kings."

"Aw, man, that is beautiful."

It's not so much that these guys are sympathetic to management as they are unsympathetic to management and the union both. Just so sick of the whole stupid war.

We sit in bumper-to-bumper traffic on the Whitestone Expressway and wonder why morale at the LaGuardia tower is so completely different than it is at the TRACON.

Lars goes out on a limb and says maybe the reason LaGuardia isn't a shithole like the TRACON has something to do with Leo, the LaGuardia tower manager on the ninth floor. "For all his bravado, Leo is still his own guy, you know?" You can talk to Leo. You can ask for a day off to go to your kid's soccer championship and not be laughed out of Leo's office. Leo isn't another FAA talking head. Leo, with his monthly pep talks downstairs in the stuffy conference room with the cardboard jammed into the windows to keep out the glare; Leo loving his power, drinking his power, and spewing it out in a fountain of sharing-the-love: "I trust you with everything I have. I do that every day. It's what I have. Trust. Because you gotta have the important parts of 'What-am-I-really-doing-here?' When you go to sleep at night and you wake up in the morning, are you confident that you've done it right? I can't help you with that. It's not my burden. It's yours. It's about safe transportation for the public. Pay attention! Are you paying attention? When bad things happen, that's what I look at. In this split second of time, what were you looking at, what were you thinking about, and why did it take you x, y, z seconds to respond? You can explain it to me, or I'll give you the chance to walk down on the concourse to a full waiting lounge of passengers, and you can raise your hand and tell them, 'Oh, I'm the air traffic controller that's going to work your flight, and oh, by the way, I have a problem with paying attention.' Look, if you think the distance is that far between your actions and their lives, you're kidding yourself. You are kidding yourself. That's what you are. Kidding yourself."

It would be complete cornball stuff were it not so frighteningly true.

The pep talks are usually only once a month on training days, required refresher courses. Then you watch movies of runway incursions at other towers and wonder what you would have done differently. Then you watch movies of all the ways the FAA is going to get-this-technology-thing-down and move away from *Smokey and the Bandit* CB radios and into, like, GPS or something awesome like that. It used to be you could go home after the movies were over, but now the FAA says you are not allowed to leave until you have put in every last second of your eight hours of training, so whatever: you read the paper or eat some crackers and bullshit about the chicken wings you had for dinner last night. Whatever. It's not *that* bad. It's no reason to alert your union representative.

The point is: the team. Whose team are you on, anyway?

"The carpool" is what everyone calls Cali and Lars and Eric and Tim, who move as a unit each day in one car or the other and hopefully not Eric's stupid little truck. They've rejoined the rest of the C team up in the tower, everyone again battling rush hour, again and again and again, the morning moves jackhammer fast. *Bonk, clunk, bonk, clunk, bonk, clunk.* Cali's craning his neck, watching an MD-80 he just launched on runway 4. *Is this asshole going to go, or what?* This is an American Airlines MD-80, which in controller language means: geriatrics. *You soaking your bunions there, buddy?* Nobody understands what the American pilots in those MD-80s *do* that takes them so long to roll. Cali watches, hopes. Up in the air, he's got an RJ on approach for runway 31, tells that pilot to square the base, which means don't cut corners, make a nice wide, square turn in the sky. *You're gonna need the extra time, dude. I'm launching an American MD-80 down here. Square the fucking base.*

"I don't think you're going to make it," Camille says. She's back here on cab-coordinator position, overseeing. It's kind of like the outfield. The cab coordinator watches the backs of the guys on Local and Ground, a second set of eyes.

The MD-80 gathers oomph like an old lady getting out of a chair down runway 4. The RJ appears first as a glimmer just past Shea Stadium, bigger and bigger until it fully reveals itself. These airplanes are headed toward each other on intersecting runways. Too fast. Too soon. Here it comes. The MD-80 is not over the threshold. . . . *Fuck.* "Go around!" Cali says into his headset, instructing the RJ to abort its landing. It's too close to the MD-80. It's too close. . . . The plane swoops down, then up abruptly, like a gull with a fresh kill.

"Go-around!" says Camille, putting everyone on alert. "We got a go-around!"

Cali asks Eric, who's monitoring all the little choppers and private planes zooming around, if he's got anything at 2,000 feet that might get in the way of the go-around. Eric says he's got nothing. Cali takes the RJ up to 2,000 feet over Rikers Island; Camille radios the TRACON, says we got a go-around you're going to have to resequence.

"Yeah, I knew it was a tight shot," Cali says to the team, apologizing. LaGuardia has *thousands* of go-arounds a year. At an airport like this, everything is a close call, everything is dependent on split-second decisions, snap judgments, jets constantly barreling toward each other. It's people, just *people*, with nerves of steel and uncommon courage, keeping the planes from bashing into each other.

"I knew it was tight," Cali says again.

"Nobody's gonna shed a tear over that shit," says Lars.

"If those guys would have played nice, it would have worked," says Joe. If the American would have rolled faster, it would have worked. If the RJ would have squared the base, it would have worked. If the TRACON would just give more fucking separation between arrivals, it would have worked. If Kennedy with its whiny-ass delays hadn't . . . Well, Kennedy hasn't really bothered LaGuardia at all yet today, but it will. It will.

Us versus them. It depends on what team you're on, and this is the team. This is the C team. This is the *family*. This is what is so awesome.

Joe stands at a computer monitor, poking it as if trying to revive a dead cat. "Yo, Tim," he says. "I can't make my touchy thingie work. Can you insert that Cactus RJ in front of Flagship?" He summons Lars. "Our touchy-screen thingie is not touching again," he tells Lars.

"Christ—"

ONE DAY, LEO, the almighty tower manager, invites me out a little gray door on the tenth floor to see the tower observation deck and to have a smoke. He's tan, square, a little bit short, a little bit rascal. "Back in the day," he says, "people paid money to come out here on this observation deck and watch aviation. Okay? There was a time when this was *interesting*. It was *important*. It was a place to be."

It's windy, hard to get a lighter to light. The sky is crisp blue, crested white. Manhattan looks manageable from here, neatly laid out as if you could weed it.

"We're not Phoenix, you know?" Leo says, shouting over the harsh growl of a launching 757. He's a big cheese. He's in charge of twenty-four towers in the region, including Newark and Kennedy, but the LaGuardia tower, such as it is, is his baby darling. "Nothing against the fine people of Phoenix," he says, "but there's *history* here. They showcased this tower at the 1964 World's Fair, okay? And Amelia Earhart, she flew into this airport. . . . So did all the early airplane builders, people that not only conceptualized aviation but *built it themselves* with their own hands. This same piece of ground is where they flew into."

He pauses dramatically. He squints toward a world beneath that is his, all his. "I make these new controllers understand the history of where they're at, okay?" he says. "Because this is a place that has a heart and soul. It's all about the great people who were here before and their stories. And the stories can be a burden on people's souls forever. I try to make my people understand that this place is unforgiving, and a mistake here will be a burden on your soul forever."

I suppose it makes a difference having a guy at the top who is all romance and conscience and chivalry, the sort of fellow who makes you want to purse your lips, wag your brow, and give him an attaboy punch on the chin. I tell him he's awesome. I never say "awesome." It's a word that invades my vocabulary only here, at the LaGuardia control tower. We turn toward the south, speculate about the choppers hovering over what's left of a crumbled Shea Stadium. We marvel at LaGuardia's new-tower-next-year; the actual empty promise has been standing right here for almost a year now. It is massive, of course phallic, a 233-foot concrete stalk. Lately, it's been draped in scaffolding, a very encouraging sign. A gigantic red crane hangs over the top, frozen in place, as if painted there.

"You're looking at $63 million," Leo says. "It's our new tower. We're moving in next year. No, they really mean it this time."

ON OCTOBER 9, 2010, the guys get their new tower, this time for real. The old tower blocks full view of the runways, and so plans are made to chop it down to four stories and use it for storage.

Over the next six months, nine controllers across the country are caught falling asleep while on duty, including a tower supervisor, on his fourth midnight shift in a row, who nods off around midnight at Reagan National Airport. The pilots of two jetliners fail to reach the Reagan National controller by radio and have to land on their own.

The FAA reviews a comprehensive set of "fatigue-prevention recommendations." Scientists, NASA researchers, NATCA leaders, and some of the FAA's own experts say brief naps during breaks are essential to enhance public safety. (Both Japan and Germany have dedicated sleeping space in their control towers.)

"On my watch, controllers will not be paid to take naps," says Transportation Secretary Ray LaHood.

Nationwide, controller errors increase by 53 percent in 2010.

The FAA continues to tweak its NextGen modernization program, "the biggest change in air traffic management since the introduction of radar in the 1950s." Riddled with software glitches resulting in a cost overrun of $330 million so far, the system is supposed to allow planes to fly closer together, increasing the number of flights controllers handle by about two-thirds, and allowing airports to be busier than ever before.

GUNS 'R' US

Sprague's Sports
Yuma, Arizona

OUT-OF-STATE RESIDENTS CAN PURCHASE FIREARMS IN ARIZONA! read the sign behind the counter at Sprague's Sports in Yuma. ASK US HOW. I asked a clerk named Ron for details. He was short, packed solid as a ham, with a crew cut and a genial demeanor, and he was leaning on a glass case filled with hundreds of gleaming pistols. "Now, these are a separate story," he said, explaining that if I wanted to buy a handgun, he'd have to ship it to my home state and I could take possession of it there. "That's federal law, that's not Arizona talking." Then he pointed to the cavalcade of hunting rifles lined up on the long wall behind him. "Any of these you can get today—or these over here," he said, leading me to a corner of the store where two young men in ball caps and a woman with a sparkly purse were admiring a selection of AK-47s.

"You have to admit this is pretty bad-ass," the one man was saying. He had a carbine shorty perched on his hip, Stallone style.

"I don't know," the woman said. "To me, it looks mean."

"It's supposed to look mean."

"They should make it in pink," she said. "Wouldn't that be cute?"

"You're shitting me."

"They should make it in Hello Kitty!" she said. "I would totally buy it if it was Hello Kitty."

"Sweet holy crap," the other man said. "That would be the worst possible death. Can you imagine? Shot dead by a Hello Kitty semiauto."

It was difficult to tell if Ron was listening in on any of this; both of us had our lips pulled back in pretend smiles. "Now, what can I show you?" he asked me while the one guy went on faking his bad death and the woman continued her torture with something about rainbow-colored bullets.

I didn't really want to buy an assault rifle, much less a handgun, but I was curious to know what buying a gun felt like, how the purchase worked, what all was involved. This was admittedly foreign turf. Back home, saying *Hey, I'm thinking of buying a gun* would be a conversation stopper, taken as either a joke or a cry for help. Nobody in my circle back east had guns, nobody wanted them, and if anybody talked about them at all, it was in cartoon terms: guns are bad things owned by bad people who want to do bad things. About the only time the people where I came from even thought about guns was when something terrible happened. A lunatic sprays into a crowd and we have the same conversation we always have: Those damn guns and those damn people who insist on having them.

I had come to Arizona, the most gun-friendly state, to listen to the conversation the rest of America was apparently having. Forty-seven percent of Americans report owning at least one gun; the U.S. is the most heavily armed society in the world. If an armed citizenry is a piece of our national identity, how is it that I'd never even met it?

In Arizona, anyone over eighteen can buy an assault rifle, at twenty-one you can get a pistol, and you can carry your gun, loaded or unloaded, concealed or openly, just about anywhere. The IHOP was said to be the only restaurant in Yuma with a sign prohibiting you from bringing your gun in with you to eat. "Needless to say, most of us won't eat there," Ron said. The assault rifles stood stupid as pool sticks on the rack behind him; they were black and blocky, with long and longer magazines protruding erotically this way and that, and to my untrained eye they looked like the sort of thing an assassin might purchase on the black market and not, as it was, at a store beside a Lowe's home improvement center, across the street from Sears.

"I'm kind of surprised you carry assault rifles," I said to Ron.

"There's no such thing as an assault rifle," he said. "These are 'military-style rifles,' or 'modern sporting rifles.'"

"But they're *assault rifles*," I noted. I knew that much from TV.

"'Assault' is one of the worst things the media has ever done to us," he said. "Have any of these rifles ever assaulted anyone?"

He went on to say I could buy as many of them as I wanted and walk out with my arsenal today. "These guns have helped our industry tremendously," he said. "They've attracted a whole new generation." Sprague's had earned a proud reputation for offering a wide selection of firearms some other stores didn't even stock. "We specialize in many high-grade guns and the politically incorrect black guns with extended magazines," the store website boasts. People from nearby California, one of seven states where assault weapons are banned, came in just to see them in person. "Is there one you want to see or try?" Ron asked. "We have a shooting range next door."

I asked him to help me pick.

"It's personal preference," he said. "It depends on how formidable you want to be."

He brought down the Colt AR15-A3 tactical carbine, clicked this and clicked that to check that the chamber was empty, slammed an empty magazine into it, and handed it to me. It felt disappointingly fake, an awesome water pistol, perhaps, or a Halloween prop, and I handled it awkwardly, like a toddler trying to figure out what to do with a fork, and Ron could tell I was uncomfortable with it.

"If you were more of a radical, militia-type person I would say yeah, an AR makes all the sense in the world," he said, "but that's not where you're coming from."

I asked if I would need to tell him why I wanted to buy a gun like that, or tell him what I intended to do with it. He squinted and smiled and appeared politely speechless. "Would you have to do what, now?" he asked.

"Well, why *would* I want one of those guns?" I asked. "What would be my reason?"

"If anyone asks, you can say it's your Second Amendment right, I guess, but beyond that . . ."

It was hard for us to find a comfortable, common starting place, but the reach was certainly genuine.

One of the things I wanted to talk to Ron and the people at Sprague's about was Arizona's infamous 2011 Tucson massacre, and I wondered when would be an appropriate time to bring it up; the massacre was, well, a *massacre*, and I feared it would dampen the mood.

A small detail in the timeline of that horrific day always stuck with me. When Jared Loughner got into his dad's car that morning to go shoot Gabby Giffords, he ran some errands first. He stopped at the Circle K on Ina Road to get something to eat. He went down to the Walgreens to pick up some photos he'd gotten developed. Then he went to the Walmart Supercenter at the Foothills Mall to get some ammo for his Glock. Something reportedly happened there. A snag in the plan. The clerk at the register, who was never identified, and whom Walmart corporate officials refused to talk about, said no. He, or she, denied the sale to Loughner, who left and went to a different Walmart six miles away, where he bought enough ammunition to fill two fifteen-round magazines and the thirty-three-round extended magazine he would unload a few hours later into the crowd over at Safeway, killing six and injuring another thirteen, including Giffords.

Why did the first Walmart clerk refuse the sale, and how? What did this person see in Loughner and where does a private citizen get the authority, or the gumption, to refuse to sell ammo to someone? These questions were never answered, if they were even asked by media providing day-and-night coverage in the bloody aftermath. The mysterious clerk at the Foothills Mall Walmart dropped out of the headlines almost as soon as he, or she, appeared. What may have lingered then for some, or at least it did for me, was a nagging sense of unfinished business. So these are the people who stand at the front line guarding America against its lunatic mass murderers? Clerks at Walmart. Clerks at sporting goods stores. Minimum-wage cashiers busily scanning soccer balls, fishing tackle, and boxes of Tide.

RON GREW UP IN YUMA and had worked at Sprague's for twenty-seven years; several of his coworkers had put in at least twenty. All of the clerks milling about the store were clean-cut, dressed in crisp buttoned shirts with their names embroidered on the pockets, and the respect they showed the merchandise reminded me of department store shoe salesmen in the old days who wore suits and used shoehorns. The store was brightly lit and impeccably clean—no dust or cobwebs on the hundreds of bobcat, coyote, elk, and other taxidermy mounted on high—and no fingerprints or smudges on any of the cases. "You have to go *fast,* in circles—it's all about friction and *heat,*" one clerk said to another, sharing tips on glass cleaner and shine. Stray scraps of paper were instantly swept up, Disneyland style, and the sheer number of clerks standing at the ready meant that no customer ever had to wait. The merchandise was arranged in boutique fashion: colorful boxes of ammo stacked like candy by the register, a library of gun books and magazines near the restrooms. There was a holster department, a gun safe department, and an optical equipment department—*OVER 75 MODELS OF BINOCULARS IN STOCK! OVER 100 MODELS OF RIFLE SCOPES IN STOCK!* There was a knife department under halogen lighting accentuating the dazzle of each blade, and a law enforcement department—handcuffs, thumb cuffs, leg irons, stun guns, Tasers—against a backdrop of stuffed sheep. Sleek flat screens ran silent footage of dramatic hunts in each corner of the store, and earnest country singers provided a storewide sound track of unrequited love, hard work, and whiskey.

The guns were in the back of the store, and this is where most of the customers hung out.

"I have six handguns—bought five of them here," an old man said to me. I was waiting for Ron, who'd gone to the back room to find a gun he thought I might like. "I have five rifles, all of them here," the man said. "I spend most of my time reloading shells. All my friends are dead." He had thin white hair and a long, sagging face dotted with age spots. "Do you know what the biggest problem with divorce is? It's the bedroom. And a lot of it's the man's fault. Like a damn rabbit, on and off."

It felt like we should have had rocking chairs, perhaps a set of checkers between us. This was one of the things I liked most about Sprague's: the general-store feel. Groups would form, strangers becoming neighbors discussing one gun or another, sharing stories. "I lost my wife in November," the man said. "Sixty years. Now my kids keep trying to get me to go live with them in California. My doctor said, 'What's your lifestyle?' I told him guns. He said, 'Stay in Yuma.' "

Ron came back carrying two assault rifles. "Hey there," he said, greeting the old man. "What brings you in today?"

"Same as yesterday."

Gently, Ron placed the assault rifles on the counter. He told me one was a Smith & Wesson M&P15, and the other a Heckler & Koch 416. They looked every bit as formidable as the AR but these were .22s and Ron said they'd be easier to shoot.

"So more like beginner assault rifles?" I asked.

"There-is-no-such-thing-as-an-assault-rifle," Ron said.

The Smith M&P15 sold for $425 and had a bright orange cardboard wrapper on its fat barrel that said *Kick Brass*. The HK416, made in Germany, had white engraved lettering on it, probably a classier look, for $529. But the Smith was lighter, easier to carry, and the orange wrapper was exciting. "I'll go with this one," I said.

"Okay, you'll need to fill this out." He handed me a six-page government-issued form, told me not to make any mistakes or else I'd have to start all over. "No cross-outs," he said.

Anyone in America who wants to buy a gun has to fill out ATF Form 4473, with thirty-six questions in all, and hand it in to the dealer selling the gun. The clerk takes the form and contacts NICS, the FBI's National Instant Criminal Background Check System (open every day of the year except Christmas), where an examiner runs your answers through a series of databases to make sure you haven't lied, and within minutes tells the clerk what to do: proceed with the sale, deny it, or delay it for three days while NICS does some deeper digging and decides later.

PLEASE PRINT.

Are you a fugitive from justice?

Have you ever been adjudicated mentally defective?

Are you subject to a court order restraining you from harassing, stalking, or threatening your child or an intimate partner or child of such partner?

Have you ever been convicted in any court for a felony, or any other crime, for which the judge could imprison you for more than one year, even if you received a shorter sentence including probation?

I stood there puzzling through the form when a guy walked up, replacing the old man beside me, and he, too, struck up a conversation. He was a man of some heft in a red T-shirt and sunglasses wrapped behind his neck, as was the fashion in Yuma. "You say you're just starting out?" he said. "You picked a good one. With the HK, you would have just been paying for extra steel you didn't need."

"That's sort of what I thought," I lied.

"I just got that same Smith for my kid," he said.

I looked at him. He appeared far too young to have a grown son.

"Wait, how old is your kid?" I asked.

"Six," he said.

RICHARD SPRAGUE, the owner of Sprague's Sports, is a slender man in his fifties with a tapered face and coarse graying hair, and he wears crisp, well-ironed outdoorsman attire. Other Arizona gun stores would not even entertain my request to visit and ask questions about selling guns and ammunition, but Richard without hesitation invited me to spend as much time as I wanted at Sprague's—behind the counter, in the back room, at the shooting range, anywhere I wished. I thought it a somewhat courageous offer, especially given that a 2010 *Washington Post* investigation spectacularly put Sprague's eleventh on a list of top U.S. stores that sold guns traced to crime scenes in Mexico. In response to the hoopla, Richard said that he and his employees were always on the lookout for straw purchasers: a person buying a gun for someone who hadn't passed the background check. "Unfortunately," he said, "some people do break the law once they leave our store."

The Mexican border was just eight miles away from Yuma, and so proximity, rather than reckless selling, was probably the truer though far less titillating explanation of the ranking. And the number crunching behind the headline was misleading: the actual number traced to Sprague's was just fifty-five out of an impressive sixty thousand guns smuggled to Mexico.

In his office overlooking the showroom, Richard had a poster-sized sepia photo of the old days, more than eighty years ago, when his grandfather came to Yuma and bought the godforsaken desert plot and put up a hotel where the store now sits with a crowded, aging suburbia having grown around it. Richard's father added a gun store to the hotel in the 1950s, then moved the store into its own building, and over the years Richard expanded and expanded it, eventually putting up a whole new building in 2005, a superstore, with a ten-lane, 25-yard air-conditioned shooting range with café seating, a separate archery range, a classroom with desks and whiteboards, office space, an employee lounge, and a vast 5,300-square-foot showroom with sturdy iron benches out front where folks can rest and Scouts can come sell their raffle tickets and cookies.

He was a busy man, with quick eyes, and he spoke of "firearms" and "the industry" in the dry, responsible way a man might discuss flood insurance. He talked more about his family than he did guns. He told me about his brother, who died an early heart-related death, and who worked in Hollywood teaching Stallone and Schwarzenegger and others how to not look like idiots when they handled those monster weapons. He spoke proudly of the long line of Spragues, and the raw weirdness of being the last of his generation left. He volunteered information about divorces and remarriages and his love for Allyson, the one who helped him get it right. He took me to his house to meet their Doberman puppy and toured me around Yuma, a cozy town of about ninety-three thousand people with a lovingly preserved adobe downtown with parks stretching along the river, where kids swam and families picnicked under the ironwood trees. This is fertile land, where the Gila River empties into the Colorado—green, sunny, warm, a winter home for snowbirds parking their bright white RVs in rows stretching miles and miles into the horizon.

Richard and Allyson took me to the Yuma County Fair, where, in a little trailer for VIPs, Richard's picture hung on the long wall of men who had served as president of the fair board. We ate pork and potatoes and corn outside with neighbors and tapped our feet to the Western Underground country band. When two fighter jets from the Yuma Marine Corps Air Station base zoomed loudly overhead, I instinctively ducked, and Richard looked into the sky and said, "The sound of freedom."

He was proud of Yuma and wanted me to like it and I told him I did. He was proud of the firearms industry and wanted me to like that, too, and I was working on it. Unlike the conversation stopper back home, here in Yuma, saying, "Hey, I'm thinking of buying a gun," was more or less presumed, like picking up dry cleaning, or getting a haircut.

Guns could be fun too. Allyson liked trap and skeet, and so one day she took me shooting. We drove fifteen miles into the desert where Sprague's operates an outdoor range, and we took turns with the long gun aiming into the sky at soaring orange clay pigeons about the size of hockey pucks. Trap (the disks fly into the distance) and skeet (they swoop in an arc across the sky) are shooting games that have nothing to do with killing anything. The clay simply goes *poof* into the air if your aim is good enough, which mine was just once out of perhaps twenty-five tries. Without the burdensome image of killing, I found shooting guns completely enjoyable. "Pull!" I shouted, followed by "Oh, shit," a pattern that reminded me of summer nights at the driving range, or swinging in circles at the batting cages.

"What's the most surprising thing about your trip so far?" Richard asked me one morning. We were driving back from a daybreak session at the outdoor range, where he had given me some beginner lessons on how to shoot my new M&P15. It wasn't hard. Virtually no recoil, just as Ron had promised, and while in that way I was satisfied with my purchase, I found that I could not let go of a feeling of disappointment, of some kind of tangled shame that had nothing to do with shooting guns, or gun ownership, but that somehow I had wimped out and bought an assault rifle a six-year-old could use. Already, by that point, I was thinking about getting another gun. I thought about the Olympic Arms Plinker Plus I hadn't really gotten a chance to examine and how much I enjoyed saying "Plinker Plus." I thought about investing in a vintage Uzi and how much fun it would be to say, "Dude, I have an Uzi."

Arizona was big on freedom and the feeling of recklessness was intoxicating.

"The most surprising thing?" I said to Richard. He was backlit against a morning sky exploding with red and pink and orange. "That's going to be hard to summarize."

"There must be something," he said.

"I guess the most surprising thing is that everyone here thinks guns are so normal," I said. I told him it wasn't like that where I come from, not like that at all.

He nodded in consideration, and I wondered if he understood. I offered him a piece of gum and he took it and for a while we just chewed and admired the passing mesquite. "Think of just the hunters," he said. "Thirteen million in this country. That's thirteen million Americans trained with firearms—the equivalent of the largest army in the world." He flipped his visor down to cut the sky. "Anyone thinking of invading this country has to take *that* into consideration."

Well, wow. Hunters? Hunters rising up? It took me a moment to conjure the image. I wondered whom Richard imagined an army of guys dressed in Day-Glo orange and hip waders rising up against. Al Qaeda? The Chinese?

I asked him who. *Who?*

He shrugged, said it could be anyone, another country, anyone. He said the whole point of guns was personal responsibility: taking care of yourself, your family, your neighborhood, your country. The more people there are with guns, the safer the society. "That's part of what has made this country great," he said. "That we have the freedom to make sure we're safe, that we have the means to protect ourselves, to be ready for even the occasional wackos that are out there."

I hadn't come to Yuma to discuss the Second Amendment, but it kept coming up, as pervasive as the constant hot sunshine. People wanted to talk about it, defend it, explain. I wasn't there to challenge the position, but I did feel like a foreigner bringing news from a distant society. *Where I come from, people don't talk about the right to bear arms all that much; we just don't.*

"The largest army in the world," Richard said again. "Bigger than China's. And if you think Afghanistan and their populace is well armed, wait till they try to come into this country. It should give you some cause for comfort."

He looked at me. I had my head jutted forward and my thumbnail between my teeth.

"That's just how I look at it," he said, and continued driving. The heat on the horizon was already visible in wobbles and waves.

YUMA HIGH SCHOOL is the home of the Criminals, and at home games the football players storm onto the field behind police cars blaring their sirens and circling the team frantically while the mascot, a giant miserable-looking bobble-headed dude in striped prison gear, runs Keystone Kop–style to whip up the fans, many of them dressed in "Crimwear," criminal-themed T-shirts and hoodies available in the school store—the "Cell Block."

The motif is on account of the famous Yuma Territorial Prison, a massive, craggy adobe landmark sitting since 1876 high on a hill in downtown Yuma and where today you can pay $5 for a tour. Yuma is proud of its prison, celebrating it in postcards and parades like the annual Yuma Prison (motorcycle) Run that happens every April. People in Yuma find it notable that in the old days folks back east regarded the Yuma Territorial Prison as the absolute worst place a convict could be sent.

The criminal imagery was simply a backdrop, of course, but it did help explain things: Bad guys were everywhere. Keeping yourself armed against them was not a matter of debate so much as a way of life, a routine as obvious as church. The bad guys were coming, and you were naïve or just plain stupid not to be prepared.

Nearly all the shoppers I met at Sprague's came in asking for something for self-protection. They wanted guns for their nightstands, guns for their purses, guns for their pickups, guns for holsters on waistbands, ankles, and bras. A guy in a wheelchair wanted a pistol to keep beside his thigh, something with a light trigger pull, because his illness made his hands weak. A tiny woman with a spray of tattoos beside her eye wanted something "big, blocky, and manly-looking" to scare off would-be attackers. An old woman with long gray hair wanted something for her kitchen drawer.

"Where I come from, people don't talk about shooting bad guys as much as you folks do," I said one day to a gathering of customers and clerks.

"You depend on the government to protect you," said a middle-aged woman dry-firing a Ruger. She was admiring the smooth trigger action and regretting her clunkier Glock. "We depend on ourselves," she said.

"It's an entirely different mind-set back east," said Kevin, a slim clerk with thinning black hair who had sold me a ticket for the Yuma Catholic High School 125 Gun Raffle. "You can get a *permit* in New York City to own a gun," he said. "That's the thing. They'll *permit* you. In Arizona we don't care. Our government doesn't *allow* us, our government stays out of our ability to protect ourselves."

But—from what? I'd never been attacked by anyone; I didn't know anyone who had ever been attacked by anyone. I follow the news, of course, and I see violence enacted all the time on TV. But

I didn't walk around in fear of getting mugged, or worse. Was this simply naïve? The people shopping at Sprague's were saying yes, yes, a thousand times yes. Anyone without a gun was inviting disaster.

I thought about my assault rifle. I did not consider personal protection when I bought it. In a bragging and joking way, I sent photos of it to people back home. I kept the *Kick Brass* wrapper on it and I tried to position it so it looked mean. I didn't tell anyone that it wasn't a gun that could easily blow a guy's head off or anything, even though it did sort of look like it could, and I didn't say anything about the six-year-old. I read somewhere that the .22 caliber is the gun of choice for Mafia hit men and that made me feel a little better about my choice. I recognized that these were almost certainly socially abnormal thoughts—feeling good that the gun you bought was indeed a killing machine—but that did not stop me from having them.

It is difficult for me to say what exactly was prompting me, or what sort of corner I was turning. Perhaps buying an assault rifle—even as a joke, or an experiment—puts you over some sort of threshold. Or it could be something about anyone's capacity to get caught up in a shopping frenzy: hang around people buying stuff long enough and pretty soon you want to buy the stuff too. I do know the gadgetry of guns appealed to me. The clicking and the clacking, little laser attachments you could add, the feel of steel so expertly shaped to fit a human grip.

Standing at the counter with Kevin, I asked him to show me something small, for my purse.

"Women always come in saying they want something small," he

said. "Then they find out how much harder a small gun is to shoot. Save yourself the time and get something big."

He unfolded a felt pad and put it on top of the glass case, then brought out a Glock 9mm semiauto. It felt solid and serious. He showed me how to slap in the magazine and how to pull back the slide. It was an unnatural action, kind of a pull and a push at the same time, and I didn't take easily to it. I asked to see an alloy Smith & Wesson on the top shelf of the case. It was wearing a little tag about being feather-light. Kevin said it was too small for me and the caliber was worthless.

"You're not going to stop anybody with a .22. It's going to poke little holes in the guy."

"He'll run off after that," I said. "Anybody would."

"He's on meth," Kevin said. "He's got your kid by the throat. It's the middle of the night and he's going to take your whole family out. He's coming after you. He's dragging your kid. *He's on meth!* He's not feeling your little .22s hitting him, I promise you. Those bullets are going right through him, and the ones that miss are going through the drywall right into the baby's room—"

I put the Smith down on the counter and shifted my weight in consideration. If anything like that happened to me, or my kid, I definitely would want something capable of blowing a guy's face off.

I paid $450 for the Glock, a used one—a bargain. Normally a gun like that would go for $100 more.

Kevin said he would ship it to a licensed dealer near my home in Pennsylvania, in accordance with federal law, and I could pick it up there. I could then go to my local sheriff's office and in the time it would take to snap my picture, print it out, and laminate it, I would be able to get a license to carry my new Glock concealed.

All of it was so easy, and that really was the only confusing part about buying guns. So easy. And yet, why should it be difficult for me to get a gun? I wasn't a criminal. I wasn't going to commit a heinous act—not unless I had to defend myself or my family. Defending yourself and your family is what good people do. Getting a gun should be easy for good people, and impossible for bad people. The only trick is telling the difference.

AT SPRAGUE'S THEY OFFER gun safety classes, five dollars each, and the guys at the counter were always eagerly suggesting them to first-timers, pointing out that actually the classes were free, since they came with a five-dollar coupon to the store. I took the "First Shots" class, which was all about handguns. Fifteen of us sat in a quiet little classroom next to the shooting range, where Richard had set up fresh coffee and cookies, and we marveled at the heft of various pistols and semiautos and passed them around like science experiments. Nic, the instructor, made us wear geeky eye and ear protection, all of which ceased being geeky when we got into the range and started shooting and hot brass shell casings occasionally popped like hayseeds out of the semiautos, and every *bang!* reverberated through your ribs and teeth and toes. All of the older guys at Sprague's complained of being half deaf from years of shooting.

Nic handed me a Ruger .22 target pistol, and he told me to stand square, lean forward, squeeze gently, and I unloaded ten rounds at a red circle twenty-five feet away. He flicked a switch on the wall, and the target came zooming toward us as if on a clothesline. "Awesome!" he said, I think, because I couldn't hear. My target showed four beautiful holes smack-dab in the coveted red zone, and six others nearby. I told Nic I wanted more bullets and he refilled the magazine.

My aim the second go was high, way high of the target. "You're anticipating the bang," he shouted. "You're thinking 'bang' and pulling up." I asked for more bullets.

My third go was terrible. Thinking about anything but "bang" when you knew "bang" was coming was apparently some centered state of consciousness I could not reach. I asked for more bullets. I thought about the enormity of responsibility dumped on your shoulders the moment you decide to add a gun into your life. You have to know how to use it, and if you plan to use it for self-defense, you have to practice and practice until the memory is in your muscles. You don't want to be fumbling, trying to figure out the slide on your Glock or the safety switch on your Ruger or trying to go Zen when your adrenaline is saying, *Fuck! I'm gonna die!*

Nic adjusted my grip, moved my pinkies and thumbs, and pushed me so my stance was way forward, unnaturally forward, and, perhaps like anyone learning a new instrument, I needed to get the damn thing right. I asked for more bullets.

I got to thinking about the attacker coming at me with my kid by the throat, how I'd have one chance to stop him from ruining everything I ever loved, and my aim got worse. There was so much head in this game. I asked for more bullets. Nic taught me how to load the magazine myself. Press on the spring, insert the little brass bullet, repeat, pull, insert, repeat, repeat, repeat. It was a pain in the ass. Imagine playing a video game and having to stop every two minutes to change the batteries. *Can't we just get back to the shooting?* I thought about buying a bunch of thirty-three-round magazines—fifty-round magazines?—for my Glock and filling them up at home in front of the TV, like knitting, so I would be all set up for next time. After the Tucson shootings, a lot of people argued that a thirty-three-round magazine shouldn't even be legal. The kind of high-capacity magazine that enabled Loughner to get off as many rounds and shoot as many people as quickly as he did was banned from manufacture and sale from 1994 to 2004, when the federal assault-weapons ban expired. Attempts to bring the law back have failed.

In those moments I could not understand why a senator or congressman or anyone should have a say over my decision to watch TV and fill large and extra-large magazines with bullets.

I stood square, shut one eye, and fired the Ruger again and hit the red zone twice. I felt like a hero. I asked for more bullets.

WORKING IN A GUN STORE is hard on your feet, and your back. There was a stool behind the counter at Sprague's and I was trying not to hog it. I sat and watched customer after customer feel and fondle and dry-fire guns, and I thought about the burden on the clerks whose job it was to dole out firepower—only to the good guys, never to the criminals and the crazies.

I saw customers get turned down, most commonly teenagers getting carded when they tried to buy bullets. You had to be at least eighteen to buy rifle or shotgun ammo, twenty-one to buy rounds for a handgun. "Sorry, man," the clerk would say. One clerk told me about drunks wanting to buy guns, drunks wanting to buy knives—he could smell them as soon as they came through the door: "Sorry, man." Another told me about ATF agents waiting out in the parking lot, hoping to nab people in the act of making straw purchases—a constant threat at a store so close to the border to Mexico, where private citizens are effectively not allowed to own firearms.

Sergio, one of the clerks at Sprague's, had some thoughts about what it felt like to work behind the counter and size up people like Jared Loughner. Sergio was quiet, small, with a broad swarthy face and a big, rugged nose. He had been in the business for twenty-five years, seventeen of them at Sprague's, and he often sat on the stool.

"You get suspicious," he said. "A woman yesterday. She was with a guy holding a baby. She said she wanted three guns, but then he did all the talking. He kept saying 'me' and 'mine' and '*my* money.' They were just bad actors. I don't mean bad people. I mean they couldn't *act.* I said to the guy, 'I think you're trying to get her to buy guns for you.' And he said, 'Oh, er, ehhh,' and he shoved the baby back at her and flew out the door."

Looking out for Loughners and other lunatics was part of the job, he said, and he didn't like that part of the job. "I remember years ago going to an ATF seminar. The agent was talking to us, the counter people, and he said, 'I need you as a front line of defense. To watch out for criminals.' And I remember thinking he was out of his mind. How can I tell who's a criminal? And I don't have any rights as far as enforcing anything, I don't have a badge, you know, what can I do?"

He could refuse a sale. That's what he's supposed to do, according to the ATF agents I spoke to, and according to the YouTube "ATF Channel," where you can watch informational skits featuring clerks doing the right thing. If a clerk feels iffy about selling a gun to someone, he or she should simply say, "No."

The ATF has little else to say on the matter, because the ATF is busy. ATF staffing for field inspection is puny, severely stunted in its growth: the number of investigators has not grown since the 1970s. (Critics blame the stagnation on gun lobbyists who are determined to keep government agencies out of the gun conversation.) A network of twenty-five ATF field divisions oversees America's 56,000 licensed dealers, essentially one for every two states. About 650 inspectors monitor how the large-scale gun stores, like Sprague's and Walmart, conduct business. Inspectors are supposed to go into each store once every three years, but are lucky if they make the rounds in six or seven, given the manpower.

NICS is designed to weed out the criminals and the wackos so the clerks don't have to. Indeed, Sergio said the background check system, which started in 1998, represented a vast improvement over the way things were done in the old days. About 125 million background checks have since been processed through NICS, with nearly 825,000 sales denied. Well over half of those denials were convicted criminals, 8 percent were drug addicts, 4 percent had restraining orders on them for domestic violence, and fewer than 1 percent had been denied a gun because of "adjudicated mental health."

In 2009, NICS did not flag Jared Loughner's application to buy a gun: he'd never been legally declared mentally ill, and so there was no official record of his lunacy.

Nor did NICS object to the paperwork submitted by Seung-

Hui Cho, the Virginia Tech shooter. He had been ordered by a court to receive outpatient treatment in 2005, and yet there was not an official record of his lunacy, either. The Commonweath of Virginia didn't report it to NICS because Virginia, unlike other states, says only *inpatient* treatment needs to be flagged, and anyway, nobody really has to report anything to anybody because NICS is a voluntary system. Agencies are under no mandate to supply information.

The system is only as good as its databases. Critics say the databases suck.

I spent the better part of the day with Sergio, offering him the stool, him giving it back, both of us sharing sore-feet stories. I saw a guy checking out an AK-47 who had a tattoo that said, *There is only one god and his name is death,* and I wondered if I should say something.

Later, when I got up to stretch my legs, a guy walked up to me. He had a military haircut and a wrestler's build and he showed me the SIG Sauer P226 9mm, an aluminum tactical semiauto he was buying. "Finally," he said. "Do you know how long I've been wanting a good practice gun?" He brought the gun up to his eye and aimed it at the wall behind me and shut one eye.

"I don't know if you ever heard of the term 'pressure cooker'?" he said. "I'm one of those people. I help everyone else. Never help myself. I don't know why I do that, because then I get mad at everyone." He put the gun down, and I could feel myself exhale, and then he went on to recall a time when he got handcuffed in a hospital after hurling a nurse who had tried to sedate him. "But the SIG is just for practice," he said. "I have a .380 auto at home. That's a sexy gun. I wanted a body stopper, so I got a Smith &

Wesson 1911 .45 caliber. I'm a pretty good shot. I can empty an entire clip into six inches. Consecutively. Head, throat, heart, gut. If you're within fifty feet of me, I'm going to take you out."

He gave me a little salute and then he went up to the front register to pay for his new SIG, and he was out the door.

I HAD TO GO HOME for a little while, and I took my assault rifle with me, and I looked forward to getting my Glock. Ron sold me a big black case for the rifle, and he prompted me on what to say to the US Airways representative who would need to inspect it and check it in.

"You say, 'I have a firearm to declare,'" he said.

"And then she'll open the case, right?"

"Probably."

"Well, what am I going to say then?"

"You don't have to say anything."

"I promise you, she will want to know what the hell I'm doing with an assault rifle," I said.

"You tell her there's no such thing as an assault rifle," he said.

I flashed him a bored expression.

"You say, 'It's my Second Amendment right,'" he said.

"I am not going to say that—"

"Just tell her it's for recreation."

Got it. Here-to-declare-a-firearm. It's-for-recreation. I practiced during the four-hour drive to the Phoenix airport. The case was in the backseat, splayed out long as a napping teenager. When I got to the Avis car rental return place, I pulled it out. It was so . . . long, and when I finally got it all the way out, the Avis man with the little handheld receipt printer looked at it. I looked at it. We looked at each other. Words tumbled out of me without warning. "It's a saxophone," I said.

I should have said trombone, I thought, the whole way to the restroom, where I had to try to fit the damn thing with me into the stall. It was weird to pee with an assault rifle wedged up against your shoulder—it just was—and to roll with it out in front of all the hand washers watching was unpleasant.

Owning an assault rifle is embarrassing. The closer I got back to my real world, the worse it got. (The US Airways representative, for her part, was professional.) I did not talk about my assault rifle when I got home. I stuck it in the basement with many locks securing it in the case. It felt like a dumb souvenir you got in some exotic place, some Zulu headdress that seemed fetching at the time.

The Glock was different. I received it within days of my return, got my conceal / carry permit, and put it in my purse. I went food shopping with it. I took it to the bookstore. At first it simply felt dangerous to have it there beside me, like a secret, but in a vaguely delicious way, like having pot in your back pocket in algebra class. But this was a gun. It was heavy. It was inside a little nylon holster and it bounced around the bottom of my purse, where I got spearmint gum on it. I worried constantly about losing it or someone stealing it from me. I became unduly attached to my purse. I brought guacamole to a potluck and had conversations with parents and tried to pay attention, but all I could think was *Jesus Christ, I have a gun in my purse.* Everything got complicated. Was I supposed to tell my kids about it? The only thing I'd ever told them about guns was guns were bad and people shouldn't solve problems with violence and guns were bad, bad, bad. Now I had one in my purse. "Do not touch Mommy's purse, there's a gun in it." I could not bring myself to say that, so I didn't, and instead kept my purse locked in the car at night until I got a gun safe: the "biometric" lock opens only at the command of the fingerprints you program into it. I lugged the gun around town and to the community pool. You can't swim if you have a gun in your purse. You can't leave your purse on the lounge chair and you can't ask the neighbor's kid to watch it for you. I worried constantly about not knowing how to use it, not being a good enough shot. I looked up shooting ranges in my area; the hours conflicted with work, and piano lessons, and dinner. I needed to buy practice ammo, and body-stopping ammo, and, according to my gun owner's manual, I would have to empty and reload the extra magazine that came with it and switch it out every few months—something about the springs losing their spring if I failed to comply.

At the university where I work, I park in an underground lot that is nearly abandoned by the time I'm walking through it at night. More than once over the years, I have thought about carrying Mace. It was back-to-school season and now I had a gun. I could keep my hand on it while I walked and be ready for the worst. I thought about whether or not I could really shoot an attacker: Was I capable? I decided I could, although maybe just in the leg or the foot, and that one threat alone—walking through a scary parking lot—justified my decision to carry a gun. "I'll have it with me at night after class," I said, defending my decision to a friend.

"Class?" he said. "You're taking a gun to class?"

Yeah, that didn't sound right, so I checked.

No guns allowed in school. It turned out if I took my gun to the one place where I felt it made sense to have it, I would be breaking the law. Utah is the only state in America that explicitly allows guns on college campuses, although legislation to permit them has been debated in at least eighteen states since 2007—ever since Seung-Hui Cho went on that shooting spree at Virginia Tech. Armed teachers and students could prevent that sort of massacre, some say.

ON MY SECOND TRIP TO YUMA, I got into a productive discussion with some clerks and customers about shooting sprees. We were gathered in the middle of the store on a quiet Thursday, chatting beneath the $4,500 Barrett Model 99 "Big Shot" sniper rifle, while Clint Black sang about being back home in heaven. The Barrett was the most powerful gun in the store, capable of firing .50-caliber armor-piercing rounds—gigantic bullets as long as a human hand that were packed with enough firepower to penetrate solid walls and pick off a target one mile in the distance. (There was also a semiauto version for $10,000, but these were on back order.) The gun was perched on a display stand high above the others so you could walk all the way around and admire it, like any work of art.

"So how about the Tucson shootings?" I asked our little group, two clerks and four shoppers, all male. "I imagine that was a difficult day around here," I said. I thought it an obvious statement that translated roughly to: *Surely Loughner's killing spree must have given you pause, forced, as you were, to face the dark side of an America that allows for its citizens to own guns.* But that's not what anybody heard.

"The lines were out the door."

"Well, not out the door, but I remember this place was packed."

"Not as bad as the day after the election, though."

"Oh, God, no!"

"Ha, ha, ha!"

"Ha, ha, ha!"

In fact, one-day sales of handguns in Arizona jumped 60 percent on the day after the Tucson shootings. It was not a time to reevaluate a blithe attitude toward anything, but rather time to hurry and stock up in case the government made its next move to take privately owned firearms away, leaving law-abiding citizens defenseless against the criminals and the lunatics.

"Mostly it was people wanting Glocks. The 9, like Loughner had, but really all the Glocks."

"It's so ridiculous. It's *sad* really."

"A story like that just gives the liberals more fuel."

"It's so *scary*."

Everyone in the group agreed on these points in the most casual and obvious way, sort of like people at a grocery store railing about the rising price of beef. I asked them, then, about a more recent event, right there in Yuma, when Carey Dyess, seventy-three, drove his silver Mazda to the home of Linda Claton, his ex-wife's best friend, and shot her in the face. Then he killed Theresa Sigurdson, his ex-wife. Then he drove over to some other houses and shot more of her friends: Cindy and Henry Scott Finney, and James Simpson, all of them dead. Then he drove into downtown Yuma, where he walked into the office of Jerrold Shelley, the attorney who had represented Sigurdson in the divorce. He shot Shelley dead, then drove off to the desert and killed himself.

"Oh, man, that guy was running around and I didn't even have a gun in my shop!" one in our group said. "I got so scared I went home and got my Judge. A .410 pistol. It was all so unexpected. He didn't announce himself. Walked in, shot people, walked out. He must have had tiny bullets—did you see her neck?"

"Had to be a .380."

"We saw a lot of snowbirds come in for pistols after that. Old women who had never even touched a gun before."

"Then did you hear the other day some guy back east shot up a pharmacy? That's probably why I want one of these little shorty shotguns for my truck. He just wanted pharmacy stuff. He wanted his drugs."

"For his wife. She needed pain drugs."

"Something like that. I think it was in New York. Right where they have gun control. He killed, like, four people."

"The problem is, liberals are more *feel* than think. They don't understand logic and so what the hell can you even do with that?"

"It's just so scary."

I was surprised to hear them use the word "scary" to describe those who, back home, tend to describe gun-toting people as "scary."

Nobody talked about the victims of the Tucson shooting, and the only mention of the neighbors shot by Dyess was the size of the bullet holes in a woman's neck. If there were any victims at all to be singled out in the discussion, it was these people here, threatened by tighter gun laws and a government determined to impose them.

"The anti-gun nuts say the motivation is to combat crime. That's what they tell you. But I don't believe that. Put it this way: How do you control people?"

"Despots, tyrants, dictators. Someone who has control over

other people is one of those. I do not believe any of them are naïve. Have you read any Marx?"

"It's not gun control. It's *people* control. If you can control firearms, you're not going to have people rising up in revolution."

I thought about the 13 million hunters rising up to defend America against an invader, a concept that seemed almost charming and heroic now that I was imagining an America under attack by its own government.

"So the military comes in and what are you going to do? Go after them with sticks?"

"Everywhere now, it's all an anti-gun maneuver. These liberals think, 'Well, if we get all the guns away there will be no crime, no one will get shot, everybody will live in harmony.' That's how stupid they are."

The conversation was interrupted when a young guy in Bermuda shorts walked up and said he was interested in looking at the Barrett.

"The *Barrett*!" one of the clerks said, while the rest fell silent as if to take in the sound of the words, and we all looked up at the magnificent black sniper rifle.

I WENT OVER TO THE RANGE to blow off some steam and to release my mind from the endless loop of stupid-scary.

The range was like a bowling alley, only instead of renting shoes you rented a gun. You had to have a friend with you. This was a precaution against suicide, the thinking being a friend would talk you out of it. You could also bring your own gun, no friend required. Whole families came to shoot together, Friday night was ladies' night, and people had birthday parties here.

A young guy came out of the lanes, carrying the target he had just shot up. "Ahhh, that feels better," he said, taking off his ear and eye protection. "*Whew!* Re-*lax*-ing!" He had sweat on his brow and he grinned up at the zombie targets hanging on the wall that I was quietly admiring. You could buy one of those targets to shoot at instead of the same old boring concentric circles or classic bad-guy silhouettes.

"Oh, God, aren't those awesome?" the guy said. "Me and my boys came and shot the hell out of the Paris Hilton zombie." She was wearing big white sunglasses and a pink miniskirt and she was carrying a zombie Chihuahua. "My one boy shot out her cell phone," the guy went on. "And he's, like, 'Well, she can't call for help now!' We just have fun with it. Shoot out her earrings. Take out her dog. Me and my boys having a good time on a Saturday night."

"Boys?" I said. "You have boys?" He did not look old enough to have any sons at all, and I was not prepared to handle the image of one more armed six-year-old.

"My *boys*!" he said. "My *friends*."

"Oh, okay," I said.

I kept thinking about neighbors. You have this crazy family living next door. One day you go over with a pie, figuring if you just confront the crazy, you'll understand it and find acceptance. Then you discover all this time they think *you're* the crazy family. The more you try to explain yourself, the crazier you sound, and if you stay there long enough, you probably will be.

These were burdensome thoughts, and I wanted to get rid of

them. I rented an Uzi, fully automatic, a machine gun. I chose the male zombie. I think it was supposed to be a lawyer. He had a briefcase. I aimed for his left eyeball and pulled the trigger. The patter of thirty-two bullets lasted maybe three seconds, and then the eyeball was gone. The release felt like one gorgeous, fantastic sneeze, and the satisfaction reminded me of cold beer.

BEEF

R.A. Brown Ranch
Throckmorton, Texas

There once was a bull, an astonishing bull with a handsome wide muzzle, stunning scrotal circumference, and a square frame solid as a sycamore. He was the son of Cherokee Canyon, the grandson of Make My Day—a noble pedigree. The cowboy who designed him—who chose the semen, selected the dam, prepared and inseminated the uterus—named him Revelation. "We don't intend to present this bull as divine," the cowboy would write in his 2005 sale catalog, "but we do count it as a blessing to have raised him." The cowboy, although a salesman by nature, was nevertheless not one to speak in hyperbole. He believed in his heart that Revelation, just a year and a half old, could become the most storied bull in the history of the Red Angus breed. Finally, after decades of tinkering, might this be the masterpiece?

Once a year, in October, the ranch welcomes buyers. People come from all over the U.S. to Throckmorton, Texas, in the north-central part of the state, where the R.A. Brown Ranch has been selling breeding cattle for more than a century, and where as many as eight hundred head will go at auction in a single day. Fathers, sons, grandsons—the ranch has passed through five generations, cowboy to cowboy. Donnell Brown, forty-one, is the current cowboy in charge, and at the 2005 R.A. Brown Ranch Bull, Female & Quarter Horse Sale, he sold Revelation to a Houston businessman with a weekend ranch for $12,000.

In time, the bull could turn out to be worth more, much more. Top breeding bulls—once their semen is proven to produce prime calves—can go for well over $100,000. Donnell retained the rights to half of Revelation's semen. In the breeding business, the buyer gets the animal, but the seller typically retains an interest in the genetics—the true treasure. It would be two years before anyone would know the quality of Revelation's progeny, still just embryos in the bodies of select cows.

Donnell Brown wears ironed creases on his Wranglers, a starched plaid shirt with long sleeves, and a white hat with the brim cupped obediently up—not some floppy, haphazard shape like *East* Texas cowboys wear (cowboys who, sadly, don't seem to know any better). The spurs on his boots bear his initials, but he does not wear jingle bobs—those dangling silver beads Arizona cowboys wear (cowboys who are embarrassingly all flash and pizzazz). No, cowboys in Throckmorton consider themselves *West* Texas cowboys: starched and ironed just like cowboys are supposed to be. Donnell is tall, slim, with a quarterback's build and the deep-blue determined eyes of a man who is hanging on with all his might for the ride. No sin. No pride. No giving up on the four life goals he set for himself at age twenty-three: *Get to heaven; be the best possible husband and father; be healthy and happy; pro-*

duce the most efficient beef cattle in the entire world by converting God's forage into safe, nutritious, delicious food for His people. He wears a clean, straight mustache above a constant intelligent smile.

Two years after he sold Revelation, Donnell's dream seemed to have come true: the bull's babies were measuring staggering scores. Donnell knew that the weekend rancher from Houston didn't quite know what he had, so he called him to explain.

"A superstar," Donnell told the rancher, teaching him, as he often has to do, that a bull in today's marketplace is like a football player in the NFL draft, complete with a long roster of stats. He told him that Revelation's progeny were showing beef marbling scores that were off the charts, breathtaking rib-eye areas, and carcass fat depths over their twelfth ribs that were things of glory. It would be a near miracle to produce a bull capable of passing on even one of these super stats—but three of them?

"You should *syndicate* Revelation," Donnell advised, offering to bring the bull back to the R.A. Brown Ranch, where it would enjoy higher visibility, the conditioning of an athlete, and Donnell's help in selling shares so that, in return for investing, many could profit from the sale of Revelation's semen and progeny. Word spread fast. Donnell and the rancher sold seven shares of Revelation for $1,650 apiece and had a list of fourteen more ready to pony up. In no time, Revelation was sure to become the most valuable Red Angus bull in history.

And so, of course, Donnell was feeling something resembling pride when he went outside on a routine cattle call one warm October morning in 2007 and looked around the east holding pasture. Not pride exactly, because obviously Revelation was God's creation, not really Donnell's. But still. He felt blessed. That was it: he felt very, very blessed to be the man God had chosen to bring a bull like Revelation into the world.

"Come on, bulls!" Donnell cried. He sprinkled sweet grain on the brittle prairie grass, and the bulls gathered, as bulls do, like children after the big piñata spill. All of them but one. "Come on, bull! Come on, buddy!" Donnell called to the slacker lying some twenty yards away. It was Revelation. "Hey!" He went closer, and closer still, and that's when he saw Revelation lying there motionless, like some dumb lump of clay. "Come *on*, buddy!" Revelation lifted his head in acknowledgment. But he could not get up. Donnell bent over to find that his right back leg had been mangled, most likely in a fight with another bull, a battle for turf or just a boyish tussle for fun. Revelation was lame, and a lame bull was worthless. A lame bull would be sent without further adieu to the packinghouse.

"No," Donnell said. "Please God, no."

THE AVERAGE AMERICAN at the backyard grill who cares to think about the steak sizzling before him may imagine little beyond the packinghouse, where meat is cut and shrink-wrapped, or perhaps the feedlot, where beef cattle fatten up on corn on their way to market. But those are only two steps—relatively short and highly industrialized ones—in a long process. Before they ever get to the feedlot, cattle live the lives their bodies were built for: grazing alongside their mothers on endless pastures at ranches called "cow-calf operations." These are the places vacationers pass on highways beside flat Ohio landscapes and the gentle hills of Iowa and the Nebraska prairie and the vast plains of North and South Dakota, Utah, New Mexico, Montana. Cows! All those cows! Beef is the largest single segment of American agriculture, a $72 billion industry. It isn't like pork, isn't like poultry. Commerical pigs and chickens live their whole lives in massive, industrial-sized barns. Beef, at least in its beginning stages, will never be produced that way because the simple fact remains: All cows eat grass. You need land to grow calves, lots and lots of land. You need people devoted to a lifestyle. Beef production is unlike any other agricultural industry in that it has remained utterly dependent on the family farm—over one million of them in the U.S. Most of these are small operations with fewer than fifty head, and are manned by the same people who sing in the church choirs and run the school boards and football leagues that knit the fabric of small towns like Throckmorton. Many are weekend ranchers with day jobs who are attached to the land and need grazing animals to keep the pastures mowed. Only a few make serious money at it: cattle operations bring in an average gross income of $62,000, the lowest income of any type of farm.

The R.A. Brown Ranch belongs to a subset of these ranches that specialize in breeding. These are the "seed-stock providers." Whether a steak is delicious—richly marbled, not too fat or too lean—has less to do with the cattle than with the people who breed them. Choice steaks are ultimately determined by their designers, like the cowboys at the R.A. Brown Ranch. These are the people who stand at the beginning of the beef production chain. They are the inventors, the tinkerers who choose the genetics that determine the qualities of America's tenderloin, rib eye, sirloin, filet mignon, and burgers.

April marks the earliest days in a commercial cow's life, and arguably the happiest. The calves at the R.A. Brown Ranch, just six to eight weeks old, have been tagged and now wander freely over the scruffy desert hills where the sunrise is so red it fills the sky with stripes of crimson and turns all the cowboy hats pink. Jeff, a young guy with prematurely salt-and-pepper hair, wire-rimmed glasses, and an easy laugh, has the back of the cattle drive, while Casey and Cameron take the flanks. Without warning and for about the fourth time this morning, Jeff breaks into song: "*We three kings of Orient are, / Bearing gifts we traverse afar, / Field and fountain, moor and mountain, / Following yonder star. / Oh, oh . . . !*"

"Dude!" Casey calls back to him. "Stop! Just . . . stop." Slim, trim, and serious, Casey's supposed to be in charge of this drive, moving about two hundred calves and their cows steadily over the hilly terrain back to the ranch, about eight miles away, for some routine doctoring.

Jeff cannot get the song out of his head. There's a goofy quality to him, an unselfconscious enthusiasm for cowboying that belies the whole rough-and-tumble spirit of the thing.

"You are so in love," offers Cameron, the cowboy with the movie-star looks: jet-black hair, square athletic shoulders, and eye-catching dimples.

"I did *not* say I love her," says Jeff. Jeff wants a wife, a fact he is reticent about with no one. He lives with his dog, Boss, in the bunkhouse on the ranch, the only unmarried cowboy here. The three cowboys are dressed alike: white hats with the brims bent identically up, buttery leather chaps, stiff coiled ropes clapping from their saddles, muddy spurs. The net effect is startlingly quaint. *Cowboys?* This is not some dude ranch where parents take the kids for some reenactment of the past. This is an intact cowboy culture that in fact exists all over America, if you know where to look. Here is a slice of Americana virtually unchanged in the last century, practically Amish in its tenacious grip on the power and glory of tradition. There are some places in the country where four-wheelers and pickups and even helicopters have replaced the loyal quarter horse as the vehicle of choice for cattle drives, but not here. Not in Texas. This is less a matter of a romance—although there is plenty of that—and more of necessity. Rugged, rocky terrain blanketed with mesquite and prickly pear is largely impenetrable to bulky trucks and anything with tires. Hooves, out here, simply work best. Likewise the cowboy costumes: Ride through thorny mesquite without chaps and long sleeves just once and you get the point. The sleeves also protect against sunburn and the hat shades the face and acts as an umbrella in the rain.

Out here on the range there often are no other context cues—just cows, horses, ropes, songs, giant sky and prickly pear, buffalo grass, big bluestem, Texas wintergrass—and so it's easy for a cowboy to lose sight entirely of what century he is, in fact, in.

Moving a herd of cows is not a difficult task, especially Red Angus, notoriously gentle and polite. (For a good time, try wrestling up some Brahmans.) Jeff, Casey, and Cameron keep the cattle in a clump, occasionally waving their arms, letting out a "Wheeet, wheeeet" or "Get on now, gals!"

Jeff: "I never said nothing about love."

Casey: "Okay, then shut up about it."

Cameron: "You've known her for a whole six days."

Jeff: "*Eight*. She's awesome."

The cowboys whistle through their teeth, slap their chaps, and the cattle move as one, a rumbling blanket of rolling amber, humming their lazy cow songs: "*Aaaaroooom, aaaroooom, aaaroooom.*"

Beef, even in this century, is still personal, is cultural, is *cowboys*. Cattle intended for market (the males) stay at cow-calf operations like this one for about six months grazing alongside their mothers, and are then loaded on a trailer and taken to auction. From the auction barn they head to cattle hell: the feedlot, where they join as many as 100,000 others in tight quarters gorging on a corn and antibiotic mash intended to make them obese. It has become a fact of the modern industrial steak: if people want to be able to afford it, this is the way it's going to be. It takes too long to fully grow cattle on grass, and America doesn't have enough grass for all that cattle anyway. Cheap corn means affordable beef.

The mature calf lives at the feedlot for another six months, gaining as much as three and a half pounds of flesh per day. What walks in as 800 pounds will be sold as 1,200 at just over a year old. The margins are stunningly slim: feedlots make about $3 per head. The feedlots sell to the packinghouses, where the invisible, holy transfiguration takes place: animal becomes meat. It is an act of determined ignorance and shrink-wrapping, untouched by sentimentality, as old as mankind and updated to maximize profit. The packinghouse is where beef finally goes corporate. The big four, Tyson, Cargill, JBS Swift, and National, slaughter nearly all of America's beef.

America eats 27 billion pounds of beef a year. That's about 62 pounds per person, or about 3 ounces each day. We show no signs of slowing down. Demand has increased 20 percent in the last decade alone. This is, in part, a function of population growth and in part a function of food science and the efforts of the seed-stock providers: our steaks keep getting tastier.

Beef is low- and high-tech simultaneously. Past necessarily coexisting with future. Because of the cowboys and because of the science.

On the day he found Revelation lame in the east holding pasture, Donnell stood there feeling sick. Gut-sick like a man watching his house burn down, or a groom at the altar waiting for a vanished bride. In the silver liquid-nitrogen tank up in the ranch's artificial insemination center, he had about one hundred "straws," or doses, of Revelation's semen—hardly a gold mine. The most prized Red Angus bull in the world—his very own creation—was now lying at his feet, worthless.

Even the bravest, most proficient semen-collecting cowboy can't get good semen from a lame bull: the stress of injury affects both quantity and quality. (Collecting semen from a bull is a straightforward task: Put a bull in a pen with a teaser cow or a teaser horse—a bull will mount just about anything—and wait a few minutes. A cowboy stands near the bull with an artificial vagina, a kind of warm water balloon, and when the bull begins to ejaculate, the cowboy reaches in and redirects the bull's penis into the artificial vagina. On average, a good bull will make two hundred doses for breeding from just one ejaculation, so it's worth it.)

Donnell took his cell phone off his belt clip, called his wife,

Kelli, back at headquarters, the small red house, with the goat pen outside, where Donnell grew up and now lives with Kelli and their two teenage boys, Tucker and Lanham.

"Oh, Donnell," Kelli said, taking in the horrible news. A bull-breeding aficionado, Kelli proudly serves as president of the Red Angus Association of America, and at the ranch she's marketing maven and sturdy voice of wisdom. She told Betsy, Donnell's sister, who works in the office, too, and soon the cloud of grieving engulfed brothers, spouses, kids.

In the end, Donnell decided, no, he would not give up on Revelation. No. He would try to save that bull. So he hauled Revelation away in a trailer and drove five hours to a veterinary hospital near Austin, and it was there that he learned Revelation had two torn ligaments, the anterior cruciate and the medial collateral in his right rear knee. "Nothing we can do for him here," the vet said, pointing Donnell to specialists at the Kansas State University, eleven hours away, and so Donnell got in the truck and drove farther east. Like Barbaro, the famous racehorse, if ever there was an animal worth going the extra mile, and mile, and mile, it was Revelation.

"We can try to construct a new knee," the Kansas vet said, with only vague encouragement in his voice. "Sure, we can try."

DONNELL'S PARENTS, Rob and Peggy, used to live in the red ranch house, but in 1998 they retired to the fancy home in town with the big columns out front, just as Rob's own parents had done before them. For her part, Peggy laments leaving the ranch: she misses the cowboys and their songs and their shenanigans. Before she married Rob, Peggy's name was Peggy Donnell, and that's how Donnell got his name.

Rob, now seventy-four, is famous in the beef world; he played a vital role in creating the steak now sitting on America's plates. Rob came of age when the Hereford was the cattle of choice for the U.S. beef industry—a reliable, thrifty breed with far more muscle than the Texas Longhorn that had preceded it as America's main beef.

At Texas Tech, young Rob learned of a brave new world. "Continental breeds!" he said to his father, R.A., when he came home with his degree in agriculture in 1958. Breed a Hereford with, say, a Brown Swiss and get a larger carcass with, perhaps, the same quality meat—or better! Rob had other ideas, other breeds, many other dreams. A man of tradition, R.A. would have none of it. Not until he was virtually on his deathbed, in 1965, did he give young Rob the reluctant blessing to crossbreed. Within days of that blessing he died of a heart attack, creating the legend of the ranch: If R.A. hadn't given his assent, the family never would have enjoyed its explosive success in creating better and better meat.

Young Rob got to work. He crossed a Hereford with a Brown Swiss and, sure enough, he got cattle fully one hundred pounds heavier at weaning rate, with the same heartiness as Hereford. *Brilliant!* he thought. But the market did not quite agree. The problem was the cattle looked ugly, not uniform in color like the good old-fashioned amber Herefords. Some came out brindle, some gray, and some had . . . *spots.* Coat color has nothing whatsoever to do with carcass quality, but even so, Rob's cattle were discounted at auction because they looked like freaks.

So Rob got back to work. He bred and he bred and in 1975 mixed a Simmental with his Herefords. That solved the color problem. A year later he added Simbrah to that hybrid, to create cattle with heat tolerance. He added Red Angus for marbling. He got a planeload of Senepol from the Virgin Islands to add a gentle demeanor. Surely the market would embrace the concept of tenderness and quality grade in a heat-tolerant animal with a good disposition.

In 1989 he trademarked his unique hybrid the "Hotlander," a breed still popular among connoisseurs.

By this time Donnell was all grown up, himself in college, studying genetics. Texas Tech. It is the way of cowboys in and around Throckmorton: so many of them having been raised there, playing six-man football for the (2005 and 2011 State Champion!) Throckmorton Greyhounds. ("It's not the dog in the fight, it's the fight in the DAWG!") Guys like Donnell have a postgrad gig already lined up if they want it—family ranches that need them. But even Donnell had to have a business plan—something to add to grow the ranch—before he could rise up in the ranks.

Donnell said, "Dad," when he came home with his degree in 1993. He said, "It's better to be on the leading edge than the *bleeding* edge." In some ways, his father may have been ahead of his time, Donnell thought. He was creating superior beef, absolutely, but not necessarily beef the marketplace *understood*. Donnell brought science back from college, but mostly Donnell brought *marketing*.

Never a place for subtleties, the market understood: Angus. Aggressive marketing by the American Angus Association has, over the past quarter century, made "Angus" synonymous with "best steak in the world." Specifically Black Angus, even though, without the hide, a Red and a Black Angus carcass are indistinguishable. But the American Angus Association promoted Black, and so in today's marketplace, solid-black cattle, for entirely aesthetic reasons, bring top dollar.

"We have to create the meat that people want to *buy*!" was, and remains, Donnell's main point. Rob agrees, of course, but on the other hand he has the soul of an inventor and can't stop thinking of awesome new things to try. The father is the boy in this relationship. Donnell: buttoned-up, doing the right thing, selling it with a smile. Rob: trial and error and fun.

Donnell redirected the R.A. Brown Ranch—which still offers its Hotlander composite—away from fancy hybrid breeds and to an Angus focus with a twist: to become the premier *Red* Angus breeder, and have the superior genetics to prove it.

And he had those superior genetics in Revelation. *He had them.*

FOR A YEAR AND A HALF, the vets worked on Revelation's leg. Surgery and rehab, surgery and rehab and surgery. Finally, and for the last time, in August 2008, the vet shook his head: "No."

"Okay, then," Donnell said. "Okay."

"It was like a close friend dying of cancer," he says today. "You're almost relieved when it's over. Almost."

He did not say good-bye. He is not a sentimental man. He sent Revelation to the packinghouse, where the bull got converted into 1,200 pounds of hamburger. Sometimes now he wishes he could have saved Revelation's head like a deer's and mounted it. Sometimes he does think that way.

But mostly he thinks about Revelation's ear. He saved a notch from Revelation's left ear. He sent it to the ViaGen cloning lab in Austin, and there it sits, on ice.

NOW, JEFF. Jeff used to work in a packinghouse and he hated it. "A whole lot of crazy dudes running around with sharp knives." Unlike Donnell, Jeff is a free-floating cowboy without predicament or a predetermined set of lifelong goals. "I just wanted to be a cowboy ever since I was itty-bitty," says Jeff. He doesn't have a family ranch to inherit; in fact his father is an insurance salesman who long ago escaped the ranch of his ancestors and for years begged Jeff to grow out of his silly boyhood cowboy dream. It didn't work. A man is what a man is. Jeff went to college to study agriculture, cowboyed part-time all through college. He got the job at the R.A. Brown Ranch two years ago and he's building his cowboy résumé, getting his name out there.

Jeff: "I'm sorry I keep talking about her. I'm really sorry, guys. But hey, it's a big deal to meet a girl. We don't see a lot of girls. . . ."

Cameron: "Eight days, dude. *Eight* days!"

Jeff: "I know—"

It's hard for your life to really gain traction without a wife. Jeff met the new prospect at church. He had been going to that church for nearly a year and was ready to quit. ("I'm, like, are there no girls here?") She's real nice and real pretty, but the main thing is she lives just thirty-six miles north. He wants a wife who won't make him move anywhere he doesn't want to move to. The main problem with wives, as he has seen time and time again, is that after they get the cowboy to marry them, they make him stop cowboying.

Jeff will never stop cowboying, and neither will Casey or Cameron or any of the other dozen or so who work at the R.A. Brown Ranch. People who don't understand, or who think small, wonder why a guy would choose to work twelve-hour days out in the constant Texas dust in a long-sleeve shirt and thick leather chaps on a sweaty horse for maybe $2,000 a month rather than, say—especially in Texas—off on an oil rig where he could make quadruple that with no experience and barely an education.

It is a stupid question, to a cowboy. It would be like asking why a rattlesnake doesn't go off and be a coyote instead. It's who you are. It has nothing to do with money. (And listen—cowboys don't *do* grease, or machines.) A cowboy is more like a poet: driven by a passion as old as the hills and the dirt, and one that has nothing whatsoever to do with the world's economy. He will find a way to live the life no matter what. He will talk of individual freedom and America. He will understand that a man's character is shaped by the landscape in which he rides—or doesn't ride. He will smell the dirt and escape to his essence. He will look out into the tawny range under an endless sky and ponder everlasting life. He will listen to cowboy freedom songs on the radio and thank America. He will look forward to meeting Jesus. He will wake up each day at dawn, just like the songs preach, saddle up his horse, and ride.

"Get along, girls," Cameron says, his horse walking so slow he could fall asleep. The cattle drive back to ranch headquarters will take two hours at this rate. It would be more fun if the cattle would act out some. To liven things up, Casey practices his roping using Jeff's horse, Badger. Specifically, using Badger's back leg as his target. Soon Cameron joins in the challenge, the two lassoing high and then snapping their wrists with a *thwack*. Neither Jeff nor Badger cares one bit, Badger calmly lifting and shaking his leg each time it gets snagged. Jeff has somehow moved on to singing "Twinkle, Twinkle, Little Star," and Casey wants to strangle him.

"Hogs!" Cameron shouts, spotting a group of perhaps ten wild hogs scampering between the mesquite, little black buggers, ugly and aggressive. Cameron reaches for the rifle he carries on his saddle, but the hogs are too fast. Wild hogs in this part of Texas are a menace, rampant. Cameron is by far the best hog shooter here, or so he claims, repeatedly. On a whiteboard in the saddle house they keep score and every year Cameron wins by a mile.

"This year none of your hogs count unless you bring back at least a tail," Casey tells him. "*At least* a tail. You have to have proof."

"You guys are such losers—"

It's nearly noon by the time they make it back to the ranch and steer the cattle into a paddock. Then, with whistles and whoops and their obedient horses charging and cutting, they separate the cows from the calves.

To achieve uniformity and to maintain quality control, Donnell likes all his cows on the same estrus cycle. One at a time the cows come through a metal chute, Jeff tapping with a prodder from behind, and one at a time Cameron and Casey rectally insert the progesterone plugs. Each one has a blue string hanging out for easy removal in a few days. The progesterone will keep the cows from coming into heat. When Donnell says he's ready, the cowboys will pull the plugs and give each cow a shot of prostaglandin, resulting in ovulation. Prostaglandin on, say, a Tuesday means each cow will be in heat by Wednesday from about 2:00 a.m. to 2:00 p.m., so one of the cowboys will put on his arm-length plastic gloves and insert a straw of semen carrying some 20 million sperm cells with an artificial insemination syringe called an AI gun.

George, who has cowboyed here for fifty-seven years, is by far the best with the AI gun. "He has a gift with his hands to know how to feel rectally into a cow that most people don't have," Donnell says. George will expertly feel the reproductive tract with one arm, then with the other guide the gun through the cervical rings (the tricky part) and deposit the semen at the opening of the cervix. It takes maybe sixty seconds per cow, and every cow on the ranch, 1,300 in all, is bred that way, as many as 400 in a single day.

The superstar cows—the genetically superior—are put on a different regimen. AbiGrace is the Browns'—and the breed's—rock star in this category. She'll be overstimulated for maximum egg production, inseminated with choice sperm. The resulting embryos, as many as a dozen, will be flushed and frozen. Those embryos could be sold for more than $1,000 a pop on the Internet if Donnell chooses, but usually they get put into surrogate cows—proven moms that don't, let's say, have the genetics to be worth breeding. AbiGrace can then be stimulated to make more embryos, and more still.

Without scientific assistance, a mature cow will produce just one calf a year. With embryo transfer, AbiGrace can crank out twenty-five.

In a week's time, about 65 percent of the artificially inseminated cows at the R.A. Brown Ranch will become pregnant. A bull will be let loose to impregnate those that didn't conceive the AI way. In nine months the newborn calves will drop to the ground, and the process repeats.

All in all, as far as cowboy jobs go, Jeff likes this whole seedstock gig well enough but is not too crazy about all the science. It's not the disgusting part that bothers him, the insertions and goo and glops. It's all the test tubes and the computers and all the shots and record keeping. *Really?* He dreams big. He dreams of working on a million-acre ranch, like in Nebraska or Montana or someplace, where they call the cattle in just twice each year and a cowboy is handed a can of beans and told to get on out and don't come back until he's got 1,200 head moved in for doctoring.

It's hard to know how a wife fits into a dream like that. Hard to know.

CLONING REVELATION is a big decision, and Donnell doesn't know what to do. He has never cloned a bull before, never imagined himself stuck in the mud of such profound uncertainty. For about $20,000 an exact genetic replica of Revelation could be engineered in the lab and soon enough be out there grazing on the silver bluestem. Actually, technically, Donnell could order up two new Revelations, or twenty Revelations, or more.

Donnell stares at the horizon a lot. All day in his truck, like so many days in his truck, hundreds of miles a day, sometimes, to look at bulls, pick up cows. "There's the question of playing God," he says about the cloning decision, "and there's also just the business model to consider." His hair is cropped close, matted tight to his head from years and years of cowboy hats. He wears sunglasses on a neoprene strap, always at the ready. "Like I tell my dad, 'It's better to be on the leading edge than the bleeding edge.'"

He's just returning from a ranch in Coleman, Texas, where he transferred seventy valuable Red Angus embryos into some surrogates. He's back at the ranch, headed down to the AI center to check on the action there. Lots going on today. Spring at the ranch is always nuts like this. He parks his truck. He notices a splotch of dried mud on his starched jeans. He takes out a knife he keeps clipped to his belt, unfolds it, and scrapes that mud right off.

The AI center is a modest white tin barn surrounded by a catacomb of pens and clanking red gates. It's positioned at the far end of the ranch, flanked by shady hills providing cool comfort to hundreds and hundreds of Black Angus bulls. Atop the hill, a lone oil derrick bounces its lunatic head, up and down, up and down, as if davening. Inside the main event is the mighty gray metal chute, a monstrous contraption that can calmly hold a cow or a bull and, with the benefit of hydraulics, squeeze and restrain it. Once in place, a cowboy can do what he needs to do: inseminate, castrate, brand, palpate.

Today, a freelance cowboy who specializes in ultrasound technology is here with his machine, which is connected to a computer, which is connected to a thumb drive, which contains the information that will eventually be uploaded to a lab in Iowa. Technicians there will run a program translating the pictures the cowboy transmits into numbers.

"Howdy, sir!" Donnell says, all smiles.

"How's your boy?" the cowboy says. "He's playing ball next year?"

"Yes, sir, Tucker's looking to play quarterback," Donnell says. "We're mighty proud."

"I'm about through with these bulls," the cowboy says, grabbing an electric shaver. "About a half dozen left. Seeing some good scores." He shaves some hair from the back of a 926-pound young bull, squirts a shot of lubricating oil on the hide, then gently places his ultrasound wand over the spot he knows to be just between the twelfth and thirteenth ribs. The picture that emerges on his computer screen is unmistakably and perhaps unsettlingly an actual rib-eye steak. Clear as a plate of beef at Outback Steakhouse.

"Nice marbling," Donnell says. "Okay, *real* nice."

The cowboy takes pictures of the rib eye, then gets a shot of the bull's back fat. All carcasses are trimmed at a quarter inch of body fat, the industry standard, so you're hoping to see that score low and marbling high. The complete ultrasound takes less than five minutes, and when the cowboy is through he pulls a lever, releasing the squeeze on the bull. The bull roars out while another, with a great clank and clatter, thunders into the chute. Once processed into numbers, the data will go to the Red Angus Association of America, where anyone with a computer can look up the stats of any animal registered. Determining a cattle's worth used to be more mysterious. Just a few decades ago, it was a matter of human cow-sense—a combination of showmanship, gossip, and excitement whipped up at the county stock show. A seller would fatten up his bull, scrub him, brush him beautiful smooth, apply hair dye and hair spray as necessary, and parade him in a circle and hope to win the blue ribbon. The winning bull would thus become famous and could command the highest stud fees for the year. That tradition continues today, but mostly for fun: What cowboy does not want to win the Fort Worth Stock Show and get his photo taken right there alongside his bull in front of a green velvet drape?

Determining value now happens on spreadsheets. A cowboy like Donnell can pull them up on his BlackBerry: the ACC (accuracy) of the EPDs (expected progency differences) of one bull versus another and one cow versus another. A herd's full set of EPDs reads like endless pages of NASDAQ offerings, a chart of numbers expressing the relative values of carcass weight, marbling, rib-eye area, fat thickness, maternal milk, cow energy value, calving ease, birth weight, weaning weight, yearling height, scrotal circumference—fourteen traits in all—that each bull's progeny has been statistically predicted to achieve.

EPDs can be difficult material for the weekend cowboy to master, but for a modern seed-stock producer like Donnell, the information is gold. Breed a better bull. Get a dam with the best EPDs for calving ease and cow energy value and breed it with a bull with the best EPDs for marbling and rib-eye area and maybe weaning weight times yearling height (an online "EPD Mating Calculator" can help with this task) and see if you can't just produce perfection. Tweak with the next generation, try again, and again.

And then one day you achieve glory: you find you have created something no cowboy has ever before created. Of course you name it Revelation. And of course, if it goes lame, you do everything in your power to save it. And of course if you lose the battle and have to send it to slaughter, you . . . clone it?

To date, no more than a thousand cattle have been successfully cloned in the U.S., and the market reaction has been mixed. People aren't sure they want to eat cloned beef. People just aren't sure.

But this is Revelation. This is a historic bull. Donnell would need the approval of all seven ranchers who own syndicate shares in order to clone the bull.

Late one summer night, he sits at his computer, and he types an e-mail to all of them, and he reads it over to make sure it sounds right. He pauses awhile. Nothing to lose by just putting the question out there. Nothing to lose by just asking.

AND NOW IT IS OCTOBER, and a beautifully wet one at that. Throckmorton averages just twenty-six inches of rain a year, and so drought is a constant and real concern; all this precipitation feels like a tremendous blessing, providing green blankets of wheat and refilled water holes everywhere. It's been a productive year. All those cows Jeff and Cameron and Casey and George inseminated last April have just been pregnancy-tested, and the results forecast a promising spring birthing season. The R.A. Brown Ranch 35th Annual Bull, Female & Quarter Horse Sale is just a few weeks away. The leadoff bull is Turbo, son of Destination, great-grandson of Cherokee Canyon, great-nephew of Revelation. He has impressive EPDs—the highest inner-muscular-fat score of any bull in the sale.

"Turbo charge your program," Donnell wrote, on page 67 of the 2009 sale catalog. "Thrust your program to the forefront of the fastest-growing breed in America with Turbo." He expects the bull to bring $25,000, plus an average of about $3,000 apiece for the five hundred others.

And if all that isn't enough good news, the Throckmorton

Greyhounds are once again in first place. *Undefeated* through seven games with Tucker Brown as quarterback.

Donnell, Kelli, and just about everyone in Throckmorton is blissfully possessed by the victorious Dawgs, dressing in purple and gold each Friday night, waving banners, texting play-by-play action to relatives in faraway towns. Posters of individual players decorate the walls of restaurants, and in churches worshippers ask God for one more victory, one more, one more. Kelli is the kind of mom to wildly cheer her son on, but she is also the kind of mom to never count the number of points he scores. "I count his *assists*. When he comes off the field, I tell him how many times he helped other kids score."

And if all that isn't beautiful enough, Jeff has a new girlfriend. Actually, two. No, the eight-day relationship did not work out. Whatever. Now there is Hannah and now there is Sara. Each knows about the other. Because Jeff is honest. He is honest. Hannah is pretty much perfect in every way, lives not too far away, but she's busy as a tick. The Sara situation makes no sense whatsoever. She and Jeff have nothing in common. Sara lives off in the metroplex, goes to happy hours and movies. She has never even met a cowboy before Jeff. No *sense*! How is it that they talk forever on the phone? *Forever.* They laugh. They never want to hang up. She visits. He's honest. He says: "There is Hannah." He says: "I'm Christian and you're a Jew. How would that deal work out? What would we do with our kids?" He says: "I'm not moving to no Metroplex." He says: "I'm a cowboy with cowboy dreams."

He thinks, *No sense whatsoever*, and finds himself calling her again.

Sara drove all the way up from Dallas last night to visit Jeff and to bring him a present. This morning, up at the saddle house, Jeff is telling Casey and Cameron about it, while the three tack their horses, lifting, tugging, patting flanks with affectionate slaps.

Jeff: "It's not that I don't *like* it! I'm just saying: What does a city girl know about a cowboy shirt?"

Cameron: "You should have just told her thank you."

Jeff: "But I didn't *understand* it. I was *confused*. I'm, like, '*Huh?*' It had these shoulder-flap deals. I'm, like, 'What are these *for*?' "

Casey: "You should have just said thank you."

Jeff: "I told her it was soft. I said it was real nice fabric! It's probably designer something. She said she got it from some top-notch store. Norbert's?"

Casey: "*Nordstrom's!* They got a big piano playing all the time in that store."

Jeff: "A piano?"

Cameron: "Guys, let's just drop this whole stupid subject—"

Jeff: "Well, I can't wear something with no shoulder-flap deals sticking up—I feel bad. I think she thought it was plaid and so it must be a cowboy shirt. I feel real bad."

Donnell walks up.

"Morning, gentlemen!" he says. "Ready to roll?"

"Yes, sir," Cameron says. "We'll get her loaded here in a moment."

No matter how neat and tidy Cameron and Casey and Jeff look, Donnell always looks at least three degrees neater and tidier. He has on his dark dress-up jeans and a special starched shirt, solid beige, that bears the embroidered brand and insignia of the R.A. Brown Ranch.

They're headed to a rodeo, five hours away, for working cowboys only—not those flashy athletes you see on TV who rodeo for a living. This is ranch versus ranch, all the cowboys bringing to the arena the skills they actually use each day out on the range. Roping, doctoring, milking, bronc riding. (You would never find bull riding at a ranch rodeo, because no self-respecting working cowboy would ever have reason—or be stupid enough—to climb on the back of a bull.)

Jeff will ride bronc tonight. On the one hand, it's an honor to be the bronc rider; on the other hand, it's what you give to the young guy with no kids and no wife. Just, well, in case. Jeff is pleased to be the bronc rider for the R.A. Brown Ranch. It gets his name out. It's something to put on his cowboy résumé.

They will take separate trucks, Donnell alone in his, because the others know better. Donnell can easily turn a five-hour trip into a ten-hour trip. *Easily.* He likes to visit. He likes to stop and chat with customers. Today he'll pass out sale catalogs and hang posters of Turbo at sale barns, feedstores, anyplace that looks good. He has a roll of tape in his truck.

Soon he is alone on Highway 183. A pickup approaches in the opposing lane and he raises two fingers, waves. He will do this over and over again, every truck he sees, until he reaches a town with too many to greet. Then, on the other side of that town, he will wave again, truck by truck. On and on it goes: he drives, waves, gets his eyes locked on the horizon.

All the investors have said yes, have given their approval of the plan to clone Revelation. Sometimes Donnell wishes one of them had said no. Sometimes he does think that way. Sometimes it's easier when God takes choices *away* from you. It's up to Donnell now, up to him to call the cloning lab and pull the trigger. He has not yet done so.

His dad said, "No." Actually, his dad said, "Nah," as in, *why in the world would you spend all that money on some dumb clone?* It's funny. Because his dad is the tinkerer. The one who always wants to try awesome new things, and Donnell is the one clinging to good, conservative sense. You'd think their positions would be reversed.

But here's his dad's point: A better bull is on the horizon. Something even more amazing than Revelation will come along, so put your faith and your prayer and your energy there. In the future. Not the past.

It's a tough one for Donnell to get. He's a cowboy. A cowboy holds on to tradition, to history, to all that is known and correct. It's good to look forward, of course it is. But it's hard to look forward when the past was so perfect.

He may still decide to clone. He may not. Instead of idling, stuck in the mud of indecision, he tries to think: Revelation plus AbiGrace. The top Red Angus Bull. He has the semen. The top Red Angus cow. He has the eggs. And now he has the resulting embryos in sixteen surrogate cows. Next spring, when the calves drop to the ground, he'll see what he gets. He'll see.

Anyway, right now, he wishes he thought to bring a staple gun. That was dumb. Because tape won't stick to a corkboard. And that's the only place here at this particular feedstore where he's allowed to put a poster. And there are no extra tacks. Other posters of other cattle are using up all the tacks. And he isn't going to take another man's poster down; he is not a man to take another man's poster down.

He needs a staple gun, so he finds a Super Walmart and pulls in. He parks the truck. He has on the spurs he heroically won riding bronc at the 1989 Texas Ranch Roundup rodeo. He has on his fancy embroidered shirt. He again notices a splotch of dried mud on his starched jeans. He again takes out the knife he keeps clipped to his belt, unfolds it, and scrapes that mud off. He reaches into the back of his truck, grabs his hat, the handsome black felt one he brings out each fall. He puts the hat on his head, positions it low, walks tall, and listens to the gentle jingle of his spurs.

In this way, all dignity and elegance and fight, a cowboy enters Walmart on an October afternoon full of steam, the way of sun after rain.

THE RIG

Pioneer Natural Resources Oil Rig Oooguruk Island, off the Shores of Alaska's North Slope

TooDogs is on the run. "Catch me later," he'll say each time I approach, and then he disappears for a day. There are not a lot of places to hide. This is a six-acre island, 250 miles above the Arctic Circle, a few miles off the shore of Alaska in the Beaufort Sea—nothing but white ice, ghostly steam, cold steel. The temperature outside is 38 degrees below zero, and now the wind is kicking up.

"Hey!" I say, finding TooDogs upstairs in the camp smoke room, where he's leaning, peering out a window. Outside, snow blows horizontally, a curtain of weather obscuring his rig, Nabors 19AC, standing tall on the other side of the island, about a half a football field away, lit up in the darkness. It's a royal-blue and yellow tower, platforms and blocks of machinery stacked high over the hole where the drill enters the ocean floor. TooDogs, the "toolpusher," built the rig. A toolpusher is a guy who builds a rig, runs the drilling operation. I'm not yet sure how he earned the rig name TooDogs. Some say it's because he can get as angry as two dogs fighting; some say it's because he's part Blackfeet Indian and there's

an old joke about a boy of similar origin named "Two Dogs Fucking." (He spells it TooDogs, not TwoDogs, because, he says, "that looks like shit.")

Not everyone here has a rig name. Having a rig name is neither a sign of notoriety nor longevity nor respect. Some guys, like Turtle and Kung Fu and Brain and TooDogs, are simply destined.

"You hear that?" TooDogs says, leaning his head toward the window. "*Brrr. Brrr.* That's torque."

He's a burly guy, a Weeble that wobbles but won't fall down, at first glance kind of a clone of so many others here: mustache, wire-rimmed glasses, cap, Carhartt coveralls, bedroom slippers. About ninety people live out here on the ice, nearly all men, some of whom wander around in their pajamas, since it's a twenty-four-hour operation and maybe they're just popping out of their rooms to brush their teeth. No boots are allowed inside camp, a snug set of frozen trailers holding glorious heat, and fresh food that's trucked in over the ice roads once a week, and two beds to a room, and stalls of clean showers.

"You know what time is for?" TooDogs asks me.

"What it's *for*?" I ask.

"It's to keep everything from happening all at once," he says.

I look at him, nod politely. He drags hard on his cigarette.

"Can you imagine the alternative?" he says, and for the first time I notice that his eyes are a deep steel blue, there is a white scar snaking between them, and the saying on his cap reads: HUNT HARD . . . IN ALASKA. He makes his eyes big, and his face gets red, and the scar appears whiter. "The alternative?" he says. "*BOOM!*"

Now I'm staring at him.

"What?" he says.

"I guess I never thought of it that way."

"It's something to remember when your stuff gets cluttered," he says. "You know, when the stuff in your head gets cluttered?"

He says his stuff has been pretty cluttered this hitch. A tangle of thoughts—family, money, work—clogging up his mind. He says it's no big deal. He says it's all workable. "Sometimes I just think my give-a-shit spring is about to bust."

He looks out the window, listens again to the torque, the growl of motors trying to spin the drill bit through rock. "The hole's talking to us. It's tight. *Tight. Brrr. Brrr.* I can't believe it."

I suggest he take me over there, tour me around, and show me what's going on. No one goes to the rig without TooDogs's permission. "I've been asking for days," I point out.

"Maybe tomorrow," he says.

I tell him I'm getting bored with the chase.

"You just have to learn my traplines," he says.

"Traplines? This is a rig reference?"

"Traplines," he says.

"Oh, it's a fishing term," I guess.

"Traplines!" he says. "Like a trapper has a trapline?"

"Wait, we're talking about hunting?"

"It's just an *expression*! Jesus, woman. *Gawd!*"

"Please show me around the rig," I say.

"Tomorrow," he says, and he tells me he has to get going, says good-bye, and heads out of the smoke room. I follow him, three steps behind, as has become our practice.

He has lived in this camp, on and off, for two years, ever since the island was built. How do you build an island to put an oil rig on? You wait until the ocean freezes. You can't dig water, but you can dig ice. Dig to the bottom and excavate a foundation, about eleven acres in all. Find a source of gravel—in this case, a pit ten miles away—because you need a lot of it. Crews built ice roads and started hauling. They kept hauling, 20,000 truckloads, traveling a total of 400,000 miles, the equivalent of about sixteen trips around the world. They had to hurry. They had to get it all done before the ice roads melted. They dumped gravel, dumped and dumped, sculpted a six-acre rectangle out of it, then got to work on a retaining wall: more gravel—8,000 sacks of it, weighing 13,000 pounds each—one on top of the other, *bam, bam, bam,* a barrier to fight back the summer sea. They had to hurry. They had to connect the island to shore, six miles away. They dug a trench, a crazy-long trench, in which a subsea flow line would carry oil. It cost $500 million to build this island, not to mention the brawn of constantly revolving crews of as many as six hundred people working in temperatures cold enough to kill.

I have listened to engineers explain all this, and overall it has been hard not to look at them and think: *My Lord, America needs oil.*

For his part, TooDogs is not overly impressed. "A rig is a rig," he says.

I am still three steps behind. I have learned it is the only way to keep his attention, or what little of it he offers. "Sometimes it's best to just turn the thinking off," he says. "Cut-and-dried. The best way to live is cut-and-dried. Just make up your mind and move forward."

He has toured me around certain areas of the camp this way, often pretending I'm not here. I throw questions up at him; he halfway turns his head and halfway answers, then offers tidbits as if to tease entrance into a complicated mind. "I've been married for twenty-eight years," he says. "We didn't speak for a lot of years. Resentment. Could be. Not on my part. I was an asshole." He says he's a loner, a person who hides, deals with the world only in manageable chunks. It seems an unlikely analysis when I watch how loved he is here, how all the guys depend on him, how he's the glue holding so much of this operation together, a fact he readily if regretfully recognizes. "I'm the dad," he tells me. "I'm the mom. I'm the jailer. I'm the bail bondsman. But mostly, I guess, the dad."

We zoom down the stairway, squeaky clean and bland beige like so much of this place. On the whole, the camp has the cozy feel of a college dorm, or perhaps the too-cozy feel of a submarine. The extreme temperatures make the outdoors nearly as inaccessible as the deep sea. You have to pile on about twenty pounds of arctic gear just to walk outside, where the only thing waiting is darkness. Always darkness. We are so high atop the globe the sun doesn't shine for fifty-six days in the dead of winter, and this is February, mid-death. Madness is a topic of conversation in the camp. How to avoid it. How to bring other guys out of it.

I follow TooDogs toward the dining hall. We pass the loud, uproarious sound of a fiddle playing "Come All Ye Fair and Tender Maidens" spilling from behind the bedroom door of the man they call Kung Fu. Some people like the music, some complain it sounds like a dying cat, but nearly all appreciate the calming effect the fiddle playing has had on Kung Fu.

TooDogs quickens his pace. There is a sneaky quality to his walk, a slinking. I ask him how old he is. "Just turned fifty," he says.

I applaud him for answering a question so directly. "That was really good."

"Shut up," he says.

We come upon Turtle in the hallway, a small, fleshy kid with the constant appearance of someone who hasn't quite woken up. "It sucks being young," Turtle announces. "Do you know my feet are actually still growing?"

"No, I didn't know that," TooDogs says.

Turtle has brassy orange hair, a messy mop matted down on one side, sticking out on the other, and so very . . . orange. He's a roustabout, basically a janitor, the lowest worm on a rig.

"Did you clean your room?" TooDogs asks him.

"That's my plan-forward for tonight," Turtle says.

"You have to clean your room and you have to *bathe*, Turtle," TooDogs says.

"Did you know Jason is *not* married to a black stripper named Onyx?" Turtle says, "and he does *not* have a pole in his garage for her to practice dancing with?"

"Yeah, I knew that, Turtle," TooDogs says. "I knew that."

"He had me believing that for an entire *year*," Turtle says. "*A year!* I hate him. I don't know why I'm even friends with him."

"Go clean your room," TooDogs says.

"It sucks being young," Turtle says.

"I am going to bed now," TooDogs says. "I am going to my room, and I am going to shut my door."

THE ISLAND IS NAMED OOOGURUK, an Inupiaq word meaning "bearded seal," an animal plentiful on the shores of Alaska's North Slope. The Slope is where the Trans-Alaska Pipeline starts, where the crude gets pumped up from more than a mile inside the earth, then gets sent on the eight-hundred-mile journey south to

Valdez, Alaska, where the pipeline ends and tankers come and load the crude up and deliver it down the coast. There, in places like northern Washington and Long Beach, California, it gets processed into the fuel America now so grudgingly remembers makes the world go round.

People have known for thousands of years that oil was abundant on Alaska's North Slope, a vast tundra, flat and treeless, on and on and on, from the foothills of the Brooks mountain range to the Arctic Ocean, an endless, unchanging landscape bigger than Idaho. For centuries, native Eskimos cut blocks of oil-soaked tundra from natural seeps to use as fuel. In the 1920s, explorers arrived and began poking holes. In 1968, they discovered Prudhoe Bay State No. 1, the largest oil field in North America and one of the largest in the world, and a year later the adjacent Kuparuk field, the second-largest. Today, five of our ten largest oil fields are on Alaska's North Slope, where twenty-four separate fields pump out about 16 percent of our total domestic oil supply.

A person can't just drive around the North Slope, visit the locals, stop in at a burger joint. There are no locals, no burger joints, no houses, no cities, no churches, no billboards advertising radio stations playing hit songs. The gateway to the oil fields is the town of Deadhorse, where the airport is, and where security restricts passage to anyone but the 3,500 workers who fly in and get bused to camps in rotating hitches that can last anywhere from two weeks to six months.

It took nearly a year for me to gain access to the Slope. The corporate giants who control the fields—BP, ConocoPhillips, ExxonMobil—are famously private about what goes on up here. Rarely do stories of Alaska's oil emerge unless there is a freak accident to talk about, usually a spill. "At a smelly site just off a gravel road," wrote a reporter for *USA Today* in August 2006, "workers in oil-drenched coveralls tote vacuum hoses and thick towels across a patch of blackened tundra. A lone caribou grazes in the distance." It was a bad year for BP, when a dime-size hole in the pipeline caused by corrosion sent nearly 5,000 barrels of crude spilling out across the snow, and so of course there was a lot of news coverage of stinky oil and filthy workers sucking and slogging. It was indeed hard not to side with the winsome caribou—to project onto it all manner of gloomy thoughts about the greedy nature of the human race. And so that conversation goes.

Pioneer Natural Resources—the company that built the island where TooDogs is in charge of the rig and Kung Fu plays the fiddle and Turtle fake-hates Jason for lying to him about being married to a stripper named Onyx—allowed me to come to the Slope to have a different conversation. Pioneer is the first independent operator to produce oil on the Slope, a market cornered by the three majors for its entire history. In many ways, it represents a glimmer of economic hope. Everyone knows the oil up here is running out; production is declining 6 percent a year, down from an all-time high of 2 million barrels a day in 1988 to 700,000 today. But everyone also knows the oil isn't really running out—it's just a lot harder to get to. It is a common story in the saga of natural resources, whether you are talking coal or gas or oil: The big companies suck out the easy, vast reservoirs, and then in come the little companies nimble enough to pick away at the leftovers.

The ongoing debate over whether or not we should be drilling for oil in Alaska, onward to the Arctic National Wildlife Refuge to the east—from the environmentalist perspective, from the thirsty

SUV perspective, from the climate change perspective that has us all debating a whole fossil fuel shift in paradigm—typically leaves out one factor: We *are* drilling for oil in Alaska, every hour of every day for the past thirty years, drilling in some of the most extreme conditions on earth, where the windchill can easily reach minus 98 degrees, so cold that you have to leave your pickup running twenty-four hours a day or you'll never get it started again, where it is pitch-dark for nearly two months each winter, where people live without families, without homes, without access to so much of what most of us think of when we think of what it means to be human.

Who are these people, and how do they get the oil out of the ground? It seems, on its face, an embarrassingly simple question, and maybe that's the point. Crude. Petroleum. We process it into gasoline, asphalt, plastic, fertilizer. We fill up our cars with it, drive on roads made of it. We use it to make all those soda bottles and all those Baggies holding our lunches, the foam in our mattresses, the padding in our running shoes. The vegetables we eat are protected from bugs by it. We travel because of it, drink out of it, sleep on it, wear it, eat it, whine about how much it costs, argue about it, hate needing it, love it, kill for it. It is our most ubiquitous natural resource, the juice that made the past century possible. How we get it in the first place would seem to be a fundamental building block in our understanding of what it means to be a citizen of the world. And yet here is an industry and a culture that is as alien to most of us as the moon. An *abstraction*. It's not like steel towns, or farming communities, or fishing villages, or any of the places where local industry and economy and culture bleed into and inform one another. There is no county fair exhibiting

North Slope rigs, no crowning of an Arctic Oil Queen, no famous country music song celebrating a guy's heroic deeds on the tundra. There is no blending of Alaska oil field culture with anything resembling real life. Workers go home to Anchorage or Fairbanks or Dallas or Mobile, Alabama, or Jackson, Mississippi. You can live anywhere and work here, and when you go home your wife and your kids and your neighbors will have no idea what you are talking about. They will never see where you work unless they get a job here and become part of the invisibility. Even in Alaska—where oil accounts for 90 percent of the state's revenue—there are no souvenirs, no postcards, no talk on talk shows about what's going on up on the Slope. The situation wouldn't be so odd, perhaps, if we really were talking about the moon, where presumably nothing actually happens. But here is the stuff, the fuel, we're so thirsty for, and here's where people are fighting the worst kind of elements to get it. The longer I stayed on the Slope, the more I wondered how we can be so disconnected from people we're so connected to.

Construction of the island had just been completed when I first visited in the summer of 2007, and a lot of the people from the Dallas corporate headquarters were there marveling at it and feeling optimistic and remarking on the weirdness of the word "Oooguruk." We took a boat over from shore, and we wore hard hats and orange vests and safety glasses, and as we toured around the island, one of the workers stopped to show us a polar bear cage, a giant jail-like structure. There were ten of them placed around camp.

"Wait, why do you put the polar bears in cages?" a guy from Dallas asked.

"The cages are for the *people*," the worker answered. "You see a polar bear, you ring the alarm, and jump in the cage."

Even in summer, when the temperatures got up to 60 degrees, and herds of caribou ambled quietly over the marshy tundra, and the sun never went down for months at a time, life on the Slope seemed extreme. All that alone time. Nowhere to go. Stuck in a camp, little to look forward to other than food and a phone call home. But nothing could have prepared me for life on the Slope in winter.

The temperature, on the day I landed in Deadhorse in February, was 45 degrees below zero. I worried about what that might feel like, wondered if the clothing I'd been provided—thick overalls, massive parka, enormous gloves and boots—would really do the trick. I geared up and felt like an astronaut. I bounced out of the plane, squinted as if preparing for a punch. I felt nothing of the sort. For the first three or four seconds, cold is just . . . cold. Nothing spectacular at all. Then my glasses seemed to freeze to my face, and I took a breath and felt a sting in my lungs that might have been instant ice but probably wasn't. Within minutes, my cheeks, chin, and nose began to ache, first the skin and then . . . muscle? I had no other way of understanding that weird sort of ache. Soon I learned to aim the hood of my parka, lean my head so the fur trim would catch the wind and steer it away. Every little bit helped. I started admiring animals with very bushy fur.

Deadhorse is a place that greets you with the emblematic architecture of the Slope. Nothing is lovely, nothing is charming, nothing is intended for anything other than hard use. Modular corrugated-steel Conex boxes serve as office buildings, machine shops, a hotel, and a general store decorated outside with a cartoon drawing of a dying horse with its tongue hanging out.

The two-hour bus ride to Oooguruk, over the ice roads, was a visit to a post-apocalyptic world, an endless industrial landscape without the humanizing effect of pedestrians. We saw a musk ox. The heater on the bus barely worked, and so the guys huddled into their parkas and shivered but did not complain. Oooguruk is six miles off the coast, on the western reaches of the Slope, and so by the time we drove over the Arctic and into camp, there were no signs of other rigs, other camps. No neighbors at all.

The camp, a series of Conexes all stuck together, was rather luxurious in the scheme of things. Inside, a few conference rooms, a weight room, a movie room, a dining hall. Bedrooms were overbooked, I was told, so my bunk for my two-week hitch would be in an "overflow area." Aaron, a welcoming guy on the operations team, offered to escort me there, leading me through camp and out the back door, which opened back into the bitter air—and into a polar bear cage.

"Follow me," he said, unhitching the thick metal latch, and we went out the other side of the cage into the frozen night.

"So my room isn't attached to camp?"

"Oh, a lot of guys stay out here," he said.

We hurried down a narrow pathway of crunching snow, toward a long building resembling a boxcar that had a series of freezer doors with numbers spray-painted on them. He gave the door marked 305 a shove and it opened just fine. There was warmth inside, plenty of warmth, and a fluorescent light over a bed with a sheet and a blanket. No sink, no bathroom—all of that was back at camp, and so I'd have to go outside, back in and back out of the polar bear cage, and into the main camp if I wanted to use it. Aaron said he'd try to scare up a two-way radio for me to keep in here, in case I got stuck. He said sometimes the snow blows and piles higher than the door, and if that happened, he would come and dig me out.

"Now, guys are going to mess with you and tell you you're sleeping in a bait box," Aaron said. "Because you're sort of polar bear bait out here? But look, the bears are out hunting seals this time of year, up where the ice is broke, so it won't be a problem. And really, it's a lot quieter out here. Very peaceful."

Then he left. I stood there. I stood there and tapped my foot. The room smelled strongly of Lysol. There was an extra can of it provided on a shelf. There was a window with a blue blanket covering it, nailed in place. There was nothing else, just a new kind of aloneness. I've known silence before, and I've known solitude, but nothing quite like this. It was the kind of alone maybe a monk feels, or someone in solitary confinement? No, that wasn't quite it, either. I stood there utterly cut off, a person in a tiny bubble of warmth, out on the ice, beyond tundra, beyond good sense, a freezer door away from a solid white wilderness, a place I figured even God forgot.

Aaron was right about the peace, right about the quiet, right about the bears not showing up, but it was all that he didn't say that kept me guessing. All that no one on Ooogurük ever seemed to say: *This is ridiculous.* Was life out here not an absurdly desperate way to make a living?

For days I would try to sympathize, offer a compassionate ear, try to get at how these people survived the cold, the remoteness, the working conditions, the time away from home. I suppose I was prepared to pity them. I wanted to understand how they'd gotten themselves into this mess.

I was getting nowhere; I couldn't seem to phrase my question in a way that made sense to anyone.

One night in the dining hall, a guy turned to me and said, "You don't get it. We *want* to be here. We haven't been sentenced here. We choose to be here. We are happy here."

TooDogs runs a fair rig, a respectful rig, where standards are high but no one is going to chew your face off for no reason whatsoever like what happened to him all those years roughnecking. All those years. *And all those years before that*. A lot of terrible shit, excuse his language. But a lot of terrible shit happened to TooDogs even before he ever got on a rig and started roughnecking, way back home on the reservation in Montana. Let's just say more shit than any kid should have to deal with. And listen, when he hives up the way he does, it has nothing to do with allergies. It's memories. It's just bad memories popping up on his skin, and it only happens if someone touches him, so people here learn, they just learn, never to touch TooDogs.

He says none of it is a big deal. He says it's all workable. "You can't control anything. Have you ever tried? See how messed up it gets? So just let 'er lay."

I have no idea what day it is. No one here speaks of Monday or Tuesday or Wednesday or Thursday. What would be the point? Every twelve hours is the same, working or sleeping, working or sleeping. Time blends, blurs, all but disappears.

A lot of people I meet on the Slope have a history they're running from. They're running from families that don't work, that they can't make work, that fail them, that they fail. Kung Fu has been in and out of jail more times than he remembers. Stubbs, a recovering drunk, keeps finding and losing the Lord. Willie, one of the young ones who rarely speaks, has a mom at home who beats him. Alaska has always been a place people flee to; the Slope is a place you flee to after you have fled to Alaska. A last chance. For some, it's redemption. For others, salvation.

By now I have spent a good many hours over on the rig, a series of stairs connecting platforms, rooms with roaring motors, pumps, pipes, long avenues of wellheads, bright blue and bright red and bright yellow—it is like the biggest, loudest, most colorful furnace room you ever entered. An oil rig, no matter if you are talking Alaska or Texas or Saudi Arabia or Iraq, is most famously recognized by its tall and mighty derrick, which is the support structure holding the drill. The reason it's so tall—in this case, 183 feet—is to enable drillers to add new sections of pipe as drilling progresses. You keep adding pipe so you can reach deeper and deeper into the earth. The drill bit paves the way, turning clockwise, grinding down. (The scale of all this is much smaller than most people imagine: the drill bit ranges in diameter from six to thirteen inches; the pipe is as small as three inches. An oil well is a remarkably skinny hole.) The people on the rig orchestrate a constant parade of steel pipe, moving it, positioning it, connecting it, sending it spiraling down. They never see the oil itself, never smell or touch it—except in the rare case of a spill or an explosion or some other catastrophic event. The disconnect is absurd, or perhaps holy: the goal is to find that which must remain unseen.

The torque, over here on the rig, has gotten worse. Way worse.

The torque is on account of the top drive trying to turn the drill bit and the drill bit refusing.

"We're stuck," TooDogs says to Rod, his immediate boss, the "company man" who typically spends most of his time in his office behind a computer. The torque has brought Rod over to the rig.

"We are not stuck," says Rod, who also goes by Colonel Klink, after the guy on the old *Hogan's Heroes* sitcom whom he resembles, sort of. "We are 'temporarily detained.'"

"Dude, we're stuck," TooDogs says.

They're sitting in "the doghouse," the heart of the action, command central. It looks like the pilothouse of a ship, only instead of overlooking the sea, everyone is watching the rig floor where the drill should be turning 80 or 120 rpm but isn't. Kung Fu is standing out there looking at the hole, waiting for action. Beside him, the man they call Brain, because he is the only college-educated guy on the crew, is motioning to Andy, the driller, who sits in the doghouse at the console. Mostly Brain's motions say: *What the hell is going on?*

Andy leans into his microphone. "We're *temporarily detained*, gentlemen," he announces to the men on the rig floor.

"Thank you, Andy," Rod says.

"Jiminy Christmas," TooDogs says. "You two should date."

TooDogs and Rod have worked on so many rigs together over so many years, they can't help but relate like brothers. "Rod's hole, my rig" is the way TooDogs describes the division of labor. While the toolpusher is in charge of the iron and the crew and the tone and the humanity of the drilling operation, the company man's total focus is the hole being drilled, an infinitely complicated, invisible place full of mystery and challenge and all the tools the toolpusher sticks down into it. The company man is the guy who reports back to the bosses in Anchorage and Dallas on the morning conference calls, discusses the day's plan-forward. TooDogs goes to the meetings, too, but he doesn't usually have to talk, and one of his favorite sports is watching Rod click his pen and yank at his eyebrows and get all red and irate about how dudes at desks don't know shit compared to guys on a rig.

The drill bit isn't the only thing going down the hole. It's just the tip of the "drill string," which contains the tools, or "jewelry," the drillers need to keep the whole assembly stabilized, to help it get unstuck if it gets stuck, and to read the rock formations that might help explain what the hell is going on down there. The oil is sitting somewhere down there in pockets, trapped, along with gas, within microscopic pores of rocks in underground formations. It flows under its own pressure, sort of like soda in a can. Pop the cap and the gas escapes, and the oil comes with it.

Long gone are the days when oil wells went straight down like drinking straws. Directional drilling technology allows drillers to go down, over, up, snaking any which way through the earth and landing in ever sweeter sweet spots, reaching horizontally as far as four miles from the rig. In the old days, a single vertical well exposed about 200 to 300 feet of oil reserves. Now drillers can reach more than 20,000 feet of reservoir rock with one well, significantly reducing the footprint above ground, which in turn reduces costs and, in this part of the world, scarring to the tundra. If a person could see under Ooguruk after all forty wells here are completed, the picture would be a spiderweb of looping wells.

Stubbs, who works downstairs in the mud pits, comes into the doghouse to ask a question about the torque. "Something's really fucked-up with the number one pump," he says. "You seeing that?"

"We're seeing it," Rod says. "We're feeling your pain."

Stubbs is a thin man in his fifties who moves as if life has offered nothing but wear and tear. He takes off his hard hat to scratch an itch, and I notice that he has, oddly enough, the same brassy orange-colored hair the kid called Turtle has. I notice, too, that Jason, the welder, has the same color hair. There is something going on here with hair.

"I think we lost a blower on the number one pump," TooDogs says to Rod. "I think it's the blower."

"Well, it's down," Rod says. "We can't do shit without circulation."

The two are staring up at the monitors in the doghouse, sitting on a cushioned bench. Turtle has mysteriously appeared.

"Turtle?" says TooDogs, summoning the young roustabout over to the throne upon which he sits. "Turtle, I have a question."

"What's up?" Turtle answers.

"Come closer," TooDogs says.

Turtle moves.

"Closer."

Soon the two are nose to nose and TooDogs speaks. "Why-are-you-*here*?"

"I wanted to hear what you guys were talking about," Turtle says.

"*You don't get to do that*," TooDogs says. "You're supposed to *work*, Turtle."

On some rigs, a lowly roustabout would never speak to the toolpusher, let alone the mighty company man, but this rig is different. Some old guys learn to break the cycle of abuse, while others don't. It happens in all walks of life.

"Turtle, Turtle, Turtle," says Jason, the welder, who is here contemplating how to design a bracket to hold a computer monitor at the proper height for Andy, who has been complaining of a stiff neck. ("Would you like me to make it *decorative*, boys?") Then he begins singing, just loud enough for Turtle to hear, "The Turtle Song," a ditty he made up for the guys to sing on the plane ride out of Deadhorse, which they often do.

Turtle, Turtle, shake your little tail.
Turtle, Turtle, shake your little tail.
Wrinkle up your little nose. Hold a snail between
your toes.
Turtle, Turtle, shake your little tail!

"He's singing 'The Turtle Song' again!" Turtle shouts to TooDogs. "I hate him!"

"*Shake your little tail*—" Jason goes on.

"Criminy," TooDogs says. "Andy, do something about them."

THE SLOPE OPERATES on a 24-hour clock, 365 days a year: Christmas Day, New Year's Day, every hour of every day, there is never a moment oil isn't being taken out of the earth. The typical shift is two weeks on, two weeks off, although many people stay considerably longer than that, earning bragging rights and more money than they can figure out how to spend. There is nothing to do here but work. Everything over eight hours in any given day is overtime, except on weekends, when it's all overtime all the time. A kid like Turtle just starting out as a roustabout can easily pull in seventy grand. "That's stupid money for a kid right out of high school," Turtle tells me. "That's insane, stupid money." For a while, he thought he'd work a few years, save everything, and pay cash for college. But then he started buying motorcycles. And computers. And just anything he felt like. And now he looks at his dad, a Slope toolpusher making 250 grand, and he thinks, *Forget college.* His dad has a house in Florida, has a giant hot tub connected to his pool, custom-built in the shape of Mickey Mouse's head. "It's awesome," Turtle says. "It's the best overspent project ever."

I meet a twenty-three-year-old electrician who brags of having no high school diploma and who last year earned $140,000. Charlie, the guy who builds the ice roads, once stayed on the Slope for seven months straight and, legend has it, saved every check, went home to Fairbanks, and bought a new house. With cash.

The trick for a lot of guys who work here is to figure out how to go home and not spend all their money on booze.

There is no alcohol allowed anywhere on the Slope. A person getting caught with it will be run off for life, no questions asked, no second chances. Everything here is flammable. One mistake and you could blow the place up. When an oil field worker boards the plane in Deadhorse to go home, he will more than likely order as many drinks as the flight attendant permits. Many of the younger guys I meet say they don't stop drinking for two weeks, until it's time to get back on the plane for the Slope. Many of the older guys I meet have spectacular addiction-and-recovery stories they try in vain to impart to the younger guys.

After their twelve-hour shifts, most of the people on Oooguruk eat and go to bed. "There-is-no-where-to-go," they keep pointing out. They're tired. The company had a pool table in the camp for a while but tossed it after no one used it. I never see anyone in the movie theater. I learn of parties, such as they are. Guys gather in the dining hall for ice cream, or chocolate chip cookies they nuke for twelve seconds.

For a lot of guys, home is harder than the Slope. I hear this story over and over again. Somewhere along the line, an endless loop of anguish sets in: the Slope is an escape (from home) which many speak of longing to escape from (to go home), only to discover they need to escape (from home.)

It is certainly not the case for everyone. There are plenty I meet who are building satisfying careers here: engineers and geologists, medics and computer technicians, people who speak of learning to bracket their lives into manageable two-week chunks.

But it's the people on the front line, the roughnecks working the rig, who command the most notice. (Nearly all the people on Oooguruk are subcontracted by other companies. The roughnecks work for Nabors Alaska drilling company.) "Roughneck" is a specific term for a job on the rig crew, one rung up from roustabout, but also a generic term used for anyone who survives the job and graduates to pit watcher, derrick hand, driller, toolpusher, company man. In the same way a general will always think of himself as a soldier, a roughneck is a roughneck is a roughneck no matter how high he climbs in the hierarchy of a rig. "It's the same anywhere you go on the Slope," a guy on the construction crew tells me. "The roughnecks think they're *the shit*. They parade around like this whole place is about them. We put up with it because they're the ones getting the oil. If they don't get the oil, we all go broke." Perhaps, then, there is a kind of indulgence; roughnecks are allowed to be, maybe even expected to be, eccentric and tough: in and out of prison, Harley guys, hard-hunting guys, men who *strut* their badass selves for all to fear.

Of course, there is also the need for a certain amount of guts.

A rig is an unforgiving steel tower, rife with peril: stuff turns, fingers get lopped off, arms, a couple of years ago a leg. That was over on Nabors 14E, where TooDogs was punching wildcats into the ice. Tim, a roustabout, couldn't see through the steam in the pit room that night, couldn't see where he stepped: into an auger that sucked him in. TooDogs reached, grabbed, but it was too late. Both legs sucked in, the guy up to his hips in the machinery, screaming, not knowing his left leg was already cut off, the right wrapped around the auger shaft. It took rescuers seven hours to cut him out. TooDogs held him. Gently wiping his forehead, talking to him the whole time like any dad would talk. They jammed a stick in his mouth for the final cut, flew him out of there to the hospital, eight hundred miles away in Anchorage.

Roughnecks live terrible shit like that, the kind of constant shit that can bond a man to another for life, like combat soldiers who easily shrug off each other's madness.

AT BREAKFAST ONE MORNING I run into Kung Fu, who brings his Bible here each day, opening the doors of his makeshift church for fellowship.

He is a clean-shaven man with an enormous bodybuilder's

chest he displays proudly beneath a tight white T-shirt. He has full sleeves of intricate tattoos: eyeballs, crosses, shamrocks, skulls, peacock feathers. Today he's wearing an American flag bandanna, and he's drinking his pre-workout stimulator, a vitamin concoction his mom cooks up in her health food store in Fairbanks.

"Love should be the only motive in what we do in the name of the Lord," he is saying to Stubbs, who has joined him.

"You're a *preacher*," Stubbs is saying. "You're going to be a real preacher someday! I'm telling you, man—"

Kung Fu thinks he is taking care of Stubbs, and Stubbs thinks he is taking care of Kung Fu. Stubbs has worked on the Slope for twenty-two years and he has been sober now for about a year and a half, a fact he attributes in part to TooDogs, who always forgave him after prison, always welcomed him back—but mostly to Angela, the first woman in his life who didn't steal his money. Kung Fu is not nearly so far along on the sobriety plan, but Stubbs is helping. When he's home in Anchorage, Stubbs will call Kung Fu at least once a day to make sure he's still sober. He also checks in with Zack, the derrick hand, and he also calls Turtle to see if he got dinner, which he usually didn't, so he drags Turtle over to his house for chicken.

Bible fellowship is ending and I wait quietly for the two to finish prayer.

"That-is-the-shit," Stubbs says. "Man, you got it going on."

"Amen," Kung Fu says, and Stubbs heads off and Kung Fu takes a swig of his pre-workout stimulator, smacks his lips, and then leans in to tell me a secret. *"You must listen,"* he says. *"I'm serious."* He tells me to never, ever log on to www.infowars.com from my *home* computer because the site contains top-secret information about the enemy and the enemy will know I'm onto them if I use my home computer.

I ask who the enemy is and he blinks, as if changing channels. He smiles wide, shows me his teeth. "That to me is probably one of the most incredible things I have," he says. "All my natural teeth."

I ask him about the Slope. I ask him why he came to the Slope.

"It made me a new man," he says. "I was leading a hard-core whopper-stopper lifestyle. Like, for instance, you're looking at $180,000 worth of plastic surgery. I ended up getting jumped by an outlaw gang. I won't name any names. I was going to open a strip club, Lords of Liberty Motorcycle Militia, bikes and guns and strippers, and then in the back I could have my meth lab right there. That was my dream."

Instead, he got a chance to get a Slope job two years ago. It was something of a divine rescue. He got the name Kung Fu almost as soon as he arrived. He would walk around doing sword kicks, dive rolls, just spinning all over the place in that way he has of trying to expend excess energy. It was a little weird, but not so unmanageable in the hallway back at camp. But on the rig floor? He started going all kung fu over there too. It upset Andy, who is stressed out enough just trying to make sure his young roughnecks keep the casing connections going without getting themselves killed. You can't have a guy out there doing flying scissor kicks. You just can't.

"Dude," Andy said on the phone to TooDogs, who was over in his office at camp. "We have to do something about Kung Fu." It was not the first time the two had had the conversation. TooDogs went over and saw for himself, saw the ninja performance, saw all the guys just staring at the karate dude going apeshit with his act.

TooDogs walked onto the rig floor, stared at him with those steel-blue eyes. "Kung Fu," he said. "Come over here." Kung Fu did as he was told.

"What the hell are you doing?" TooDogs asked him.

"I want to be Spider-Man," Kung Fu answered.

"I beg your pardon?"

"I had me a dream about yon derrick," Kung Fu said, in a fake Irish brogue. "I wish to climb the derrick, because derrick hand is my destiny. Can I be derrick hand?"

TooDogs stood speechless for more than a moment. He looked Kung Fu long and hard in the eye to see if there was anything *in* there, anything in his brain to work with. Kung Fu had already been run off three rigs. It would be easy enough to run him off this one.

And whatever TooDogs saw, he saw. If there is one force that drives TooDogs, it is a kind of cavernous compassion, a well of empathy that never seems to empty. Maybe because of all the forgiveness he's still working on getting, or maybe it's just the way he's built.

"All right, my man," TooDogs said. "You are going to be my project. You are my poster boy. I don't know what's tripping your trigger. But we gotta find a way to de-tune you if you're gonna stay on my rig."

It is still touch-and-go for Kung Fu, who, with TooDogs' encouragement, started bringing his fiddle to the Slope. And his vitamins and his Bible. Lately, he has been trying to rename himself "Brother Brian," which isn't sticking.

In the dining hall, where Kung Fu and I sit and talk, he finally reaches clarity about life for himself on the Slope. "You get two weeks of room and board," he says. "You wake up. *Bam*. Food's ready. *Bam*. Clean sheets, towels. Everything's taken care of. It's like rehab. It's like *vacation*. And then you get a fat check. It's, like, can you believe they actually pay us to do this? I mean, *come on!*"

He begins laughing in a way that doesn't seem right, doesn't seem joyful, and then in a minute he is crying. *"Oh, Brian Matthew Regan, put it away, Brian Matthew Regan! Repent! Repent!"*

TooDogs appears, holding an empty cup. All he wanted was some orange juice, but now he's walked into this.

"Help," I say to TooDogs.

"Dude," he says to Kung Fu. He grabs hold of one shoulder and shakes him. *"Dude!"* But by now Kung Fu is lost in sobs.

TooDogs sits with him and I excuse myself. "This is a rig," I hear TooDogs say repeatedly. "This is just a rig."

A STUCK DRILL IS NO WAY to start a hitch. Rod just came in yesterday, and he's getting a bad feeling about this well, ODS K 33, also known simply as 33. It costs anywhere from $5 million to $20 million to drill a single well, more if you get stuck for any length of time—it costs at least a quarter million a day to run the operation—and considerably more still if you get so stuck you have to give up and cement off, leaving $3 million worth of equipment on the drill string behind.

At this point, the bit has reached 8,491 feet, a measurement indicating distance but not necessarily depth. It's moving—or it *was* moving—at about a 68-degree angle through the earth, headed toward oil, or so everyone hoped. The challenge in drilling is that so very much of it is a matter of blind faith. The tools the toolpusher sticks down the hole send signals up, information about pressure and torque and weight, all of which gets translated into numbers on computer screens, which TooDogs and Rod and the engineers back in Anchorage look at as they rub their chins and fret. The whole invisible journey is guided by nothing but a joystick.

"The hole's real ratty," Rod says to TooDogs over in the doghouse. "I'd like to backream and run a walnut sweep, is what I'd like."

"Getting in and out, that's what we gotta worry about now," TooDogs says.

"You mean on the backreaming?"

"This hole has seen eleven-pound mud."

"Everything above us has seen a 10.7. It's already swollen in."

"We'll know that when we go back in and get the wiper out of there."

"Bottom line, right now we don't know shit," Rod says.

"Can't do shit without circulation," TooDogs says.

"We're stuck."

You can't drill without circulation. Think of, well, sex without lubrication. So much of drilling seems borrowed from sex, although no one ever says it. In all its phallic glory, the drill enters the earth, spinning clockwise. It squirts "mud" as it goes. The mud comes out of the middle of the drilling assembly and out into the hole—or "well bore"—the drill makes, and then back up to the surface. The mud, a carefully concocted mixture of water and gels, is the key to just about everything. Not only does it provide lubrication for the drill, but it sends the rock you're chewing—the "cuttings"—floating up and out of the hole. Also, the mud provides pressure, keeping the well from collapsing. Think of diving into the ocean: the deeper you go, the more the ocean pushes you up. The earth works the same way: the deeper you go, the more forceful the pressure. To keep burrowing deeper, drillers increase mud weight, forcing the hole to stay open. It is a delicate balancing act. If the mud weight is too heavy, they'll bust open the wall of the well bore and get a blowout. A blowout is when the well explodes, often taking human bodies and usually the rig with it.

"Basically, you're trying to fool Mother Nature," is the way one guy explains drilling to me. "You're trying to get in her, and she's trying to push you out. You keep her open with your mud, and you ream deeper."

He draws me a picture. He never once makes the joke. Not so much as a wink.

After more talking and fretting and coming back to the same point—you can't do shit without circulation—TooDogs comes over to me. "Okay," he says. "Put your stuff on, because I'm taking you back over to camp."

I tell him I don't want to leave.

"We're fixing to start jarring. You can't be here when we're jarring. Now! Let's go."

I put on my parka, head down the rig stairs with TooDogs, whose big, blocky body is so nimble on these steps. He leads me quickly across the yard; we go through a polar bear cage into camp, and he deposits me in the mudroom. "Stay!" he says. His face is red, and his scar is getting white, so I know he's serious. I put on my slippers and head to the dining hall and eat some surprisingly fresh shrimp salad, feel surprisingly sad about getting run off the rig. It's hard to leave that place, hard to miss out on the unfolding mystery of what the earth is hiding.

Some construction guys come over to cheer me up with news of an arctic fox hanging out by the incinerator.

"That's cool," I say.

They tell me about various polar bears they had to chase off the island last fall with the dozer, about how fun it was to see them dive back into the sea.

Soon, a distant *BOOM!* explodes from over on the rig, followed by a *BOOM!* You can hear it all the way over here in camp. Jarring involves hydraulic pistons deep inside the earth, tools in place on the drill string to help a driller get unstuck. *BOOM!* And thirty seconds later, *BOOM!* One hundred thousand pounds of drill pipe pulled up and then let loose, *BOOM!* Jarring is full of violence, the derrick shaking and moaning after each *BOOM!* I head to the smoke room, where the view is better, and wait an hour for the guys to come back, to tell me about their success jarring, their success beating Mother Nature at her foolish game of "No!" *BOOM!* I wait two more hours in the TV room, then back to the dining hall, the smoke room. There are only so many places to go. After four hours, I give up and go back to my bait box and try to sleep. *BOOM! BOOM!* All night long.

It bothers me that no one here states the obvious. No one says, "Isn't this kind of like sex with a girl who won't put out?" In the same way, no one here talks about the living conditions, the crazy remoteness of the island, the cold. How can the temperatures not be a constant topic of conversation? How can "Jesus H. Christ, it's COLD!" not be a daily exclamation?

In the morning, I step out to greet a windless dawn. The cold is not a slap so much as a squeeze. The rig is quiet now, a hush of exhaustion. I think about limitation, surrendering to all that can never be. Soon the sky welcomes the sun, briefly cracks open with fierce stripes of red. The world, as far as the eye can see, turns pink. I think about the loneliness out here, so acute and thick. The remoteness. The aloneness. The twenty-four-hourness. Men in slippers. Constant. Shrimp for dinner. Blinking. Changing channels. Madness earned. I look out into a white sea rolling on and on to the horizon, all frozen lumps. I think about the moment the ocean froze, having simply stopped moving mid-wave.

ONE DAY I pull Jason aside and ask him what is up with the orange hair. He is perhaps the least tortured orange-haired soul here, a third-generation Slope worker, thirty-three years old.

"It was supposed to come out 'Sandstone,'" Jason tells me. "Like the picture?" He is a boxy man with thin eyes that can't help smile even as he pretends to scowl. "We didn't leave it on long enough, so it came out more orange."

"So you guys just sat around one day and dyed your hair?"

"Pretty much," he says. He tells me there were six or seven of them in the room, that Brain had already shaved his off, and so had Kung Fu.

I'm trying to picture this, and the thing is, I can. I can see these guys, a collection of misfits who so easily fit together—I can see them sitting in a room, acting like teenage girls with their first box of hair dye.

"It was a Clairol product, I believe," Jason tells me. "Nice 'n Easy?" He tells me his wife, who is not a stripper named Onyx but instead a hairdresser, got it for him to bring to the rig. He speaks lovingly of his wife, tells me he's a family man with a nice house in Anchorage with an actual white picket fence, and he tells me about the hot rod in his garage he built when he was sixteen out of a '64 Ford shortbed. He's now rebuilding it with a nine-hundred-horsepower motor for when his oldest son, Joel, gets old enough to drive. Then he's going to build another, out of a '55 Fairlane, for Justin. Slope life, for Jason, is just about money. Providing for his family. The trick to survival on the island, for him, is just a matter of entertainment, torturing the gullible new kids, torturing the dude who walks around with perfect hair.

"You know Melvis, don't you?" Jason asks. "With the hair? Don't call him Melvis to his face, by the way. But you know who I'm talking about?"

The thing is, I do. There is a man who walks the rig with suspiciously pretty hair. He is a man who admits to getting highlights put in—says his wife makes him do it—which is bad enough. But the question on everyone's mind about Melvis is: How come when he takes off his hard hat his hair springs back to its perky Elvis position, while everyone else walks around with normal, sticky hard-hat hair?

"You *know* he uses product," Jason says. "You *know* he must."

"I'm gonna say yeah," I say, discovering in Jason a kind of fabulous gossip.

The group hair dye was a way of *communicating* to Melvis. A way of saying: *Your hair is weird*. They did it last hitch, hung out in Jason's room and applied the Nice 'n Easy, and the next day they showed up and paraded by Melvis. "At first he thought it was a compliment," Jason tells me. "TooDogs had to tell him, 'Dude, they're making fun of you.'"

"Poor Melvis," I say.

"Yeah, well, poor Turtle," Jason says. "He now thinks he's blond. He's, like, got a whole rock star thing going with that hair."

"It's not a good color," I say.

"It's a fucking *joke* color," Jason says.

"You have to tell him."

"I know. I know."

TooDogs loves his wife severely. *We're soul mates. We dream together. Sometimes. Not lately.* He thinks of her as his anchor, and as the angel who saved his life. Actually, technically, the angel came to her and told her: "He is going to die." She reported this to him. Shortly after that, TooDogs woke up on the steps of a detox place. He was maybe thirty. He doesn't remember getting there, only knows he dragged himself there. His drug habit by then was heroin to take the edge off cocaine.

TooDogs thinks his wife is the only person in this world who really knows him, but then again she doesn't know him at all. It's confusing. A big clutter in his head. Lately, he's been wondering, *Was it worth it?* He'll call her, as he does each night, and ask. She'll say, "You're thinking too much. Quit it."

Lana, his wife, whom he rarely refers to by name, takes care of everything back home in Sterling, about two hours south of Anchorage. A Slope widow, that's what women like her are called. She raised all four of the kids pretty much on her own. He made it home for each of their births, that part he managed. But not a whole lot else. He thinks he wasn't a good father. He was never there. He has a lot of regret over that, over thinking the money part was the most important thing. Then sometimes he wonders if they even wanted him there. If she did; if she does. She's got her life, and he's got his. He's scared of his kids being grown now, and he thinks she could fade away. Or lose interest in him. Not really. Because he put everything in her name. The house, everything. So if they get divorced, she can't take anything from him. Because she's already got it. That, he thinks, is another weird one.

It wasn't always this way. In the beginning, being a Slope worker, it made him a tall man. His wife would meet him at the airport after each hitch, bring the kids. He loved seeing them from the plane, bouncing in the window of the airport. They'd crawl all over him. Torture him with hugs. He'd hive up. *Oh, it was all right. It made me feel like a rock star.*

In those early days, when he was still in his twenties, he reunited with his own father, who had taken off when he was a kid. They even worked on the same rig together for a little while. They called his dad Spinner Hawk. They were just starting to gel as adults. It was a chance to get some answers, maybe, to understand some of the bad shit that left him with hives. Maybe his dad saw what was going on back then. But by now his dad was deep into alcohol and drugs. One day, TooDogs got a call. "I'm at the end of my rope," his dad said. TooDogs tried to get over there, but it was too late. *I found him. Oh, yeah. You open the door and you feel life go through you. I knew he was gone. I mean, like, hair standing on end. I felt my hair blowing back. His spirit was bouncing around in there pretty severely. I found him in the bedroom. Shot himself right through the head. So.*

TooDogs started running pretty hard after that. The Slope was safe. To him it was, and is, one of the best lives a guy could have. Things break, you fix them. It's all hands-on. It's all workable. Being married is hard. All the touchy-feely. *Way hard. I can love, but I have to work at it real hard. Because love is a touching deal. The kind of love on a rig is easier.* He thinks he's probably a better father to the roughnecks than he is to his own kids. *I regret leading a double life. I do regret that.*

The worst part about the detox place, where he stayed for thirty days after the angel came, was he had to hug everyone. Every morning, by the coffeepot, they made him go around and hug. The weird thing was he started to like it. *I was raw. I was a newborn kid.* For the first time in his life, he found the courage to touch people. To this day, he still touches everything. *Everything.* Like, if he walks by a tree, he has to feel the bark, or even just a mailbox or a big fleshy sunflower. He has to touch.

He is working on *being* touched, but really, he's not optimistic.

He didn't use health insurance to pay for detox. He figured it wouldn't stick if someone else paid for it. He drained his retirement account, like $100,000, all of it in hundreds, put it in Baggies. He went to the dealers he owed, counted out more than $60,000. "Ignorant, ignorant, ignorant," he said with each bill. He had to feel the money leave his hands to make everything stick.

He has been sober ever since, not a drop of anything in like eighteen years. He still feels like a piece of crap for having been a junkie. He's less angry now than when he first came out of detox. When it got real bad, he would go to the rig with a sledgehammer and pound on the iron, just beat until he couldn't beat no more, then sit down and ponder.

He has never hit a person out of anger, or madness, or whatever twisted shit causes people to beat on innocent people. It has to, he thinks, be a sickness or something that makes someone constantly beat on a little kid. There has to be forgiveness and forgetting. *Forgetting.*

Howard Hughes couldn't be touched. It's a for-instance. It's okay. It isn't, but it is. The violence led me to become a better person. I'm trying to justify it.

You can't dwell on the past. You can't get anything back. No, all you can do is improve yourself. Make yourself into a better person. He wants that severely. *Severely.* It's what he works hardest on. Pretty much constantly.

For years he worked out on the ice, wildcatting. Bait boxes on sleds, dragged fifty miles out on the ice. He'd build the camp, build the rig, drill the exploration wells, wouldn't leave until the ice started melting. He'd be gone sometimes from like November through May. He loved it. That sounds crazy, but he loved it, minus 50, minus 70. He would just stand there and think: Mother Nature at her finest. If he went outside with his hair wet, he could snap it off.

He discovered humility out there. He would stand in the cold and look up at the stars and say, *Okay, I am a tiny piece of nothing down here on a vast frozen sea.*

Life on Oooguruk, compared with wildcatting, is practically vacation. Two weeks on, two weeks off, a camp like this? It's luxury living. It gives him more time at home. It's hard to adjust to all that time at home. He has a shelf in a closet. He puts his shaving kit on the shelf. He has one drawer. He has a Harley, a four-wheeler, a snowmobile, a fishing boat, a couple trucks. It's hard to be a human being. That's why he likes mechanical stuff.

His one son, Ray J., started roughnecking. TooDogs gives him advice. "Buy all your toys first," he tells Ray J. "Your relaxation, get that lined up first."

With oil prices the way they are, the money in drilling is crazy, crazier than ever. A toolpusher like TooDogs could go anywhere in the world. There's a rig in Kazakhstan that wants him, another in Calgary, another in Sydney. It would mean long hitches again, being away for months at a time.

The thing about his wife is, if she would say, "Stay home," he would. He ran it by her a few times. That's what he told her, "All's you have to do is give me the nod." But she didn't. She has this wave she gives him at the end of his fourteen days at home. "See ya!" He knows she's kidding. He knows she is. It's funny, he thinks. *Am I lonely? No. Am I? Yeah. It could go a lot of ways. I could be lonely, but then I get covered up with family and I break out in hives. Some things a guy needs to work on.*

CHARLIE, THE GUY WHO BUILDS the ice roads, is out there widening them. A warming trend—we are up to minus 20—can mean a blow is coming. A phase-three blow, the most severe, means you can't see ten feet in front of you. Nobody goes anywhere during a phase three, which can last a week or more. No one is allowed to work—if there's an accident, they won't be able to get you out of here—so guys sit around and watch movies and curse the ennui.

"There's a good chance we'll get stuck here for a few days," TooDogs says to me.

I make the point that getting stuck has been a theme this hitch.

"It's not always like this," he says.

Jason comes in carrying the masterpiece he has finally finished: the bracket to hold the computer monitor at eye level for Andy.

"Ta-dum," he says. It's a thick iron chain, each link welded together to form an S shape.

"Awesome," Andy tells him. "I'm so glad we waited for the decorative version." Applause goes around the doghouse, and the installation begins at once. "Whoa, what are you doing there, cowboy?" Andy says when Jason nearly knocks over the monitor. Andy holds the monitor. Brain offers to help snake the wires, lies on his belly, but can't quite reach. TooDogs pushes Brain's butt with his foot, inching him forward while helping Andy balance the monitor. Jason drills the hole standing on Brain's back to reach, while Turtle reaches around and, using TooDog's arm as a brace, hands Jason the screws.

"Okay, now nobody laugh!" TooDogs says.

And so they do. Jason is the first to tip, then the others. They could be college kids setting up their first dorm, or they could be boys building a fort; it could be any snapshot of brotherhood, of love's incorruptibility.

Nothing is going right. Normally, it takes about 30 days to drill a well. Nearly 2 weeks into 33 and there's no end in sight. Seven hours of jarring freed the drill that night I sat in my bait box listening, but then the next day, or night, or maybe day, the MWD, the tool that sends the signal that tells them which way to turn, abruptly lost its pulse. They lost thirty-six hours to that calamity, about $300,000 to the company. They pulled it up out of the earth, thousands of feet up, and found three small rocks lodged in the mechanical parts of the tool, freezing it up. How did the rocks get in there?

Rod was upset. He sat the crew down in the conference room, put the three rocks on the table. "Hopefully, we're not pumping rocks in our sweeps!" he bellowed.

Stubbs, who is in charge of the mud pits, wondered if it was his fault, looked down. Zack, who is in charge of Stubbs, sat there furious. *They keep clean pits!* TooDogs sat there thumping his fingers while Rod vented. He could see Zack seething. That kid took pride in his work. That kid had come far. *Kids!* It's not their fault they come here so inexperienced. Not like in his day, when you grew up playing with nuts and bolts. These kids start out here and they don't know which way the fucking drill bit turns. TooDogs has to teach, righty-tighty, lefty-loosey. "It's just like a beer bottle," he'll say to them. And they're, like, "I don't use a screw top, I drink premium." He'll think, *Jiminy Christmas.* He'll start even more basic. "Your focal point is these," he'll say, showing his hands and his feet. "Make sure these don't get broke." He builds from there. He'll take one guy's spot, like a pipe racker, and have him stand back and watch. Then he'll let the guy do it, step back, and critique him. It had been a lot of work, growing this crew. A lot.

"Well, whatever you're doing, it's not working!" Rod went on in the conference room. "Obviously it's not working! Them rocks cost us a lot of money! A lot of time!" He was sort of making the same point over and over, sort of losing the guys with each repeat.

"Look, we're not smoking anyone here," TooDogs said, interrupting Rod.

Rod looked at him. Well, yes, he was smoking someone. Or he was trying to. There was a pause, a tilting of heads, two parents trying to get their act together. "A lesson learned," TooDogs said. "*Everyone* step it up. Take the time you need to do your job right, all the way, full-on, nobody cutting corners on *nothing*. That's for everybody in this room."

"A lesson learned," Rod said, retreating.

The next day they hit gas. Gas is not a workable deal. The gas units in the well were spiking dangerously above 1,500 units. They had to quit drilling, increase mud weight to keep the gas contained, but not too much, so as to avoid fracturing the formation, but enough to control the gas, which could, if it got out of control, blow up the island.

Nothing is going right. It won't matter for long. They will all leave soon, if the blow doesn't come, and a new crew will come, and the problems will continue, or not continue, the drill will go on turning, or not turning, until they come back in two weeks and continue drilling, or not. This hole, the next hole, the next hole, pick the rig up and move it to another oil field, another set of holes, there is no finishing, never an ending, on a rig.

ONE EVENING IN THE DINING HALL, there appears the beauty of prime rib. Prime rib means: Sunday. It's a Slope-wide tradition in every dining hall, every camp. It is about the only certain time marker. Sunday gets people thinking of Wednesday, change-out day, going home. Prime rib has a way of reminding people of time again, of something on the horizon.

"Drink beer, drink whiskey, chase women, go out in the woods and kill stuff" is how one of the guys describes his time home after leaving the Slope.

"Keep yourself alive, that's it."

"Yup."

"Instead of trying to fit everything into a weekend and feeling like hell till the middle of the week, we get to spread it out."

"That's where we're lucky."

"Yup."

When he goes home, Turtle's plan-forward is to buy a new motorcycle, his third. (He will drive it out of the dealership in Wasilla and immediately get a speeding ticket.) Kung Fu is going to visit his dad in Sacramento—a somewhat scary notion, seeing as Sacramento is where he was fixing to locate Lords of Liberty Motorcycle Militia, his strip club/meth lab. A lot of memories there. (He will end up back in jail with his face bashed in but, proudly, not his teeth.) Stubbs has no big plans except for helping Angela, his fiancée and the first woman who didn't steal his money, take care of the seven mentally disturbed people in their home. "They have disorderments," Stubbs tells me. "They think they see shit. You try to make them happy." Other than that, Stubbs will hang out at Go Cash Bingo, where no alcohol is served and where he plays seventy-two cards for $14. (He will continue an eight-month losing streak.) Andy plans some quality time with his fiancée, who is game for anything and who will most definitely come with him to hang out with Jason at Humpy's bar, where, hopefully, the waitress wearing a harness carrying Jell-O shots will offer to suck and blow, which Jason will more than gladly partake of, many times over. "Suck me! Blow me! On your knees!" Jason will get more than roaring drunk, and so will Andy, but Andy will hold it better. (Andy will plan a bachelor party, a weekend of gambling and topless girls in Vegas. Jason will announce his intention to attend the party, and his wife will abruptly file for divorce.)

TooDogs doesn't know. He's eager to leave but not eager to go home. The Slope is the only place he feels he has any control. "It's good to have that, good for a person to have a place he can go to feel safe. But what a fucked-up place to feel safe."

The king salmon aren't in yet, so he won't take out his boat. Lately he's been staying an extra night in Anchorage, to de-tune before driving home. He likes to shop. *He loves to shop.* He likes to people-watch. His daughter is graduating high school, and he'll go to her graduation and clap. Pretty soon there will be a free bedroom in his house, and he dreams of turning it into a man cave. He's picturing tongue-and-groove, probably like a herringbone pattern? Abstract shapes. He's thinking a desk. A stereo. Probably a couch. Plus his knickknacks, a collection of animal skulls, a collection of crystal balls.

THE MAIN THING everyone cares about, ever since prime rib, is the blow. Getting stuck on the island. But the blow doesn't come. The night before change-out, duffel bags get piled in the hallway by the mudroom, symbols of freedom. My flight out of Deadhorse is earlier than the others'; the van driver tells me to be ready at 4:30 a.m.

TooDogs gets up early to say good-bye. "I figured I might as well come out," he says. He offers to carry my stuff. "Looks like you're free," he says, standing in the mudroom.

"Looks like you are, too," I tell him.

He says it's no big deal. He says it's all workable. "I'm a machine," he says. "It's what I am."

I have learned not to argue. He sits with me while I wait for the van driver. The mudroom is utterly quiet this time of day, no one in here banging locker doors or kicking off boots. Just the buzz of fluorescent lights overhead and the faint sound of TooDogs thumping his fingers on the bench. He's already dressed for his day of travel, wearing clean blue Carhartts, same HUNT HARD cap.

"A loving family is way better than anything you can create up here," he says finally. "I did make that clear, right?"

I tell him I think so. I tell him there's a kind of love up here, too, though.

"I'm talking about a *real* family," he says. "You know what I mean. *Gawd*, woman."

"All right."

"But I can only *handle* this one," he says. "Does that make any sense? It's not a bad thing. It's kind of sad. But not."

I look at him, nod. He's clean-shaven for the first time I've seen, the stubble noticeably absent. He trimmed his mustache.

"What time did you get up?" I ask. "You're all *clean*."

He says he did laundry. He watched a fishing show. He listened to Clint Black.

"Do you know what the life expectancy is of a roughneck after they retire? Did I tell you about that?"

I tell him no, we didn't cover that.

"They give up," he says. "Two old guys I worked with didn't get their first retirement checks. Both just up and died before the first check came."

We sit in that thought for a moment.

"I'm thinking: broken heart," he says.

He shrugs, continues thumping his fingers. I cut him off before he can say it doesn't matter, that it's all workable.

"That's not workable," I say.

"No," he says. "That's the whole deal. It's not."

We say good-bye. He calls to make sure I get home safely, apologizing for worrying: "That's just the way I roll." Days go by, weeks, a few more hitches. He gets a Father's Day present from his kids, who all put together to buy him a tepee for the backyard, eighteen foot around. Kind of a man cave, but not. As touched as he is by the gesture, he can't help but wonder if they want him to move out there for real.

He gets a big job offer, a chance to be a company man, just like Rod, except off on rigs all over the world. He'd be gone months at a time again. He tells Andy about it, wonders how, if he took the job, he would tell the rest of the guys. He tells Andy he feels like he'd be abandoning his children if he left the island. He tries to explain that kind of sorrow to his wife. "You said you wanted to improve yourself," she says. "This is improving." He calls Jason, invites him to shoot archery at a shooting range. From twenty yards away, Jason hits a fake moving bear. From the same distance, Jason then hits an arrow *into* the arrow on the still-fake moving bear. TooDogs tells him he's sorry he hasn't been more of a friend during all the divorce stuff. Jason says, "Quit it." TooDogs tells Jason about the job offer and, like everybody else, Jason says, "Take it."

On the last day of his very last hitch on Oooguruk, TooDogs pulls Turtle aside. "I didn't think much of you when you started," he says to Turtle. "But you're turning into a real good floor hand." Turtle recoils, nearly weeps, then leans in for a hug. TooDogs hesitates, takes an exhausted breath, but finally opens his arms and cradles Turtle's head. "This is a rig," TooDogs says. "My God, this is just supposed to be a rig."

He does well as a company man, so well he gets quickly promoted, and promoted again, until finally the offer comes to go all the way to the top, to become a corporate superintendent, one of the smart guys on the other end of the phone, yelling at the idiot roughnecks to get their drill unstuck, move faster, stop wasting the company's money. On his first day of work in management, July 13, 2010, TooDogs is fifty-two. He walks into his office in Pittsburgh, Pennsylvania, and his heart abruptly stops beating, and he is gone.

SPUTTER

I-80, Exit 284
Walcott, Iowa

She had 44,000 pounds of warm beer in the trailer, and when she hit the brakes, she could feel the beer slosh forward. *Wake up, girl. Wake up!* (She had been dreaming, or pre-dreaming, imagining herself kidnapped, dead and famous and featured on *Nancy Grace.*) She slapped her cheek, shook her head. She turned to channel 19 on the CB, opened the window, smacked her other cheek.

That was when she got the idea to go topless. Who knows where a fool notion like that even comes from? *I have to do something to wake up.* Manning the eighteen-wheeler with one arm, she wiggled out of her shirt. *That's what I'm talking about.* She unhooked her bra. *Whoo!* Flung that bra into the back of the cab. *Whoo, girl! Whoo!* she said to herself, the hot air blowing on her breasts and the thrill of adventure refueling her. This was just north of Columbus, Ohio, on I-71 at around 3:00 a.m. on a blistering summer night, and Shannon Smith, aka Sputter, was back in business.

She got another idea. She flicked a switch on the dash and, bang, on came the cab lights, exposing her soft brown body to the night.

Hello, fellas! (Hey, they probably needed to wake up too.) She didn't wave, didn't even look in the direction of the passing trucks, but instead grinned smugly, a pose that definitely enhanced the overall effect. "Northbound naked chick!" they said to each other on channel 19. Stuff like that. "Nice rack, Air Ride!" one guy said as he passed. *Oh, please.* She did not think she had anything even approximating a nice rack. (So that was sweet.) She righted her posture, thrust her chest forward like a confident old hen, and she drove clear on up to Cleveland like that, two and a half hours away.

"But I still listen to channel 19 even though I have the satellite now," Sputter says to me after she gets finished telling the topless story, as if the point of the whole thing is to explain the radios on her dashboard, and not to take my imagination to all the places it has just taken me.

"Well, I can't believe you did that," I say.

"Oh, we help each other out all the time," she says, as if keeping the guys awake were the other point. It is the middle of July, solidly hot, and she has her shiny black hair in ribbon curls on top of her head. "Girl, I can't even express how happy I am you're here," she says. "Aren't we having an adventure? I feel like we're sisters already! Do you? *Do you?*" She has buttery-smooth skin, round, sturdy features, and the steering wheel is so large, she uses it like a shelf to rest her elbows on. She's put a half million miles on this rig—an International 9400 Eagle, royal blue, with a 500-horsepower Cummins ISX engine, ten speeds on the floor, and an air-ride suspension system.

She's at home here, her body gently jiggling with the rhythm of the road. She tells me she started long-hauling at twenty-three, just as soon as she was old enough to get insured; it was her dream ever since she was a little girl watching her daddy, a heavy-machinery mechanic, who spent all his days under the hood. She would make a noise with her lips, a sputtering sound, and he would sing to the tunes she made up, and somewhere in that transaction Sputter, now thirty-five, got her nickname.

"Well, I bet he's proud of you now," I say.

She looks at me. "He didn't want me driving a big old truck," she says. "What kind of father wants his baby girl out driving a truck?"

"Okay, but—"

"Girl, just sit back and enjoy the scenery."

We are somewhere west of Chicago, coming off some exit, merging onto some highway; everything about the expansive Midwest thoroughfares—the diesel stops and fast-food joints and weigh stations—has collapsed into a collage and I have given up trying to keep track. We started our zigzaggy journey about five hours ago at an abandoned Kmart parking lot where Sputter keeps her truck near her home in west Cleveland, and we're bound for Walcott, Iowa, and the Iowa 80, the world's largest truck stop, where the thirty-first annual Walcott Truckers Jamboree starts in a few days. Along the way, we'll drop off a load of factory-new farm tractor rims, pick up a box trailer full of feeding troughs, and another of beer—and haul whatever else Rob decides, based on the bid offerings on his computer back at the Landstar dispatch station in Kalida, Ohio.

Sputter is excited about the jamboree. She wants to show me the very best of her world. She has told me legends of glamorous lights and tricked-out trucks too ornate to believe. "*You will see some chrome!*" She has a magnanimous way that invites the whole world into her inner circle, and like most people, I have tumbled easily in.

To say that I'm glad I did would be a vast understatement. I almost didn't make it. I almost canceled this trip. My mother has just died. She was eighty-six. She was ill. It was expected. "A beautiful death," my mother would have said of it. My father held her. He was eighty-eight, ill, his heart literally breaking. My sisters and brother and I had been at this for months, and now it was my father's turn to die. People said: "Oh, how beautiful, your parents dying in each other's arms." We said: "Not really." He lasted ten days. Exhausted, spent, we postponed his funeral a week while the extended family reassembled. I cut out of there, went to Cleveland. I knocked on the door at Sputter's house, leaving all that behind.

"Thank God for Wonder Hangers," Sputter said, greeting me. We had been planning this meeting and this trip for months, and she was excited. "Do you want to see what these things have done for my closets?" she said, holding the hangers. She lives in a second-floor duplex that might have been spacious but it was too jammed with stuff to really tell. She seemed nervous, unsure of what to say. I have no other explanation for the tour of the closets. "The problem is Michael, my boyfriend," she said. "He shops more than a woman. . . . Wait a minute, step over that. Wait a minute! See, all that's his. All *that's* his, and all this. Michael, he just loves to buy clothes. Look at this! Look at this. What is this? A hundred forty-two dollars' worth of stuff in this bag. I bet he won't even remember he has it. He wears a police uniform every day, so I really don't see the need. He's an officer in the housing authority, like the projects? Cuyahoga. He's not scared there. I'm scared for him. But I love to hear the stories. Because you wouldn't believe what people call the police for. But I'm nosy that way.

"Now we'll move on to the other bedroom. Close that door. Again, most of this is his stuff. Girl, please. All this! This is his stuff. That's his stuff. Clothes baskets. I bought him those storage things for more room."

It was a turbulent tour of her apartment, her life, all of it coming at me tsunami-style. "Michael wants a wedding at the beach," she said. "Can you believe that? I want it at a haunted house. Because I love Halloween. We're at a standoff. I'm, like, *the beach*? I'm not this beach girl dressed in white, all the people dressed in white. I think I'm more tomboyish than this girly girl he thought he met. I don't know where he got that. Beats me. Beats me." The apartment was hot, and she carried a hanky and continually dabbed her forehead and her neck.

"Look at this," she said, sorting through her dresser. "I get cards from him. 'For the one I love.' I'll send him to the drugstore to buy me some medicine, like some Alka-Seltzer or something, and he comes back with stuff like this. Stuff like this. It's a rose, a singing rose. Singing cards. You know. He just sees stuff and buys it. I asked him before, 'Why do you do that?' He said because growing up he couldn't afford it. Yeah, but be a little bit more sensible now, I mean, *come on*.

"Now you have to meet my cats," she said, leading me to the living room, where a woman was sitting watching *Wheel of Fortune* on TV. "This is Elaine," Sputter said. "My sister."

"Hi," Elaine said.

"Okay, here's Hurt," Sputter said, picking up the tabby from the couch. "He was a stray. He was in a cat fight. When he would try to walk forward, his hind would raise up and he would go backwards. I took him to the vet, they amputated his tail. He had a big hole in his side. But he healed!

"My other friend, a Siamese cat, lives in the attic. His name is Ghost. Him and Hurt don't get along, so I have to keep them separate."

Elaine sat watching. She was backlit. She held the remote up and softened the volume on the TV. "So you're going to ride with Sputter?" she said, and I smiled and nodded.

"Have you ever done it?" I asked her.

"Ride in *her* truck?" Elaine said, waving the very notion away from her face. "My favorite truck is a Peterbilt."

"Oh, so you're a truck driver too?" I asked.

"No, no, not me," Elaine said. "I just love Peterbilts. I collect them. And even my e-mail address is Peterbiltforyou."

"Peterbilts are classy," Sputter said, sitting down with her cat on the couch and pulling my hand to take a seat next to her. "But not even in my top three. They're real heavy-duty trucks, don't get me wrong. They pull real good."

"Best truck on the road," Elaine said. "I just always loved Peterbilts, even as a little kid."

I felt I should offer something, but I never knew people even *had* favorite trucks.

"Elaine works with the elderly," Sputter said, and then she put her face up to Hurt and began her good-byes in hushed tones.

"The elderly?" I asked.

"Alzheimer's, wheelchairs, you know, the *elderly*," Elaine said. "Sometimes eight hours, sometimes sixteen." She was taller than

Sputter, I could tell that, and she had a calm demeanor. "It makes for a long day, especially when the moon is full," she said. My impulse was to say, "Hey, we have a lot in common!" but then I thought no, we don't; my parents were dead, so I was no longer in that line of work. Elaine told me about a dying old lady whose hair she washed, and she told me about a crazy old man she danced with every day, and when I asked her if she liked her job, she said she did.

"Girl, you're covered in cat hair," Sputter said to me, and she came at me with a lint roller. She rolled my arms and my legs and my back until she was satisfied that all signs of Hurt and Ghost were off me, which I did pause to think was funny, if not disturbingly convenient, and then we all went outside and got in Elaine's big Ford. Elaine drove us to the Kmart lot and she told Sputter she owed her one for the favor, and that was how our day began.

THE HORIZON PULLS us farther west, and we listen to country music, and Sputter alternates between singing along and telling me stories and complaining about Michael.

The sky is without clouds, flat cerulean blue, and the Toyota passing in the left lane has four bikes attached to a rack, one with pink streamers flapping helplessly. When you are in a long-haul truck, you are in a zone above, a shared space high above the rhythms of vacation, commuting, visiting. When you are in a long-haul truck, you are in a moving neighborhood above all that, and having nothing to do with it.

There are precious few women truckers out here, a fact Sputter finds surprisingly little to say about. She thinks of her fellow truckers as brothers. Good guys. Ornery. *Brothers* to tease, but also to protect—everybody united in the massive, complex call to haul America's stuff. Cookies, soup, juice, carpet, umbrellas. She tells me about some of the stuff she's hauled, a list as random as it is thought-provoking. A trailer full of Clorox bleach, ketchup and mustard packets, mail, oxygen tanks, caskets, fireworks, plastic eating utensils ("that come in the pack with the napkin, salt, and pepper"), tissue, paper towels, cardboard, huge rolls of paper, books, sales inserts for newspapers, bundles of shredded paper and aluminum cans, paint, cat litter, dog food, toys, GARBAGE ("Yes, actual stinky trash"), brand-new garbage cans, TVs, DVDs, camcorders, Whirlpool products, plant pots, military equipment ("ammunition, tank parts, and wooden crates"), glass freezer coolers, oil, batteries, hydrochloric acid, white powder calcium, liquid chemical solvents and solutions, aluminum ingots, powder coating, fifty-gallon drums ("empty and full of car-wash liquid"), totes (also empty and full), cleaning products, plastic beads that are melted down to make bottles, all kinds of auto parts (crankshafts, bumpers, rims, engines for big trucks and the motor for the Ford Mustang, doors, gas tanks, windows). "In 2009, I had the pleasure of hauling the body for the 2012 Ford Explorer to be crash-tested. So I got a sneak peek."

It's rare to sit and contemplate cargo, to say nothing of the people hauling it. *Stupid trucks. Why are there always so many trucks? Can't somebody do something about all the goddamn trucks?* We travel on turnpikes in sedans and minivans, trying to ignore the monstrous rigs with which we are forced to share the road. That there are people up inside those rigs, big and little lives moving about, rarely occurs to most of us, or if it does, we'd just as soon they all go away. Never mind that we are dependent on these people, 3.5 million truckers delivering 69 percent of the stuff we buy—$670 billion worth of stuff. We know the stench of diesel fumes, the splash on our windshields that only an eighteen-wheeler can throw at us, and somewhere in the periphery we see shadows of dudes at truck stops hunched over coffee and pancakes and eggs. We know, but we don't know at all. Our grocery stores are stocked fresh every day, Home Depot has all the latest colors of paint, and Amazon ships two-day, or one. How all this stuff moves about the landscape, gets from here to there to us, is not our concern any more than how the furnace in the basement blows heat into our bedrooms. Except that furnaces don't have lives. There is no befriending a furnace.

"Now don't laugh," Sputter turns to me and says. "But I'm kind of proud of the way I'm taking care of these stupid tractor rims we're hauling." She says it's hard to explain. She says responsibility has always scared her, seriously, almost like a phobia. "Other than that part of it, I think I would make a great mom."

We chew on that one a while.

"I wish Michael was more like my father," she says, then. "My father, like me, is a laborer. Change the oil? I do it myself. Not Michael."

"I suppose everybody has different skills," I say. I have no idea why I'm defending Michael.

"How does laziness even form in a person?" she says. "*How?* That's what I can't get a grasp on."

We think on that one too, flip our visors down almost in unison when the sun shoots us blind. We pass a billboard for McDonald's apple pie and discuss its merits.

"One time I hauled a whole truckload of cherry pie filling to New Jersey," she says. "Oh, man, I smelled cherry the whole way there. That was a treat. Then I got stuck in New Jersey. That was the worst." With so much of the manufacturing happening in the Midwest, there's way more stuff going toward the coasts than coming out of them. If Sputter had it her way, and usually she does, she'd just stay in the Midwest, going from plant to plant to plant. "Like now I'm taking these tractor rims, and then another day I'll be picking up huge tires, and then maybe a whole trailerload of front grilles. Same thing with car parts. One day steering wheels and then the next fenders. It's like everything is in bits and pieces all over the country and I'm hauling it so people can put it together. It makes me feel like I'm part of something."

Already for the third or fourth time today Gretchen Wilson comes on the radio and Sputter reaches and turns the volume up. *"I don't waste my time on / Manicures and spray-on tans, / And I don't pay no never mind / to the calluses I've worn on my hands . . ."* She slaps her thigh as she sings, and belts the chorus: *"I work hard, I play harder, / I'm a good-timin' American daughter . . ."*

She raises her hand for a high five. "That's it, girl! That's it!" With that, she lets out her Sputter laugh, a rolling boom that requires all of her. She can just as quickly cry. Anything about innocence violated, a dead animal, an orphaned child, will make the tears pop. I have already decided not to tell her about my parents, not because of her characteristic fragility, but because of the acuteness of my own.

"So, do you like my truck?" she asks.

"Oh, I do," I say, politely.

"I mean, I know it's not a *Peterbilt*," she says.

"This isn't considered a fancy truck?"

"It's kind of like a Pinto," she says.

She doesn't own it—as most drivers don't anymore. The era of the independent owner-operator largely ended when fuel prices began going crazy in the 1980s, giving way to a system of fleet owners—like Rob back in Kalida—who own all the trucks, hire the drivers, and do the dispatching. Fleet owners work sort of like restaurant franchisees, contracted by one of the bigs, Con-way, J. B. Hunt, or, as in Rob's case, Landstar. Sputter gets her weekly paycheck from Rob, who provides full benefits, and she gets paid a percentage of each haul she makes, split among her, Rob, and Landstar. She takes home about forty grand a year.

When Sputter first started hauling for Rob, he wasn't too sure about her. To begin with, he wasn't used to seeing black people in the middle of Ohio. And a woman? She could sense his reluctance. She knew he would just need time. Now they're like family and he spoils her. Every time Rob buys a new rig for the fleet, he offers it to Sputter before any of his other thirty drivers—it's been her turn for a new truck for two years now—but she says no, a thousand times no. A truck, she tells him, is like a pair of jeans: it takes a long time to get it molded to your body just right. Rob lets her take off during the worst of winter because she's afraid to drive on ice. He honors her request to keep her routes within the Midwest. He knows how hard it is to find—and keep—a good trucker, and he knows he has something special in Sputter.

In the era of no jobs, jobs, jobs, long-haul trucking is one place were there are jobs aplenty—about four hundred thousand openings at the moment, and thousands upon thousands expected on top of that in the coming years. It is by any measure an industry in crisis, a culture America can't afford to have collapse. Image-wise, the postmodern trucker isn't who a trucker was back in the days of

B.J. and the Bear and Burt Reynolds and *Smokey and the Bandit*. The 1970s was the trucking heyday, at least as far as pop culture went. But even before that, starting way back in the 1940s, truckers were cool and mysterious. Here was the new American cowboy, the maverick carrying the torch of freedom and mischief and cigarette butts flicked to the wind.

That's all gone now. Now it's just a shitty job. You're gone all the time. Corporate fat cats telling you what to do, or the government saying you can drive up to eleven hours a day, and then you have to sleep for ten. Since pay is by the haul, the incentive is to break the law, fake your logbooks, which everybody does. You eat crappy food. You get lonely. You get fat.

Sputter complains about none of this, wondering only how long she can keep it up. The toll on her body—her knees are giving out from climbing up and down, down and up, into the cab. And then there is the career/family dilemma same as any woman has. "How can you raise kids and drive a truck?" she says. "Did I tell you I'm thirty-five? Did you know I was that old?" The sun is drenching her chin, a glow reflecting up.

"One minute Michael wants babies and the next he doesn't. He's fifty-one. I told him, I said, 'Michael, there's not much time left for babies.' I said, 'Let's go to a doctor and get fertilized and have as many as we can have.' He said, *'I'll give you one.'*"

LATE INTO THE NIGHT we chug slowly through the lot at a Travel America truck stop and find a space away from the harsh glow of Qiznos red and green and flashing L-O-T-T-O pink neon.

Sputter lines all three axles of the rig just so, shifts into reverse, and puts her whole body into spinning the mighty steering wheel as she backs the seventy-one-foot eighteen-wheeler into an impossibly skinny slot. It's dark over here, a good spot, and we have neighbors on either side of us, rigs rumbling. Most truckers keep the engines on all night, for the air-conditioning in the summer and the heat in the winter. People always ask Sputter if she's afraid out here all alone, and she always tells them no. The guys are more or less respectful and she can handle herself. When the lot lizards in heels and tight tops come knocking at her door, they freak out when they see she is a woman, and she tries to reason with them to go back home and find another way to make a living. *You can do better for yourself!*

She throws a switch and the truck exhales a loud, satisfying hiss. "Okay," she says with a long sigh, as if to answer. She rubs her knee. Stupid knee. They don't make rigs with women's bodies in mind. Of course not. Last year she joined an organization, Women in Trucking, which she thinks is awesome. Only about 200,000 of the nation's 3.5 million truckers are female. Most of her friends in Women in Trucking have grown kids, started doing this after. Some have husbands who drive, both of them trading off, like living in an RV together. She imagines Michael doing something like that and laughs out loud at the thought. *He-would-die!*

"Did you bring pajamas?" she asks me, throwing another switch on the dashboard jammed with dials and gauges and lights. She takes a sip of water from a Gatorade bottle she filled with tap water at home.

"You wear pajamas out here?"

"More like sweats and a T-shirt," she says. "I bring them to the shower with me and get changed."

"Then that's what I'm going to do," I say, and we crawl to the back of the cab to gather our shower things, entering a capsule of a home: a twin bed topped by a fuzzy blue decorative pillow; a refrigerator stocked with apples, grapes, and soda; a microwave; and cubbies built into the walls holding shampoo, Febreze, Lubriderm Advanced Therapy Moisturizing Lotion.

"Showers cost nine dollars," Sputter says, "but I have a membership card so we'll get a discount."

I ask her to please confirm that these are not *group* showers, not one big public room of dripping faucets.

"We're not in prison, girl!" she says, and begins digging through a canvas tote. "I bought you some shower shoes, but now I can't remember what I did with them." I tell her to stop with the gifts already. Earlier she presented me with a new set of flowered sheets and two lemon-yellow bath towels. "I want you to be comfortable," she says. "How often do I get to host a guest?"

Together we ready the sleeper cab for the night, make a little nest out of two fuzzy green beanbag chairs, and argue about who gets the real bed ("No, you!") and who gets the beanbags, and of course she wins. She sets two alarms, one to wake up Michael so he won't be late for work in the morning, and the second to remind Michael to feed her cats before he leaves. She wonders if Michael shampooed the carpets, but she knows the answer is no, so she decides not to call him.

"I wish Michael was more like my father," she says again, this time through bobby pins in her teeth. "But I guess a lot of women are like that, just always looking to replace their dad."

She insists that everything in her life goes back to her dad, watching him work on those rigs. As a child, she devoured his legend: a sharecropper who emigrated north for work, arriving practically shoeless in Cleveland, where he got the job at the garage. That job was everything to a man like him. That job was America itself. He had six kids. Sputter was the youngest. How she dreamed of climbing on his big shoulders, him parading her through town like his pride and joy. She *dreamed*. It got so she dreamed of *becoming* a broken-down old truck so that he would spend as much time with her as he did with those rigs.

"I'm going to become a truck driver," she told him one day. He said she would have to learn how to fix one before she drove it. "Well, you can teach me!" she said. (And wasn't that the whole point?) He said, "No." Then one day just after high school graduation, a recruiter from the U.S. Army called and Sputter answered the phone and listened to his pitch. "Well, can you teach me to fix a truck?" she asked, and the guy said he could. "Can you make me a truck driver?" she asked, and the guy said he could do that, too, so she went down to the recruiting office and signed up that very day.

She doesn't talk about the army, boot camp, all the hard work learning. She doesn't talk about how difficult it's been to be a black woman making it in a white man's world. She talks about being like her father, making her father proud, being a good worker, never lazy, always thrifty, changing the oil herself.

There is a boom. A pounding on the driver's side door. *Boom, boom, boom.* She moves quickly to the front, looks out. A thin man, smoking, holding a shaving kit. She cracks her window.

"Shower wait's over an hour," the guy says. "Don't bother."

"Oh, okay, thanks, buddy," Sputter shouts down to him. "Appreciate it!"

We bail on the shower, decide to get up early to beat the rush. "Oh, my Lord!" she says, checking the time. She reaches, turns the satellite radio to HLN's *Nancy Grace,* comes back and flops into the beanbags. She gathers her curls into a bandanna, hushes me. Sputter has a lot of friends on her various radios (especially infomercials; late at night she calls the 800 numbers to chat with various operators standing by), but none can begin to compare with Nancy. "He should not be out on bail!" she says to Nancy, about someone Nancy thinks strangled the niece of someone Nancy has on her show. "Why-is-he-out-on-bail?"

I put my head on the pillow with the thud of a thousand centuries. The cumulative exhaustion of these past months is so complete I think only a coma will help.

The ceiling curves low over the bed, a tight little cave, and sounds are muffled, flat and private back here. I think about how people go off to spas for peace and tranquillity after they get done with some big tragedy in their lives, to heal, to finish mourning, or to begin. A long-haul truck with a radio pumping out sad and outrageous tales of strangled teenagers can, I suppose, serve the purpose.

Finally Nancy says, "Good night, friend."

"Good night, friend," Sputter says softly, and cuts the sound.

APPARENTLY, I FALL ASLEEP. I know this only because I pop awake, thinking about Elaine, Sputter's sister. I sit up straight and fast, as you do. My eyeballs feel cold each time I blink, and the darkness is the same, open or shut. Sputter is snoring softly.

I keep going over it. We were in the living room and Elaine told me she worked for the elderly, and I asked her if she liked her job and she said she did. "Well, that must be difficult work," I said, then regretting the words as soon as they came out. I had just spent the past six months of my life dealing with women like Elaine. Always women. In and out of the assisted-living center where my parents lived out their last days. Round-the-clock care, smiling caretaker after smiling caretaker. Picking my mom up like a little bird, placing her in bed, dressing her legs, dark, fleshy fingers against pasty, thin white. *Difficult work?*

Those women were saints, we said. The patience. The kindness. The sheer endurance of their cheerfulness. It hurt too much to imagine that they might only be pretending to care—just doing a job, getting a paycheck—although that fear pressed constantly on my chest. What if they were only pretending? What if CiCi or Aletha or Pauline got home and made fun of my dad for needing his blanket just so over his toes, or cursed my mom for wetting the bed? Was that what these people did when they got home? Was that the hidden truth?

Here was Elaine, one of them. It was like meeting a favorite actor on TV. You want them to *be* their character. Please, just *be* that character. If Elaine's job turned out to be just a *job,* if she didn't love the old lady whose hair she washed, didn't adore the old man she danced with—if she made fun of the old people, or showed any lesser crack at all—I would have had to run to the bathroom to throw up.

"That must be difficult work." The words were bouncing echoes in my head.

"You have to have a soft spot for seniors," Elaine answered. Those were her actual words. "It's a calling," she said. She remained a lanky figure in shadow. "And I always have had the soft spot," she said. "I can't explain it. I just like to think that at the end of the day, or the end of their life, somebody came into their life that made a difference. And they didn't feel old or mistreated or anything like that. Someone took time with them and gave them a hug and gave them love."

I didn't say, "You're an angel," like you're supposed to say at a time like that. I didn't say it because when people say a thing like that, they don't mean it the way I would have meant it. "You-are-an-angel!" Literally, here was a person who came out of nowhere and extinguished a fire.

When I think about the women of hidden America, all the labor that traditionally falls on the shoulders of women, I think they are an enormous army of soldiers hidden in camouflage. The caretakers, the nannies, the maids, the sisters and the surrogate sisters, the mothers and the surrogate mothers, all those people tending hearts.

THE SHOWER IS SURPRISINGLY FINE, Lysol clean, a two-room booth with a separate changing area and a little red light outside to show it is occupied, sort of like a Catholic confessional. I meet Sputter afterward for some eggs in the truck stop diner and we hit the road by dawn, emerging into the day about two hours outside

Walcott and the Jamboree, according to the GPS on the dashboard. We remark on the sharp hues of daybreak—another hot one ahead!—and we talk about Michael. Everything keeps coming back to Michael.

Two years ago, Michael heard the sound of Sputter's laughter at a comedy club, and it was the laughter that drew him. Who laughed like that? Out of what kind of woman was such an outrageously joyful sound even possible? He got her phone number. She thought, *Hey, a free meal if he shows up,* and was shocked when he did. She had on her favorite brown pants and a paisley shirt, and he smelled sweet and looked cute in his workout suit, blue and shiny. "I eat chicken, corn, and mashed potatoes," she told him. "That's it." She told him she didn't trust casseroles or anything mixed together or anything unknown. She knew nothing about the kitchen beyond the microwave and she was not interested in learning. She laid down these and many other laws. Michael hung in there, worked on softening the heart piled beneath all those rules. She had never been in love before. She was afraid of losing control, of the responsibility, of being seen and being known—mostly of losing control. Eventually, she let go. She fell in love. She let him in. She wonders now if he understands how huge this is, if anyone can possibly appreciate how abundantly huge.

"He didn't show his habits when we first got together," she says. "Oh, he loved my cats. He cleaned my attic. He was cream of the crop. It was, like, 'Where did this guy come from?' But then the laziness came out. It was always in there, but it was hidden."

"I'm sure he's got a lot of good qualities," I say. I don't think I'm defending Michael so much as defending love.

Her phone rings. It's her mother. "Hey, what's up?" Sputter says, answering. Her mother wants to know where Elaine is and if Elaine remembered to put the fish bait in the refrigerator.

"Mom—I'm in Iowa," Sputter says. "I'm in my truck."

Her mother wants to know could Sputter call Elaine and ask her about the bait.

"Well, okay, sure, Mom," she says, hanging up, and then she turns to me. "You have to admit that's a little weird. Why can't she just call Elaine herself?" She's been sitting so long, she's slumping, her body filling the seat like a loaf of bread in a loaf pan.

"And here's another thing," she says. "I'm out here all alone on these highways and she doesn't worry about me. Don't you think that's odd? Shouldn't a mother worry about her kid? I'm telling you, I can't really grab her sometimes."

"It's a little weird," I offer. "My mother worried constantly." It is the first time I refer to my mother in the past tense. It feels hot, like a sin.

"Bait?" I say to Sputter. "Your mother was calling about bait?"

"She fishes," Sputter says. "I went once. I didn't like the bugs. No one will go with her except sometimes Cheryl. Cheryl is the sister I'm closest to. Ten years older. She's the head, I'm the tail. She calls me her best friend. She's got eight kids. She always talks about riding with me, but she hasn't done it yet."

She reaches for the Gatorade bottle, sips the tap water she keeps refilling at various truck stops. The soda she stocked the refrigerator with is for me; she will not drink my soda. I did not ask for the soda.

"The one I get along least with is Elaine," Sputter says. "The way me and Cheryl see it, Elaine tries to have my mom all to herself. And this is another thing about Elaine: She thinks she's a great cook. She's not. It's bland."

Josh Thompson comes on the radio and Sputter turns the volume up, bounces her chin while she sings. "*You can leave us alone.*" She pauses for this next part, looks at me, points her finger to the beat: "*We're about John Wayne, Johnny Cash, / And John Deere way out here.*"

It's an odd anthem for a black woman from Cleveland, and I wonder if it's worth pointing that out, but decide against it. We fall silent for a stretch, listen to the song. There is nothing but corn on either side of us, green and green and green touching the sky. My mind drifts naturally back. I'm trying to get the grief over with, and part of that is playing the same movie over and over again in your head. (Like the ending is going to change?) I think about the funeral and the church. Your voice is puny when you are making funeral arrangements. You may be talking or you may just be moving your mouth like a starving baby sparrow.

There isn't a lot of space for extra stuff at a Catholic funeral. Both my parents were super-Catholics and so all of that came first at my mother's funeral. My oldest sister went up to the altar to say some words, sixty years of marriage, God, love, God. I sat clutching my paper, waiting my turn. There were nods and looks and ahems, but the priest hadn't been cued and maybe the service was going on too long anyway, and he went back to praying and I never got to read the words I had prepared to say at my mother's funeral.

My parents were super-Catholics, but this was not the side of them I understood. I felt I was at someone else's funeral, not my mother's, and that was the hardest part. If I could have read the words on my paper out loud, a tiny memory—her downstairs painting, me upstairs writing, the two of us meeting in the kitchen for tuna fish sandwiches, comparing notes on the anxiety of the blank canvas and the anxiety of the blank page—I could have shown people who she and I were together, and apparently I needed the witness. The memory of wanting to read, and not getting to read, is relentless as a toothache.

My father was the funny one, and half the time the rest of them were moving so fast they didn't catch his jokes. He was slow, I'm slow; together we would sit back observing. Already I'm grieving the fact that I'll never get the funny into his funeral, not with all the other hoopla, not with all this high drama of love, sixty years of marriage, God, love, and how beautiful it is to have your parents dying in each other's arms.

He would have had something so funny to say about that. Not snide. Not mean. Just something to suggest that everyone was looking at the picture head-on, and if you tilted your head and looked at it again—ha! I know he would find something funny, or I would first, and we would laugh. Right now I can't find it. The perspective is missing. A whole way of looking just—*poof*. They say pigeons have a lens over their eyes, some special membrane that allows them to see patterns of colors and stripes in the sky, and that's how they so easily find their way home. Remove the lens and they wander aimlessly in circles and go mad.

"You falling asleep?" Sputter says to me.

"No, no, I'm good."

She asks me a favor. Will I ask Michael two questions when I meet him?

"Of course."

"Do you want to write them down?" she asks.

"I think I can remember."

"Okay," she says. "Ask him, 'When did he know Sputter was the one?' Ask him, 'What does he love most about Sputter?' "

IOWA 80, the world's largest truck stop, goes through fifty-five miles of toilet paper each month, according to promotional materials. The megaplex is set on 220 flat acres under a giant sky with parking for 800 rigs, a movie theater, a museum, a truck wash, two game rooms, an embroidery center, a vinyl graphics shop, a custom T-shirt shop, a laser engraving center, a barber, a dentist, a 300-seat sit-down restaurant with a 50-foot salad bar, and the 30,000-foot Super Truck Showroom where balcony seating overlooks The Place for Chrome®.

"Can-you-believe-all-this?" Sputter says to me. She has her camera out. She's trying to get a set of seven-foot chrome exhaust pipes into a single frame.

"You like the bent or the straight pipes?" she asks me.

"Um . . ."

"You have to pick," she says.

"But I don't—"

"Everybody has an opinion!" she says.

"Okay, bent," I say.

"Do you? *Really?* Oh, wow, and here I am all about the straight!"

The Place for Chrome® sends our reflections beaming back at us in distortions and multiples—chrome mud flaps, fenders, bug deflectors, filter housings—and Sputter stands before it all wearing her purse crisscrossed over her middle and shaking her head back and forth, and the splendor only elevates her pro-truck spirit.

"What if all the truckers woke up one day and decided to stop driving?" she says to me. "Where would this country be? *Where would it be?*"

If all the truckers woke up one day and decided to stop driving, Walmart's 617 million square feet across 3,800 stores would soon empty. The 46 million chickens, 175,000 cows, and 443,000 pigs that Tyson slaughters each week would sit stranded on some highway. Amazon's $34 billion worth of stuff would remain in warehouses, and we would continue to pump 378 million gallons of gasoline each day until the pumps went dry, and then we would all have to stay home and America would grind to a halt.

The pro-truck spirit is infectious, and at the enormous gift shop I buy two *World's Biggest Truck Stop* T-shirts for my kids, and one for my husband. Sputter buys a *World's Biggest Truck Stop* shot glass for Michael, a Peterbilt hat for Elaine, and a book, *Men Are Slobs, Women Are Neat . . . and Other Gender Lies That Damage Relationships.*

Outside, the heat has made the blacktop soft and the people slow and damp. We head toward the Super Truck Beauty Contest, which involves the personal stylings of more than one hundred entrants. Many of these trucks have names, like racehorses, or perhaps rodeo bulls—Pure Attitude, Bustin' Out, Flirtin' with Disaster. Big and small, they sit with their hoods propped open and their families in lawn chairs beside them, the people fanning themselves and offering to answer any questions you may have. Sputter has only one, over and over the same one: "Can I take your picture?"

We amble past a big rig painted bubblegum pink and all done up with breast cancer awareness ribbons, and Sputter charges up to the skinny woman showcasing it to compliment her on it. Then she reaches into her purse and hands the woman a twenty.

"No, no, no," the woman says. "That's not what this is for. This is just for *awareness*."

Sputter shoves the money into the woman's pocket. "Now, would you mind if I took your picture?"

A thick man in a red T-shirt comes from behind and announces he has a working fireplace in the cab of his tricked-out rig.

"*No, sir!* A *fireplace*?"

He leads us to a shiny blue truck called Working Class with white horses galloping over ocean waves airbrushed onto the side.

"It's a *Peterbilt*," Sputter turns to me and says, making her eyes droopy and bored.

"Bent pipes," I say to her proudly. She climbs into Working Class first and I follow, and there it is: a gas fireplace framed in shiny oak spitting a tiny blue flame over ceramic logs. The rest of the cab, fully upholstered in black padded leather, is drenched in pink and purple mood lighting swirling with the movement of a smooth saxophone sound track, and over the bed hangs a mounted statuary of horses galloping over ocean waves.

"You got yourself a love shack in there!" Sputter says to the guy as we climb back out.

"I can show you some other things," he says, his eyebrows dancing pathetically.

Sputter does not register any of it—she seems determined to save this man from his own odiousness—and his companion, a woman with long gray hair and a cowboy hat, says, "I-did-not-raise-him-like-that," and claims to be his mother.

We learn quickly that neither of them has anything whatsoever to do with the truck with the fireplace in it. (Apologies to Colin Stuart, of Harvard, Illinois, the real owner, who lovingly created Working Class.) The showman in the red shirt is simply taking advantage of the location to find himself a woman. (And the mother?)

"Okay, now let's get a picture," Sputter says anyway, holding up her camera, waving her hand for mom and son to stand together in front of the love shack.

"Lord, lord, lord," Sputter says, for much of the rest of the day as we go about visiting trucks. "Lord!" If she could take it all in she would, but she can't, and so she keeps snapping pictures to savor later. In the tired evening air at the Tracy Lawrence country music concert she stands on a hay bale to get a picture of the band, which is impossible from way back here. *"Even though he hurt you he's still the one you want."* She knows every word, so she sings and sways and bops as the beat picks up, then comes off the hay bale. "Hold this?" she says, handing me her camera.

"It was Sunday morning, I was seven years old / In the backyard playing in a big mud hole . . ." She throws her arms into the air, wags her hips, twirls, fist-pumps the sky, and the dancing makes her stick out. She may be the only black person in this entire jamboree and now she is the only dancer. She is not like these people. She is the opposite of the trucker stereotype, and in that way I suppose she is the true fit: independent, a maverick carrying the torch of the American mystique of freedom and mischief and topless nights.

People perched on hay bales eventually take Sputter's dancing as an invitation, or some kind of permission. A woman with long frizzy hair gets up, yanks at her companion; then a trim couple in cowboy gear; soon a small crowd twirls around Sputter, everybody throwing their heads back and embracing the sweat. *"Pedal to the metal, let your motor run, / 'Cause he's gonna live forever if the good die young . . ."* Fireworks unload into the sky, and all the trucks in the Super Truck Beauty Contest put their lights on display—a shower of blinks and pulsating truck lights—and then they blow their booming truck horns in unison in great cacophonous celebration. You would have never known this was an industry in crisis. The people at the jamboree rejoice in spite of their world falling apart, or maybe in the face of it; I suppose history, if it goes deep enough, can keep any culture alive and kicking.

That night, we stay at a motel instead of in the truck, and right before bed Sputter turns the TV to Nancy and she squats in front of it and has me take a picture of her and Nancy together. She asks me if I know that Nancy's fiancé was murdered way back when, if I know how hard Nancy works, and if I know that Nancy got fertilized, didn't have her babies until she was forty-eight years old.

"You nap a lot," Sputter says to me one morning, hollering back toward the bed, where I'm curled up. She tells me we're in Ohio.

Ohio?

"I'm sorry," I say. "You don't understand—I can never sleep. This is really unusual. . . ." I feel like an infant in a car seat, having thrown a life-altering tantrum and just now awakening after the subsequent soothing collapse.

Apparently, while I "napped," we drove three hundred miles, stopped to drop off our haul, stopped to pick up a load of beer, pulled over for Sputter to sleep an hour, drove two hundred more miles, got breakfast, and bought a man a cup of coffee and a honey bun because it was his birthday and he was all alone.

"This all happened?" I say, crawling to the front of the cab and trying to adjust to the harsh light.

"You nap a lot," she says. We're passing through city streets, and there are banners for a rib fest and people spilling out of church. A woman wearing a hard hat and an orange vest is directing traffic. Sputter rolls down her window, shouts, "You go, girl!" and takes in the hot breeze.

Her lips are puffy and her eyes are bloodshot, and I think she's been crying. She makes a left, and boom, just like that, we're back at the Kmart parking lot. This is now happening too fast.

A blue Chevy Tahoe comes racing toward the truck, stops abruptly. Michael. He doesn't open his door to get out. She doesn't open her door to get out. "Let's see how long he sits there," she says. We keep waiting and finally she honks the mighty rig horn. *Hoooonk. Hoooonk. Hoooonk.*

"Forget it," she says. She opens her door and climbs down onto the pavement and begins reaching into the cab for her things.

Michael has a round, welcoming face and short, tight curls. He's wearing a T-shirt with a photo of himself on it. "This is me when I was thirty-five," he says, announcing himself.

"Well, you looked good," I say clumsily. "You *still* look good—"

"I can't believe you just sat there," Sputter says to him.

"I can't believe you were honking at me," he says to her. "That's a good way to get yourself Tased."

"A good way to get you to help," she says. "Did you miss me?"

"No."

"Did you shampoo the carpet?"

"No."

"Did you see I left the shampooer out for you, right in the middle of the room so you would fall on top of it?"

"Yes."

We make a few trips carrying our stuff to Michael's car, and then Sputter goes back to the truck and fills up a small trash bag with used wrappers and cups. The heat is still fierce and the sun has the sky paralyzed in the lazy afternoon position.

Sputter is quiet on the ride back to the house, looking out the passenger-side window, bouncing her knee. She's holding her camera, all those new friends and all the splendor of the jamboree locked inside. She makes the mistake of asking Michael how the cats are.

"Oh my God, she is so out of control with those cats!" he says to me, looking up in the rearview mirror to catch my eye. "She tell you about those damn cats?"

I don't say anything. She wanted me to ask him questions. *When did he know Sputter was the one? What does he love most about Sputter?* I'm supposed to ask these questions.

"That one without the tail is spoiled rotten," Michael continues. "That's the one that barfs everywhere. I even told her, I said, 'I'll get you a brand-new kitten if you just get rid of that thing.'"

Sputter continues bouncing her knee. I want to get her out of here. I don't want to let her go back into her real world, and I certainly don't want to go back into mine. I now understand trucks. I understand wanting to never stop hauling.

When we pull up to the house, we get out of Michael's car, stand at the curb, and Sputter opens her arms and we fall into an honest embrace. Her body is soft and solid at the same time, warm and familiar. She reminds me of Lucille. I wonder how long it's been since I've even thought about Lucille. She had ribbon curls just like Sputter's. She danced with me in the basement next to the ironing board. She used Lubriderm. Lucille was the woman my mother hired to help care for her four kids when I was a baby. She was with us until I was twelve. She cracked her gum and she used that hand lotion constantly. We drove her to the bus each day after dinner and I would hold her hand in the backseat, and when she got out I would bite my lip and pray for tomorrow when I could be with her again. We would hug long and hard. Later, when I turned into a surly teenager, I would torture my mom by saying, "Yeah, well, what do *you* know? *Lucille raised me.*" I didn't mean it, but I did. I was the baby, so I got more of Lucille than anyone.

When women of my generation debate about caregiving and caretaking—Should you stay home? Should you go to work? Should you have a nanny?—I never have anything to say. Having Lucille in my history taught me all I needed to know in that regard. You could have two moms, probably four or maybe even six, and not run out of love. If Sputter reminds me of Lucille, I suppose it's because I need her more than ever now.

WEEKS GO BY. Sputter and I call, text, reminisce. Then she abruptly stops. For months I hear nothing.

"Girl, I am so sorry," she says one morning, finally emerging. "I just couldn't bear to tell you."

Her words tumble awkwardly. Michael broke up with her. One day he just up and walked out. She says she couldn't talk about it. "I'm sorry," she keeps saying. It is an odd reaction to sorrow—the need to apologize to others for disappearing into a cave ten thousand miles deep, and I understand it exactly.

I ask her what happened. Nothing happened. He packed up his vast piles of stuff, left. That was it. After two years, that was it.

She tells me about the cave ten thousand miles deep. I open up and tell her all about mine, and I thank her for taking care of me.

We talk about grieving, about how it's supposed to give you wisdom. "But how long does it take for the wisdom part to kick in?" she asks me, and we sit with that one for a while, the blind leading the blind.

She buys a rusty old Cadillac without wheels and an engine that almost works. She invites her dad to come over to help rebuild it, so he comes over, and that's what they do.

THIS IS PARADISE

Puente Hills Landfill
City of Industry, California

Herman asks me if I smell anything, and the way he says it I can't tell if I'm supposed to lie. He says he loves being part of nature, enjoys watching the sunrise, and then he says it again. "Do you smell anything?"

"Well, it is a landfill," I say, finally. I'm trying to be polite. He is old, wiry, chewing a toothpick. He's been at this for decades, always the first to arrive, pulling no. 72, the thirty-foot-long tractor-trailer full of trash assigned to him each day. Dumping is permitted to begin at 6:00 a.m., and he keeps his finger on a red button inside a panel on the truck and constantly checks his watch.

"Women smell things men can't smell," he says.

At this hour the landfill looks nothing like what most people picture when they imagine a landfill. Nothing messy, nothing gross, nothing slimy, no trash anywhere at all. It looks, perhaps disappointingly, like an enormous, lonesome construction site, a 1,365-acre expanse of light brown dirt hiding buried trash from yesterday and thousands of other yesterdays. The scale of the thing alone boggles the mind. To stop and ponder the fact that nearly fifty years of trash forms a foundation four hundred feet deep is simply to become fretful with some unnamed woe about America's past and the planet's future, and so I am trying not to do it. When fellow truckers arrive, pulling up next to Herman, the ground—so deep with trash—is so soft it bounces.

The Puente Hills Landfill, about sixteen miles east of downtown Los Angeles, was a series of canyons when people first started dumping here. Now it's a mountain. In 1953 the film adaptation of H. G. Wells's science fiction novel *The War of the Worlds* featured the Puente Hills as the landing site of the first spacecraft in the Martian invasion. Dumping started in 1965 in an area named the San Gabriel Valley Dump. In 1970 the dump was purchased by the Sanitation Districts of Los Angeles County, a partnership of twenty-four independent districts serving five million people in seventy-eight cities in Los Angeles County, and renamed the Puente Hills Landfill. Every day 13,200 new tons of trash are added. That's enough trash to fill a one-acre hole twenty feet deep. The other way to look at it is a football stadium filled two stories high.

On November 1, 2013, the landfill will be out of room, and all that trash will have to go somewhere else.

At six o'clock, Herman pushes the button. The back end of the trailer rises and 79,650 pounds of debris comes thundering out, most of it wood and plaster and nails and shreds of wallpaper. Beside him a truck is dumping decidedly more organic garbage, pungent indeed, and way down the row, off to the side, a guy is pouring a truck full of sludge, sterilized human waste, black as ink.

Herman gets a broom, sweeps his trailer clean. Unlike most of the haulers who come here—the guys who drive for the conglomerates like Waste Management with their continuous fleet of shiny green packers—Herman works for the Sanitation Districts itself, moving trash from a central dumping station in the nearby town of Southgate. Thus, his priority status. He will make five trips in a day, stopping only once to eat Oodles of Noodles and cheese crackers and a cookie. On the ride home, he eats a green apple. "I've got my routine," he says. "Every day I do it all exactly the same." He talks to me about his philosophy of slowing down, not making mistakes, same way every day, the power of ritual. Peaceful. Using this method, he worked his way up from paper picker, day laborer, traffic director, water truck diver, on and on until he found his niche. There is honor, he says, in being first each day, all those other trucks parting at the gate so Herman can get through. He is careful to note that he is the only one of his entire eighth-grade graduating class of 1954 who has not yet retired. "Why would anyone retire from a place like this?" he asks. "Why *would* you?"

Having spent more than a week at the landfill, by now I am getting used to hearing workers here, from the highest to the lowest ranks, speak like this. Concerning the landfill, they are all pride and admiration and even thanks. It seemed, at first, like crazy talk.

A landfill, after all, is a disgusting place. It is not a place anyone should have to work in, or see, or smell. This is a 100-million-ton solid soup of diapers, Doritos bags, phone books, shoes, carrots, watermelon rinds, boats, shredded tires, coats, stoves, couches, Biggie fries, piled up right here off the I-605 freeway. It's a place that smells like every dumpster you ever walked by—times a few hundred thousand. It's a place that brings to mind the hell of civilization, a heap of waste and ugliness and everything denial is designed for. We throw stuff out. The stuff is supposed to . . . go away. Disappear. We tend not to think about the fact that every time we throw a moist towelette or an empty Splenda packet or a Little Debbie snack cake wrapper into the trash can, there are *people* involved, a whole chain of people charged with the preposterously complicated task of making that thing vanish—which it never really does. A landfill is not something we want to bother thinking about, and if we do, we tend to blame the landfill itself for sitting there stinking like that, for marring the landscape, for offending a sanitized aesthetic. We are human, highly evolved creatures impatient with all things stinky and gooey and gross—remarkably adept at forgetting that a landfill would be nothing, literally nothing, without us.

In America, we produce more garbage than any other country in the world: four pounds per person each day, for a total of 250 million tons a year. In urban areas, we are running out of places to put all that trash. Right now, the cost of getting rid of it is dirt cheap—maybe $15 a month on a bill most people never even see, all of it wrapped into some mysterious business about municipal tax revenue. So why think about it?

Electricity used to be cheap too. We went for a long time not thinking about the true cost of that. Same with gas for our cars.

The problem of trash (and sewage, its even more offensive cousin) is the upside-down version of the problem of fossil fuel: too much of one thing, not enough of the other. Either way, it's a matter of managing resources. Either way, a few centuries of gorging and not thinking ahead has the people of the twenty-first century standing here scratching our heads. *Now what?*

The problem of trash, fortunately, is a wondrously provocative puzzle to scientists and engineers, some of whom lean, because of the inexorability of trash, toward the philosophical. The intrinsic conundrum—the disconnect between human waste and the human himself—becomes grand, even glorious, to the people at the dump.

"I brought my wife up here once to show her," Herman tells me. "I said, 'Look, that's trash.' She couldn't believe it. Then she couldn't understand it. I told her, I said, 'This is the Rolls-Royce of landfills.' "

"NOBODY KNOWS we're even here," Joe Haworth is saying as we make our way around the outside of the landfill, winding up and up past scrubby California oaks, sycamore trees, and the occasional shock of pink bougainvillea vine. He is driving his old Cadillac, a 1982 Eldorado, rusty black with a faded KERRY-EDWARDS sticker on the bumper. He has the thick glasses of a civil engineer, which is how he started, and the curls and paunch and demeanor of a crusty retired PR man, which is what he is now. He wears a Hawaiian print shirt and a straw hat, and the way he leans way back in the driver's seat suggests an easy, uncomplicated confidence.

"People driving by on the highway think this is a park," he says. "Or they'll be, like, 'What's with all the pipes going around that mountain?' "

In fact, we are driving over trash, a half century's worth, a heap so vast, there are roads and stop signs and traffic cops and a history of motor vehicle accidents, including at least one fatality.

The outside of the landfill, the face the public sees, reminds me of Disney World, a perfectly crafted veneer of happiness belying a vastly more complicated core. The western side, facing the 605, is lush greens and deep blues, a showy statement of desert defiance, while the eastern face is quiet earth tones, scrubby needlegrass, buttonbush, and sagebrush; the native look on that side was requested by the people living in Hacienda Heights, a well-to-do neighborhood in the foothills of the dump. They wanted the mountain of trash behind them to blend in with the canyons reaching toward the sunset. A staff of fifty landscapers do nothing but honor such requests. The goal: Make the landfill disappear by making it look pretty.

"No matter what you do with your trash, nature has to process it," Joe is saying. "Okay? Think about it." We are making our way up to a lookout point where we can get an overview of the action of the trash trucks and bulldozers and scrapers, a good show and a good place to sit and think. Joe speaks with rapid-fire speed, constantly punctuating his lessons with Groucho Marx–style asides. "Look, we'd be up to our eyeballs in dinosaur poop if nature didn't have any way to run this stuff around again," he says. He loves this stuff. He is sixty-four years old, an environmental engineer, a Jesuit-trained fallen Catholic whose enthusiasm for waste management, solid, liquid, recycled, buried, burning, decomposing, is oddly infectious. I have come to regard him as the high priest of trash.

"Instead of being up to our eyeballs in dinosaur poop, we're *made* of dinosaur poop," he says. "You know? And other chemicals. We've got garbage in us. There's a carbon cell from Napoleon in your elbow somewhere. It's all nature running things around again, a continuous loop. It's all done by bacteria breaking it down into carbon, hydrogen, oxygen, nitrogen, okay? *Think about it!*"

I tell him I'll add it to my list, which keeps getting longer the longer I'm here. Joe retired from the landfill a couple of years ago, but he comes back to consult, to visit, to help Donny, his assistant who took over his job, and to sit and marvel. He entered the refuse world back in the 1960s, when people first awakened, as if from a lazy daydream, to the notion that trash not only matters but trash *is* matter, and matter never leaves. You can burn it. You can bury it. You can throw it into the ocean. You can try to hide it, but it still exists in some form: ash, sludge, gas, particulate matter floating in the air. "It all comes back to the idea of the cycle," he says. "We're going to keep reusing the same stuff, so let's figure out how to use it responsibly so we don't choke on it."

He gives me an example. "See those pipes?" he says, pointing as we cruise up the landfill. "Those are sucking gas." The pipes are fat and prominent, about two feet in diameter, and a constant source of wild wonder. Eighty miles of pipes encircle the landfill, pulling out a deadly mix of methane, carbon dioxide, and other gases continuously produced by the fermenting trash. The pipes are connected with seventy-five miles of underground trenches and to a network of fourteen hundred wells. The methane mix is highly explosive and smelly and in the past has been an environmental nightmare. As trash continues to ferment, the methane is unstoppable. And so the pipes—a kind of landfill miracle, a technology pioneered by Sanitation Districts engineers—deliver the methane downhill to the Gas-to-Energy Facility. The methane feeds a boiler, creates steam. The steam turns a turbine. The turbine generates fifty-eight megawatts of electricity—enough to power about seventy thousand Southern California homes.

Before I started hanging out at the landfill, I had no idea we could generate electricity from trash. "Most people don't know this," I say to Joe.

"Oh, a lot of people know it," he says.

No, they don't. I have checked. I have consulted folks back home, regular trash makers, average citizens going through cartons of Hefty bags, who think little beyond "Gotta take the trash out" when it comes to the final resting place of their garbage. "People don't know we power homes with landfill gas," I say. "Don't you think people should *know* this?"

He looks at me, weary. "Why do you think I've been busting my ass at this for thirty years, lady?"

He blinks, removes his glasses, takes out a handkerchief, and wipes them clean. "That's what I did," he says. "I did nothing but tell people about what we do here. Now, how much time does society have to listen and understand? Well, the answer to that is, society's interest level is pretty low. It doesn't necessarily want to know where its waste goes. It's embarrassed by its responsibility in this arena."

Joe parks the car and we get out. We stand and peer down into the landfill, at trash, the very stuff Herman and his fellow truckers dumped earlier this morning. From this distance, the open landfill is a giant brown five-hundred-acre bowl, with a frantic line of trucks inside snorting and pregnant and awaiting release.

This is the cheapest place to dump trash in all of L.A. County, about $28 a ton, and so it is the first choice of most garbage companies. When the landfill reaches its 13,200-ton daily capacity, usually by about noon, the guard at the gate will raise a flag visible from the freeway: a sign to truckers to keep on moving and find another place to dump. Anyone can dump here, any private citizen with a pickup full of junk willing to pay the fee.

Trash gets piled in as many as three active areas, or "cells," daily. Each cell is about the size of a football field, and every hour an additional 1,200 tons of trash is put into it. A team of thirty heavy-equipment operators dances madly over the pile. Huge bulldozers, ten feet tall, equipped with seventeen-foot blades, push and sculpt the trash into rows. Then the mighty Bomags, 120,000-pound compactors with 130,000 pounds of pushing power, smash and crunch and squish the trash, forcing out air, forcing it tighter and tighter to save space. All of these machines clamber impossibly close to one another, backward, forward, over steep hills of trash, clinging lopsidedly to edges. From up here, the sounds are all roar and backup beeps echoing around the bowl, and the view is a colorful shock of red and green and yellow and white, a smash of crawling color.

One of the cells has already reached capacity, and so the scrapers have moved in, the biggest machines of all, fifty-three feet long, sixteen feet high—the wheels alone are nine feet tall—and with their big belly hoppers pick up clean dirt, and dump it about a foot thick over the cell, sealing in odors, rats, bugs, concealing the leftovers of a yesterday everyone is more than ready to be done with.

Forgotten. Gone. By day's end, there will be no trace of trash anywhere in the landfill.

The next day, the process repeats. Cell by cell, the garbage spreads across the landfill floor until it hits the far side, the edge of the bowl, and a new layer, or "lift," is begun.

A constant parade of water trucks sprays the dirt to control dust, and a team of paper pickers runs madly on foot to catch anything the wind might pick up and try to carry away—the worst offender being plastic grocery bags that can take off like kids' balloons. A chemical odor retardant is sometimes used when things get too bad, or again if the wind conspires, and there are a lot of seagulls waiting on a nearby ridge. Seagulls are a landfill nuisance because they fly away with food scraps and, as is their reputation, fight each other over them mid-flight, often losing them, and soon a lady has a half-eaten hamburger splashing into her backyard pool. For a time, engineers were utterly confounded by the seagull problem, firing off cannons to scare them away, piping in the sounds of hawks and owls—but the gulls got so used to the sounds they would stand on top of the cannons and inside the speakers. The solution was elegant and simple: tall, portable poles placed at intervals over the working face of the landfill, with nylon fishing line stretched between them. The lines disrupt the gulls' unique spiral landing pattern; the birds give up before even trying. "And I guess they're too stupid to walk on in under the wires," Joe says. He's got his sunglasses on now, and, together with the hat and the shirt and against the background of the lush foliage, he is the picture of vacation.

A more urgent and literally more pressing concern than birds in any landfill is leachate, the liquids that might ooze out. People are not supposed to throw away paint thinner or nail polish or batteries or transmission fluid or motor oil, but plenty do, plenty of it comes in on trucks, and plenty of it gets smashed and smushed, mixing with rainwater into an unpredictably toxic cocktail that, if it escapes the landfill and gets into the groundwater, could be deadly to nearby communities. And so a twelve-foot liner of clay, plastic, sand, and other barrier materials covers the walls and floor of the landfill—a diaper of the largest scale imaginable, designed to absorb and seal in wetness. Seventeen miles of pipes carry the leachate into collection areas. A team of field engineers specialize in monitoring the leachate, cleaning and purifying it. One of the ways a landfill engineer anywhere in the world earns bragging rights is if he can pour himself a glass of the leachate from his landfill and drink it.

All of this—the operational area of Puente Hills—is invisible to the public, thanks to earthen berms that rise ten feet above the working face. The scraper drivers keep adding to the top of the berm as the landfill fills, constantly building the fortress wall, so all the work goes unnoticed.

For their part, the scraper drivers refer to the berms as "visuals." The most fun you can have on a scraper, they have told me, is steadying your 155,000-pound machine over the tip of a visual barely wider than the span of your tires. Once in a while a scraper will fall off a visual, sometimes sliding one hundred feet down or sometimes hanging there, half on and half off, until a crane can be summoned to rescue it. A driver who falls off a visual will get called "Tipsy Toes" or "Tipper" until the next guy does it and earns the torch of shame.

A bulldozer or Bomag driver who manages to roll his machine over into the trash will likewise have to endure the name "Flipper."

"You should go down there," Joe says. "You should go down there and ride in the trash, get a feel for it."

MIKE "BIG MIKE" SPEISER is the most famous Bomag driver at the landfill, and some say in the world. This is only incidentally because he looks, as much as a person can, like a Bomag. He is proudly boxy, enormous, bald, and he appears as though he could crush the trash without the assistance of machinery. He is forty-five years old and has impressive tattoos: a Grim Reaper, a skeleton with a dagger through the head, a skull with flames shooting out, and a skull with horns and a bullet hole in its head. "Like the Devil got shot in the head or something," he says. "Basically."

He is a shy man who blushes when he smiles, and he is known for being a gentleman. He is famous because he won first place on compactors—a test of agility and speed—in the recent Solid Waste Association of North America's International Road-E-O in Cocoa Beach, Florida. "He is the best in the nation," a few of the operators have told me. Mike does not himself brag about the honor, but he does allow: "I am very, very good at this."

Mike and I stand at the edge of a cell of trash in motion, Bomag chugging, ready to roll. He climbs the ladder to the cab and offers his hand to help hoist me up. "The air conditioner works nice, and it's a pressurized cab, so it keeps the smells out." He shows off the air-ride feature of the cushioned seat, apologizing that there is only one. He takes the controls while I hunch behind him and hang on to his soft shoulders. We crawl slowly, as if in a tank, toward and into the cell of trash, about thirty feet deep. We are high above with a marvelous view of smeared paper plates, Target bags, egg cartons, Green Giant frozen peas, Ben & Jerry's ice cream, all manner of Hefty and Glad bags splayed open to reveal the guts of everyday American life. Effortlessly, we climb over a mattress and a TV and a tricycle and a rocking chair and soda bottles and deodorant, until pretty soon the eye refuses to differentiate the trash, refuses to register nonsense the mind can't begin to place in anything close to a meaningful narrative. We go rolling through an acre of garbage, mounds and mounds of it cracking and turning to mush under the teeth of the Bomag.

"No doubt, we make a lot of trash in America," Mike says. "No doubt. And this is a tiny piece of one day, in one landfill. But I don't tend to think about that. Mostly I think about not getting run into by a dozer."

We sink in, climb out, sink, climb. Mike keeps moving forward, pushing trash toward the edge of the cliff formed by the day's massive pile—a ledge so high you can't see what, if anything, is over it.

"You're getting close to the edge," I tell him.

"I have to get these verticals down as quick as possible," he says, and without hesitation keeps moving forward. "You worry about smoothing things out afterwards. When we're diving over the vertical you'll see why."

He chatters on about smoothing and grabbing and peeling, but the only words I take in are "diving over the vertical," which we are about to do. We are about to free-fall over a cliff of trash three stories high. I make the point that this is scaring the shit out of me.

"A lot of guys I train cry their first couple of weeks," he says.

He assures me that the Bomag is extremely agile. He says the only worry, really, is tree stumps. "One time I was coming over a vertical, and on the way down I hit a stump about the size of a car. I started sliding down the slope sideways. You just kind of hold on and gun it and try to get off of it. That one gave me a pucker butt."

We drive straight toward the open sky, and head as if on a suicide mission over the cliff. I expect a crash, a violent tumble, death, but the Bomag clings to the trash like a squirrel, and we begin our slow descent down, about thirty feet straight down, into more trash—where six or seven bulldozers zoom about, backward, forward, pushing trash, sculpting the cell.

I ask Mike who's in charge here, who has the right of way, what the pattern is, who yields to whom. He says everyone more or less figures it out as they go along. He talks about riding dirt bikes when he was five. "Experiences like that prepare you. You learn the limits of motion." Any kid who grew up with dirt bikes and four-wheelers would obviously love a job like this, he says, adding that he considers himself blessed.

Before he started working here in 1990, Big Mike worked as an auto mechanic. "I could not take the stress of that life," he tells me. Like so many of the people I meet at the landfill, he tells me he enjoys nature, being outdoors, and a good deal of solitude. We climb back up the cliff of trash to square off for another dive down, and he whistles. Then he invites me to join him for lunch later. "I mean, if you want."

BETWEEN THE LEACHATE, the methane, all the enormous equipment, the dangerous dives, the brainpower, the rotating cells, the seagull lines, the irrigation, the bougainvillea vine—all the landscaping, all the field engineers, all the chemistry—I'm thinking: *This is ridiculous. This is a lot to go through so people can continue living in denial, as if our trash has some magical way of just vanishing.* At one point, I confess to Joe Haworth that I have no idea where, back home, my own trash goes after it leaves the end of my driveway, gets hauled off in a green truck while my dogs stand on the porch and bark stupidly at it. I have no idea whatsoever, and I certainly have no sense of my trash having a destiny of such complexity and such bother.

This, Joe tells me, is a preferable situation to when trash was simple. Throughout most of history, trash was a linear concern, the end of a simple four-beat pattern: you dig up raw materials, make something with them, use the something, and when the usefulness is over, you throw the thing away. One, two, three, trash. One, two, three, trash. One, two, three, trash. The piling of trash became a concern as soon as there were enough people clustered in one place to notice it. The city of Athens is said to have organized the first municipal dump in the Western world, in about 500 B.C. Citizens were required to dispose of their waste at least one mile from city walls. This was a remarkably forward-thinking plan, especially when you consider that, zooming all the way up to the eighteenth century, most Americans were simply throwing their trash out the window into the street—and this despite the fact that trash-related diseases such as bubonic plague, cholera, and typhoid fever had been known to alter the populations of Europe and influence monarchies around the world.

Burning trash became a big deal in the late 1800s with the invention of municipal incinerators as well as the practice of putting a match to the stuff in one's own backyard. Burning trash was wonderful, magical, because it made it seem to disappear.

Throwing trash into the ocean had a similar effect, and for a while that practice joined burning as America's solution. But stinky, ruined beaches and clogged harbors prompted the Supreme Court to ban trash-in-the-ocean in 1934. Even so, it's worth noting that, thanks to lawbreakers and people in countries without regulations, a soup of plastic waste floating in the Pacific Ocean now covers an area twice the size of the continental United States. This expanse of debris, held in place by swirling underwater currents, stretches from about five hundred nautical miles off the California coast, across the northern Pacific, past Hawaii, and almost as far as Japan. Scientists are still trying to figure out what to do about that one.

Joe Haworth grew up in downtown Los Angeles, and he remembers burning trash as a boy. "Everybody had a backyard incinerator," he tells me. He's sitting on one of the gas pipes on a lower ledge of the landfill, under an oak tree, taking in the shade. "I remember looking at the wax melting off the milk carton, thinking, 'Oh, that's really cool.' We put the ashes in a bucket, and the city would haul the ashes away. You'd separate the food scraps. They'd be taken to the pig farms. Then we had a mayor, Sam Yorty, saying, 'Hey, if we throw all this stuff together, we can make it easier for the housewives, make it simpler for them; let's put it all in one big can and haul it away.'" The story delights him, as so many stories do, and he bangs on the pipe to animate this next part. "Sam Yorty was elected, and housewives were bashing trash lids together, saying, 'Bless you, Mayor Sam!' Yup. Look up Sam Yorty. Y-O-R-T-Y."

And so, the urban landfill, which in the beginning was a dump on the edge of town. When the pile got too high, someone would light a match to it and make room for more. And more. And more. Volume became an absurdly huge problem, with the dawning of the baby boom and the quantity of trash exploding in the crazed TV-dinner consumerism following World War II. In 1955, *Life* magazine heralded the advent of the "throwaway society."

Burn all that trash in a crowded place like Los Angeles and you contribute to the most famous smog problem in the world. In 1959 the American Society of Civil Engineers published a standard guide to "sanitary landfilling." Instead of burning trash, the idea was to bury it. To guard against rodents and odors, the guide suggested compacting trash and covering it with a new layer of soil each day.

And so, the modern era of trash.

Joe Haworth and his college buddies were studying civil engineering at Loyola Marymount University at the time. Joe had not yet had his trash awakening, although he and his engineering friends, infected by the idealism of the time, the dawning of the environmental movement, were getting excited about . . . sewage.

"The whole nation's plumbing was coming apart," he tells me. "It was literally going to pieces. It was like the mayor's idiot son ran the local sewage treatment." There was no thinking. There was just expediency: Dump the crap into the river. In the big-picture tradition of the Jesuits, a professor at Loyola was urging Joe to do something with his life. The professor told him about sanitary engineering. He said there was a future, something big, bigger than anyone could imagine, and a chance to do something good.

There was no EPA yet. There were virtually no federal laws concerning pollution. Oil tankers were regularly dumping crankcase oil into oceans, air pollution was literally killing people—ninety-six in just four days in New York City—and in Ohio the Cuyahoga River burst into flames five stories high from floating chemicals.

And so, the awakening. In 1962, Rachel Carson published *Silent Spring*, a cry of ecological radicalism meant to awaken a public lazily dependent on the chemical control of nature. The book ignited the first serious public dialogue about the dangers of pesticides and other chemicals. Ed Muskie, the famously cranky U.S. senator, championed a national environmental policy, pushing the

Clean Air Act, the Clean Water Act—much of the work born of his disgust over the polluted rivers in his native Maine.

In 1970, President Nixon created the EPA.

The modern environmental movement was nothing without sharp young minds capable of inventing change. Funds became available, traineeships at places like Stanford, Caltech, MIT. The best and brightest, including Joe, got free rides to study trash. Joe went to Stanford. "A lot of us felt the obligation to go into public service," he says. He kicks the dirt. It all seems so adorable now. Boomers changing the world. What happened to all that? "This was such exciting stuff," he says. "We were thinking up all-new ways of helping nature play catch-up after a couple of pretty messy centuries." It was a thrilling time to be a sanitary engineer, even as the title gradually morphed into "environmental engineer." In fact, these guys would go on to change the paradigm, inventing systems that would begin to provide relief to a planet choking on its own debris.

Joe never set out to be a PR guy. He was more or less called. So much was happening, so many innovations. His colleagues didn't have the knack for putting multipart engineering concepts into the vernacular, but Joe had it in spades. He created the information office and became a mouthpiece.

Using landfill gas to generate electrical power—that was a good example. He remembers those early days with the fondness of an old man thinking of his first kid. It happened at Palos Verdes, one of the Districts' older landfills, which was adjacent to a handsome neighborhood where a woman was complaining about her dead roses. She blamed the landfill: surely something disgusting was emanating out of that dump. She was right. Inspectors found that methane, the explosive gas they normally simply flared to get rid of, had migrated from the landfill into the neighborhood.

"So we said, 'Whoa, we gotta do something,'" Joe says, standing up now, as if trying to solve the puzzle anew. "We dug a trench near her roses, put gravel in it. We figured, well, that stuff will just come up through the gravel because that'll be the easiest road for it to travel. When that didn't work, we put a pipe in, started to suck the gas out. Then our guys said, 'You know what, we're burning this stuff now just to get rid of it. That's a pretty good-looking flame. I wonder if that would work in an engine.' So our guys then began to run it through an internal combustion engine. And it ran the engine."

It was one of those eureka moments: Use landfill gas to generate electricity! To a young environmental engineer, it was the most elegant example imaginable of closing the loop, reusing everything, making something useful out of, literally, garbage.

"One of our guys thought of putting a Christmas tree up on the landfill site," Joe says. "Not a real big one. But running this little generator on landfill gas and lighting this Christmas tree. It got attention. Because it was such a curious thing."

It worked. They built an energy station, and a couple of years later, dignitaries from around the world, including Prince Charles, came to visit the Palos Verdes landfill site to see energy come out of trash.

Currently, about 425 landfills in the United States produce landfill gas (LFG), generating about 10 billion kilowatt-hours of electricity per year. This is a green fuel, offsetting the use of 169 million barrels of oil per year or 356,000 railcars of coal. According to the EPA, the carbon reduction is the equivalent of removing the emissions from nearly 14 million vehicles on the road or planting nearly 20 million acres of forest.

All those complications of trash—the methane, the leachate, all the enormous equipment, all the landscaping, all the chemistry—have really nothing to do with enabling an irresponsible public intent on ignoring trash. That's our own deal, our own psychology. In real-world terms, the complications of trash are the human inventions and human interventions intent on closing the cycle to restore nature's severed loop.

"Think about it," Joe says, squinting in the harsh glare of the noon sun. "What is pollution? Pollution's just the wrong stuff in the wrong place at the wrong time. Any other time, it's a resource. Okay? *Think* about that."

WHEN I ENTER THE LUNCHROOM with Big Mike, he lags behind, tells me to go ahead and get started. By now I know the dynamics of "second lunch," at noon, and I wonder where Big Mike will sit. The place is stark and temporal, a large white double-wide with tables and bulletin boards and newspapers and buzzing fluorescent lights.

I head down to the long table where Steve, Wes, Patrick, Jamie, Tony, and the rest of the happy loudmouths of second lunch are diving into their lunch pails. Second lunch is almost all "Dirt," the men who run the scrapers and push dirt. First lunch, at eleven thirty, is almost all "Rubbish," the men like Big Mike who crush garbage. The Dirt crew is very gabby about the Rubbish crew. They say Rubbish is aloof, boring, and miserable. Dirt, they say, is happy, hilarious, and loving. I am trying to understand the source of these distinctions.

Each day the guys of second lunch seem excited to have a visitor in the lunchroom and, like schoolkids, talk at me all at once. "We are the biggest landfill in the nation," one of them declares.

"We have awesome equipment," says one.

"We have *eighteen* D9s."

"We have two D8s."

"Compactors? We've got five of those."

"And two D10s—120,000 pounds *each*."

"We have a D11 out at our Calabasas landfill, which is even *bigger* than that one."

"I personally don't think I've ever seen a D12. To be honest with you, I don't think Caterpillar even makes them anymore."

"They don't."

"We have the biggest machines *in the world*."

"We are number one."

Steve, a scraper driver, tall, gangly, with long blond curls, holds court at the corner table. If he is the leader of this group, it is because he can withstand constant jabbing and ridicule, mostly about his hair, with its history of bad cuts, bad bangs, Farrah Fawcett layers. Lately, the guys have been encouraging Steve to get a mullet. They have offered to pay him to do it. Steve emphatically refuses, but the image brings delight to Jamie, to Joe, and to Patrick, and somehow morphs into a discussion of the possibility of Steve one day making porn, mullet porn. There is no logical sequence to the evolution of this riff, but it takes on a life of its own, until soon midgets enter the story and the idea of Steve making midget mullet porn. The laughter is uproarious, and one guy spits out his Mountain Dew, and there is stomping of feet and pounding of tables until the lunchroom trailer shakes like a ship of drunken pirates.

I feel bad for Mike up there all alone. Mike usually eats at eleven thirty, with the rest of Rubbish, but he got delayed on account of driving me around on his Bomag, so now he's stuck here with Dirt.

I get up to go sit with Mike, but then Jamie, the youngest here, thin, clean-cut, offers me a peach, saying he picked it himself from his mother's tree, so I sit back down.

"I drove on the Bomag with Big Mike today," I tell the guys. "He dove me over verticals."

"Yeah, we saw you out there," says Wes, a guy with a wide brow wearing a Budweiser T-shirt. "Big Mike will take care of you."

Big Mike waves from across the room. He's an exception to the rule of second lunch, one of the few men in Rubbish whom Dirt doesn't make fun of. This is on account of Big Mike's win at the Road-E-O, his furthering the cause of making Puente Hills Landfill number one.

"I also rode in a rig with Herman this morning," I tell the guys.

"Herman?"

"Miserable fucker—"

"He's not as bad now."

"It was when he drove the water truck that he was really bad."

"His truck was number 6601. He would hide it."

"He was, like, 'That's my water truck! You better not touch it.'"

"He had his cowboy hat. You better not touch his hat!" They

crack up over the memory of Herman's hat. Oh, that's a good one. They are all gossip and cackle. I tell them they sound like girls.

Someone brings up rats.

"I've only seen one rat in all the years I worked here."

"Coyotes eat the rats. The only rats we see are rats that other people bring in."

They proudly agree that there are no rats at the landfill—and if there is one, it is only because it was hiding in a dumpster that got dumped. For the most part, the rats are crushed by the compactor, or the dozers, or buried alive in the dirt.

As for the occasional dead rats, these offer possibilities. Like the one time Patrick wrapped one in a soft tortilla shell, presented it to his supervisor, and said he was sick of people leaving their lunch around all the time.

Oh, that's a good one. Oh, there have been so many good times here at the dump.

All of these men are lifers, most having worked their way up from paper pickers. Steve has been here for twenty-three years, Tony for nineteen, and Patrick for fourteen. For a heavy-equipment operator, getting a job with the Sanitation Districts is considered a ticket to paradise, given the benefits and good pay—about $80,000 a year before overtime—the steady year-round work, and the fact that trash is recession-proof. Most of the crew lives far east of the landfill, sixty, seventy, eighty miles away in the California desert, commuting more than two hours each way because this is L.A. and nothing is affordable. Because of the distance, and because they have to maintain squeaky-clean driving records in order to keep their jobs, they are not the sort of guys who leave work and hang out together in bars. They vanpool together, watch movies.

They spend their days alone, speedily pushing dirt from here to there, and so, aside from their time together in the van, all they have is the lunchroom.

They tell me that any of these operators can run any piece of equipment in the yard. All of the Dirt crew has at some point run Rubbish and vice versa, and even Dirt has to concede that Rubbish is more fun.

"Crushing things," says one. "The biggest thrill at this entire landfill is crushing things."

"Crushing boats. Just to destroy a boat. Or a trailer or something like that. That's probably the biggest thrill that I can think of."

"I crushed a mobile once. What was neat about it was I didn't know it was there, but when I came up to it, I kind of tagged onto the corner of it and I must have hit it just right, because when I hit it the whole thing just flattened."

"Awwww!"

For all the joy in crushing things, the facts of the matter sometimes give these guys pause.

"You'd be amazed at what gets thrown out," one says. "Stuff that could be donated. We could write a book about the American way of waste."

"Companies throw stuff away because of taxes. Like brand-new running shoes. These companies cut all their surplus shoes up so nobody can get them. But they would be perfectly fine. They could donate them. They could do something with them."

"When I first started here, for, like, probably two or three weeks these big semitrailers were just dumping piles of brand-new computer typewriters. Piles! Sometimes there would be three trucks next to each other, dumping brand-new computer typewriters. Never been opened. Still in the box."

"Waste. Waste. Waste. Sure, it bothers you, but what can you do about it?"

"There was a time someone dumped $2.1 million here. It's buried in there."

"That is not true."

"It's true!"

"Remember when they dumped all them Susan B. Anthonys?"

"Thought it was chocolate candy, but it was real."

"That is not true, either."

"It's buried in there, I swear to God."

"How do you even *know*?"

"How do you know it's not?"

"Remember the Sears that closed down? They had their big sale. Then whatever didn't sell came into the landfill. Brand-new. Brand-new! Other customers would be here dumping, then run over and pick up brand-new chain saws."

Salvaging is strictly prohibited at the landfill. This may sound like some picky rule, but the truth is, people who are stupid enough to dive in among the dozers to grab something sometimes end up dead. Private citizens who dump here are provided a separate dumping area away from the action of the machines, but that doesn't stop them from walking over to the working cell and trying to go for the grab.

"We've had people crushed."

"Oh, yeah."

"You can't see them. You literally don't know they're there. No one is supposed to be there."

"Remember that lady that got crushed?"

"Oh, yeah."

I make the point that with all this drama, Rubbish sounds way more exciting than Dirt. Maybe Dirt is jealous of Rubbish and that accounts for the animosity?

This analysis brings jeers.

"Those guys are miserable," one says.

"They hate each other."

"No, they hate themselves."

"It's a body thing," one says, and the group agrees on that one.

Most of the Rubbish crew is in pain, or used to be in pain, or is fighting it. Typically, a man moves over to Rubbish only when his body can no longer take Dirt. Rubbish is soft. Dirt is hard. A man who spends eight or ten hours a day five days a week on a D10 pushing dirt is a man with jangled bones, achy joints, herniated disks. "Your longevity is what we're talking about," one says. Most of the Rubbish guys are old, nearing retirement, with a history of back and neck operations. "Going over to Rubbish is more or less being put out to pasture," one says.

There are exceptions. Again, Big Mike, who occupies such a hallowed place in this landfill. He drove a scraper for just two years before his back got destroyed. He had surgery, a whole year in bed, and then he returned to have a terrific career in Rubbish on his Bomag, number one in the U.S.A.

But usually Dirt means you're still young. Falling off visuals, straddling one, Tipper and Tipsy Toes. Dirt is the good old days.

These days are, of course, numbered. The landfill is scheduled to close in 2013. A skeleton crew of maintenance workers and field engineers will keep the Puente Hills infrastructure working—will monitor the leachate, maintain the gas wells and the power plant that will continue to transform methane into electricity for about thirty years. But there will be no more trash, no more trucks, no more verticals to crash over, and no more radical dirt moves on a D10. Most of the Rubbish crew is old enough to retire, while the Dirt crew will get absorbed somewhere within the enormous Sanitation Districts organization, so at least they'll have jobs.

None of the guys in the lunchroom will admit to the possibility of ever missing this dump, this history, these good old days, and yet they scheme together about their bosses getting permits to open more space in the canyons, more space for trash, more time for Puente Hills.

"It's a pipe dream," one says. "Sooner or later, you just have to face the fact that this place is about to close."

WHEN THE LANDFILL CLOSES, a Waste-by-Rail program will take over. The trash will be put in sealed boxcars and delivered two hundred miles west along the Union Pacific Railroad to the desert, to the new Mesquite Regional Landfill in Imperial County, a super-landfill said to last a hundred years.

And all this old trash will still be sitting here, fermenting, producing gas. In that way, the Puente Hills Landfill will stand as a kind of monument, the symbol of an era of new thought.

The mountain of trash will be capped, sealed, covered in layers and layers of stone and clay and soil, planted, and turned over to the Los Angeles County Department of Parks and Recreation, a place for people to play. Plans have been in the works for decades: Every time a truck dumps a ton of trash here, a dollar goes into a Puente Hills Landfill Native Habitat Preservation Authority fund. The goal of the fund is to maintain a wildlife corridor more than twice as large as the fill area. Already miles of hiking and horseback-riding trails traverse this land and even the landfill itself, separated from daily operations.

Over time, the ground will settle in odd and unpredictable ways. You can't construct buildings on a landfill, because the trash has a life of its own, much of it slowly decomposing and, surprisingly, much of it not. Trash specialists called "garbologists" have done archeological digs in older landfills and have found that, rather than decomposing, a lot of trash, due to the lack of oxygen in a landfill, is actually mummified there. Newspapers from the 1960s have been uncovered from deep inside the earth—with headlines and news items intact.

"Isn't that hilarious?" Joe says. He loves the garbologist story, the mummy idea, all the crazy surprises.

We're in the car again, marveling at the work of the landscaping guys, and he's got his arm out the window pointing this way and that like some grandpa showing the old neighborhood. "See those little pipes?" he says, motioning toward small irrigation pipes snaking all over the ground.

"More pipes," I say. "A lot of pipes." It's really nothing so surprising to see an arid landscape made lush with water flowing through irrigation pipes.

"Remember I showed you the sewage-treatment plant?" he says. He's nodding knowingly and his shirtsleeve is flapping in the breeze. It takes me a moment to make the connection he's making, between irrigation pipes and sewage—

"No—" I say.

"Yeah," he says.

These pipes don't just carry any water. They carry reclaimed wastewater from the Sanitation Districts' nearby sewage treatment plant.

"Isn't that neat?" he says.

He parks at a fence, up at the top of the landfill, just beyond the horse trails, where there is a strawberry farm. It's on land adjacent to the landfill, rows and rows of fat green plants ready for picking.

"Come see the strawberries," he says, shoving the car door with his shoulder, and it reluctantly creaks open. "Okay, now see *those* pipes?" he says.

"Oh, come on," I say. "Not the strawberries."

"Yeah."

The strawberry farm is dependent on recycled wastewater for its irrigation too.

"Isn't *that* neat?" he says. He bends at his knees and then pops up with a little clap. "You should be writing about a sewage treatment plant," he says. "That's where the action is."

There has been so much talk at this landfill about sewage, and apparently I can no longer avoid it. Joe and all the engineers here refer to it with a shrug. No big deal. This is just the way things work. Sewage water feeding flowers and strawberry plants. It has taken me a while to accept the notion that this, in fact, *is* the way things work.

"Oh, just think about it," Joe says. "What is a sewage treatment plant? It's an apology to nature for putting too many people in one place."

He pauses, gives me a moment to mull that one over. He pulls his hat down to cut the sun. "Nature isn't designed for us to live the way we do. Nature designed it more like the Native Americans had it: When the neighborhood started to smell, you picked up your tepee and went over there. There was some basic human rule that said you go *thataway*." He points with both hands moving toward some imagined exit. "Primitive societies knew that nature would ultimately reclaim all that organic material so they could come back in a few years."

Nature gave us rain, streams, rivers, and the ocean to finish the job of digestion. "This is just a straight environmental-engineering calculation," he says, heading back to the car, and he opens my door for me so I climb in.

"Just about everybody in this country has one cubic foot of digester somewhere out there finishing the job that he or she couldn't complete," he says. "Your guts start the process and nature completes it. Now, where is that going to happen? If you let our sewage from this L.A. area with ten million people float into the ocean, you would have one really beat-up ocean."

With that, he throws the car into reverse, then starts driving down the mountain. He pulls over to a lookout spot where we get a good view of the sewage treatment plant in the distance, just over the I-605, tucked into the hills. I feel I should say something complimentary, but it looks like every gray, flat, giant, boring industrial building you've ever hated for marring the landscape.

"We take the processes that occur in an ocean or a river and we do it in tanks," he says. "The same bacteria that work in nature—basically a big bacterial soup that emulates what goes on in the ground or in a river—does the whole thing in a tank in a more concentrated fashion. So, instead of taking ten days in a river, we do it in eight hours inside a tank."

There is something vaguely utopian about all of this. A beautiful landfill blooming with pink flowers, wastewater feeding strawberries, fifty-eight megawatts of electricity out of garbage and sludge, hiking trails over trash. It would seem we were talking about an entirely different planet, not our own supposedly doomed one—where the sky is falling; where, because of our gluttony, we are in danger of making one final grand mess of the place, if not melting it or blowing it up. Those are all certainly viable outcomes. But there is more to the story: There are people on this very same planet having a rousing good time fixing the place, people motivated by the thrill of repair, the simple joy of invention, and an urge to do good.

The more time I spend at the landfill, the more I get the sense that I'm in a different dimension, listening to more highly evolved beings that have been here all along but, somehow, nobody ever noticed.

I MEET UP WITH CAROL, the old lady who works the front gate and greets all the truckers who come in, starting with Herman each morning and then about three hundred more through the day. She is short, haggard, hunched over, with curls sprouting beneath a ball cap. The guard booth is a shack just big enough for Carol and her stool and her clip fan and her bag of birdseed. The shack has a back window opening to the landfill abutting it. This is the bottom of the landfill, the oldest layer of trash, nearly a half century of trash, and so trees and shrubs have long since taken over.

"I started out with just doves, and now I got, like, six different kinds of birds," she tells me. "Bright yellow, and a small one with red on its chest. In the morning I see deer, coyotes, bobcat, mountain lion, some owls, some hawks, rattlesnakes, rabbits, and squirrels. That's the whole reason I like this place so much."

It is easily my biggest surprise, to hear so many people speak of enjoying nature as part of the landfill experience. What a weird and yet perfectly sensible link.

"I hold my breath a lot when the small trucks without tops come in," she says. "It doesn't hit till after they pass. I'll say, 'Oooh, the poochie truck went by!'

"I write poetry. I have to write the words down immediately or else I'll lose them. I saw a wolf here once that inspired me. I wrote about his family. He kept searching for them and never found them. I called it 'Long Lost Love.'"

IN THE END, I tour the newest building on the site, the Puente Hills Materials Recovery Facility, or MRF. I have been resisting this place. It could be because it looks so bland and sterile, like a mint-green shopping mall or a giant municipal office building, or it could simply be because I am reluctant to face my own responsibility in all of this. The MRF is to be the starting point of the Waste-by-Rail system; it's where they'll sort the trash, save and sell the good stuff, and then send only the unusable junk out on the expensive trip on the railways. Already the sorting has started, reclaiming some of the trash that would have ended up in the Puente Hills heap above.

Nearly all of the engineers I meet boast about the MRF: how huge it is—large enough to house three 747s; how the design is environmentally friendly, with over five hundred skylights, and recycled materials used throughout the project, from structural and reinforcing steel to ceiling and floor tiles.

Joe would like to highlight his own contribution: an observation deck where the public can come through and watch. "I insisted on this," he says. "I said we have to be able to show people what's happening to their trash." He's dressed today in a green flowered shirt, khaki shorts, and tennis shoes. He is excited to be here, like a man greeting a newcomer to his fancy new mansion. The observation deck is sleek and futuristic, a long glass corridor dimly lit by runway-style floor lights. Below us, the action of the MRF: Trucks pull in one end of the enormous building, dump garbage. Dozers move the garbage to the sorting floor, where bulky valuables, wood, carpet, and large chunks of cardboard are pulled out. This is commercial garbage intended for recycling—a minuscule fraction of L.A. County's trash—but to Joe and his cronies it represents a beautiful outlook for, one day, all our trash. After the big stuff is picked out, the trash is sent via conveyor to an automated picking system and finally to the picking line, where teams of sorters—women wearing safety glasses and bandannas and surgical masks—pick, Lucille Ball style, through the trash. One grabs paper, one grabs clear plastic, one aluminum, and so on. The separated materials are baled and stacked, awaiting purchase.

"Isn't that impressive?" Joe says, hands on his hips, looking down.

"Actually, I find it pretty depressing," I say. I lean into the glass and my breath makes fog. I feel like Ebenezer Scrooge and Joe's the Ghost of Christmas Yet to Come pointing to where I'm headed: a world in which a whole lot of poor people have to pick through my garbage so the planet doesn't suffocate. I sink, as perhaps anyone would, into recycle guilt.

"I sort of feel like it shouldn't have come to this," I say.

"Oh, forgodsakes, there's no room for sentimentality," he says, leading me to a bank of elevators.

Americans recycle about one and a half pounds of the five pounds of trash they produce each day—a national recycling rate of 32 percent. This is actually not horrible when you figure that, in 1989, when a barge called the *Mobro 4000* famously carried three thousand tons of unwanted trash up and down the East Coast. looking for a place to dump, our recycling rate was just 16 percent. That barge caught the public's attention: *We have no place to put our trash!* California led the recycling charge, enacting a 1989 law that said its cities had to recycle 50 percent of their garbage by 2000. Today, San Francisco has a recycling rate of 69 percent, the best of any American city.

The goal, in the larger and perhaps mythical sense, is 100 percent. Zero waste. The goal is to stop thinking of waste as a problem and to start thinking of it, simply, as the result of a design flaw in manufacturing: we should be reusing everything. "It's just about closing the loop," Joe says as we get into the elevator. "And maybe that starts with us first just getting hold of our gluttony. You know, we still have remnants of that old reptilian brain that tells us to just keep getting more, more, more in order to be happy."

Reptilian?

"You know, a guy gets his first BMW, expects to be happy," he says. "Then he's off skiing with Bob, who has a better BMW. Damn. He was supposed to be happy! It didn't work. So now he needs a four-thousand-square-foot house. You know the story."

I tell him I don't see Bob and his buddy slowing down anytime soon. We are a nation of consumers. We can't seem to stop ourselves. We don't seem to even *want* to stop ourselves.

He does not see this as a uniquely American or even a modern phenomenon. "We're not smart enough yet," he says. "We're young. You can argue how long *Homo sapiens* have been around, but the guess is something like 150,000 years. We are amateurs at this. We have just barely gotten here in terms of the clock of the earth." The elevator stops and he holds the door open, so I go first.

"We have our physics way ahead of our psyche," he says when we reach the first floor. We head down a hallway so clean, our shoes squeak. "Like, we know how to make a lot of stuff," he says. "But the notion of responsibility? We're slower on that. The idea that you're supposed to leave the world better than the way it was when you showed up? We're onto it, but we're not nearly there. We need to be able to take the next step and realize that the world's ideas are bigger than just a bunch of stuff."

The more he talks like this, the more optimistic he becomes: people will get smarter, more conscientious, more in tune with the needs of the next generation; *chivalry will spread throughout the world!*

I apologize for not seeing it. I confess that I don't see this recycling thing really kicking in where I come from, where many people regard recycling as a quaint, retro 1990s fad. Rumor has it that there's a paper glut, that no one knows what to do with all those plastic soda bottles other than make some silly belts out of them, that all this stuff just ends up in landfills in the end, so why bother?

"In the early days of recycling, maybe," he says. "Paper goods were mixed at probably a pretty low grade where the guy had it for six months in his yard, it got wet and turned into a huge spitwad. But the higher the cost of disposal goes, the more inventive people become."

We stop in the workers' locker room and Joe finds us both a hard hat and a pair of safety goggles.

It costs $29 a ton to dump here at Puente Hills. It will cost $60 a ton to haul trash by rail out of the Los Angeles basin. "People get really creative at $60 a ton," he says. We talk about thriving markets in China: wastepaper is America's number one export by volume to China. The ships that bring all those toys and TVs in from China now return full of our old paper, which they use to pack more goods made in China. And as for making new paper, 36 percent of the fiber that goes into new paper now comes from recycled sources.

"And now there are rug companies that will actually *lease* you a rug," Joe says. "If someone spills on the little square, they pop up the square. The company takes the square back, they shave the fuzz off, they melt the plastic, make new fuzz, put it back on. Yeah. Isn't that crazy? And it's being done because of the disposal costs. It pushes backward."

I ask him if there is any squashing his optimism.

"People are basically good-hearted until put in a very bad corner," he says. "We just have to keep giving them reasons to be good-hearted—the *opportunity* to be good-hearted. You know, their inclination is to be good folks until it's gone bad on them. Then they get defensive. What's Churchill's line? If you're young and not liberal, you have no heart. If you're old and not conservative, you have no brains.

"Look, environmental consciousness is not a religious thing. It doesn't have holy precepts that say you can't touch a plastic bag or you're a horrible person. It's more: Get a grip and find a balance. Life's organic. It's smelly and gooey. Get past it. It's just science. I think as we get more people reconnected to science through recycling, we get them to understand the magic of this planet. They've forgotten the magic. The truth is, it doesn't take that much connecting to go WOW! It's like lying on your back in the mountains, looking at the stars. Being able to go WOW! And *holy mackerel!* It really doesn't take a lot of study to appreciate this place."

All geared up for our tour through the floor of the MRF, Joe pushes a door and we head in. It definitely has the feel of two airplane hangars—a massive space with a sky-high ceiling. The sorting area with its clanking conveyor belts takes up a tiny corner of the building. Trash falls into it from a hopper above and goes marching along the belts while the women watch and grab and pull at it. I stand behind a pregnant Hispanic woman snatching dirty empty soda bottles out of a heap of garbage rolling by so fast, she nearly misses a perfectly good twenty-ounce Sierra Mist.

She catches my eye and I don't quite know what to do with my shame, and so, stupidly, I smile and give her a thumbs-up.

Joe invites me out to dinner. First we have to stop home and pick up Shelly, his wife. We crawl on the crowded 605 in his old Cadillac and he looks tired, spent, and I have to think by now he is talked out.

"I just don't know about God," he says, apropos of nothing, and because he is not, and probably never will be, talked out. "I don't know about an afterlife," he says.

"Yeah, me neither," I say. The ride is smooth and the leather seats stick to my legs. This was a damn fancy car in its day.

"I'm more about that Marxist thinking that religion is the opiate of the masses," he says. "Calm the people down so that the kings can get away with murder."

"Yeah—"

"But nature certainly seems to be hinting at an afterlife," he says. "As much as I can be cynical about that sort of thing. Nature says, 'Wait a minute, now, it's all cycles.' Nature does not seem to be telling us that there's a light at the end of the tunnel and then we all go *boop*."

The sun is falling appropriately onto the horizon. We both flip our visors down. Even so, it's blinding, and we're not moving, and this is going to be a long ride home.

"The spiritual world could be just a part of the cycle that we don't yet understand," he says, opening his window to get some air, which is probably technically smog. We sit and stare into traffic.

"Of course, my wife swears that she was here before as a Spanish guy," he says. "She remembers water coming in through the portholes, the whole bit. But she's odd, anyway."

The description turns out to be an apt setup. When we finally get to the house, Shelly won't let us in because it's too messy for company, and so we sit in the backyard and sip pinot grigio, and I marvel at the odd assortment of stuff in the yard and on the porch, a crooked little fake Christmas tree, an empty pond, little ceramic dwarfs, and a fat black cat. Shelly is as tall as Olive Oyl, with a handsome face and a jet-black mane, and she chain-smokes and speaks the same crazily observant language as her husband. The two get tangled in notions, in thinking about what it would be like if there were no more people on earth, in trying to remember the names of types of frogs, or the names of saints, until one of them has to run inside and get a book to look it up.

At one point, when Joe is inside trying to find his encyclopedia of movie actors, Shelly turns to me and holds her glass up to offer a toast. "To landfill people!" she says.

I raise my glass politely.

"Aren't they the most ethical bunch?" she says. "It's *weird*. So many of them were Jesuit-trained, so maybe it goes back to that, where doing your best for the common good is a paramount principle." She takes a final drag of her cigarette, smashes the butt in an awaiting seashell. "But they approach their jobs in the most principled way. They're taking the worst two things we have—trash and sewage—and turning them into golf courses and wonderful things.

"Isn't that *weird*?" she says. "Seriously, it's like a *cause* for these people. I've noticed it from the beginning, having to go to all these dreadful conferences and things. I used to think, 'These should be our politicians. We should only elect people trained in landfill maintenance.'"

Joe comes back out. He didn't find the encyclopedia. Instead, he's carrying a journal article that reminded him of something funny. "No one knows where water came from," he announces. "Some people think it came in as dirty snowballs. Asteroids. They're not positive water started here. It may have come from space."

"Oh, he loves this one," Shelly says to me, as if to provide warning. "He is now going to tell you where molecules came from."

"All the molecules came from space," he says. "Ask any nuclear scientist about the origins of the bigger molecules: carbon and nitrogen and oxygen and all the stuff that makes up life—they were all *hydrogen* to begin with. They came out of the fusion process that takes place in the center of *suns*."

"Wait for it—" Shelly says to me.

"So we're stardust, literally," he says. "*We are atomic waste!*" He slaps the table, more satisfied with that one than he has been with anything all day.

ACKNOWLEDGMENTS

This book is a collaboration of many hands and minds, and I offer my thanks to Andy Ward for making me do it, and Jim Nelson at *GQ* for hatching the idea and providing immeasurable support. To my editor Neil Nyren for championing the project and Andrew Blauner for protecting it. To the University of Pittsburgh Dietrich School of Arts and Sciences and the Pennsylvania Council on the Arts for the patronage. To the numerous labor, management, and government organizations that permitted me such extraordinary access to their operations. To all the editors who pored over early versions—Raha Naddaf, Tom Frail, Sarah Goldstein—and the research department at *GQ* for the inexhaustible fact-finding energy. To Elaine Vitone for the searching, arranging, transcribing, and scheming, and to Amy Whipple for entering the endgame. To my girls, Anna and Sasha, for laughing and twirling and pretending to like all the airport trinkets. To Alex, my husband, for holding down the ever-expanding fort and for his unrelenting faith in me. To my parents, who didn't live long enough to read this book but who continue to inspire me to keep this gig going. Finally, to the people of *Hidden America*, who offered such generous entry into their worlds and entrusted me with the stories I hope I have rendered honorably. (I'm looking at you: Foot, Sputter, Joe Haworth, Juan, Pedro, Brian, Adrienne, Donnell Brown, Richard Sprague, and TooDogs, may you rest in peace.)

jml